AUTO ELECTRONICS SIMPLIFIED–
Complete Guide to Service/Repair of Automotive Electronic Systems

AUTO ELECTRONICS SIMPLIFIED—

Complete Guide to Service/Repair of Automotive Electronic Systems

By Clayton L. Hallmark

TAB BOOKS

Blue Ridge Summit, Pa. 17214

FIRST EDITION

FIRST PRINTING—JANUARY 1975

Copyright © 1975 by TAB BOOKS

Printed in the United States
of America

Hardbound Edition: International Standard Book No. 0-8306-4749-X

Paperbound Edition: International Standard Book No. 0-8306-3749-4

Library of Congress Card Number: 74-25566

Cover: Illustration based on Chrysler Security Alarm system. Courtesy Chrysler Corporation.

PREFACE

Electronics is the science and technology of creating and using devices in which electrical conduction takes place in a vacuum, gas, or semiconductor. Until recently, the application of this technology to automobiles has been limited to entertainment and communications units—radios and tape players. Public concern over the problems of air pollution and automobile safety is increasing—and so is the use of electronics to remedy them. For example, electronic ignitions are now standard equipment on many automobiles, and electronic seat belt interlock systems are standard on all 1974 cars sold in the U.S.

These applications are just a beginning. Soon electronics will pervade every nook and cranny of the automobile. In a recent study, it was estimated that the per-car investment in electronics would reach $70 by 1976 and $100 by 1980, bringing the total market to about $1 billion by 1980! These facts make automotive electronics important not just to the automotive industry, but to everyone.

The purpose of this book is to make automotive electronics *understandable* to everyone. To whatever extent I have succeeded in this purpose, I am indebted to the following persons and organizations who supplied technical data and illustrations:

Byron J. Nichols—Chrysler Corp.

Jim Le Veck—Nissan Motor Corp. in U.S.A.

J. M. Kendal—Chevrolet Motor Division of General Motors Corp.

Joseph H. Karshner—General Motors Corp.

L. A. Weis—Ford Motor Co.

Joseph Rutkowski—Bendix Corp.

Herbert W. Williamson—Volkswagen of America, Inc.

Earl Broihier and Marge Streit—Heath Co.

Margery Honig—Renault, Inc.

Ted Just—Hays Ignition Systems, Inc.

I especially thank Heath Co. for the circuit descriptions of their products and *Bendix Technical Journal* for much of the information in Chapter 10, which is reprinted by permission.

Clayton L. Hallmark

CONTENTS

Electronic Charging Systems

The charging system (Fig. 1-1) of the modern automobile has three components—the alternator, the voltage regulator (sometimes built into the alternator), and the battery. These three work together to supply power for the ignition, lights, radio, starting motor, and every other electrical and electronic device found in an automobile.

The source of power for operating such devices may be either the battery or the alternator—or, under certain conditions, both of them.

The continual addition of electrically operated accessories, and slower driving speeds due to greater traffic congestion, has increased the need for a usable source of electrical energy at all engine speeds.

To meet this need, a continuous-output, diode-rectified alternating-current (ac) generator called an *alternator* was developed.

ALTERNATOR THEORY

An alternating-current generator, or alternator, converts mechanical energy into electrical energy. It does this by utilizing the principle of electromagnetic induction. Any conductor carrying a current produces a magnetic field around itself. A changing magnetic field may produce an emf (electromotive force or voltage) in a conductor. If a conductor lies in a magnetic field and either the field or conductor moves, an emf is induced in the conductor. This effect is electromagnetic induction.

Cycle

Figure 1-2 shows a suspended loop of wire (conductor) being rotated in a counterclockwise direction through the magnetic field between the poles of a permanent magnet. For ease of explanation, the loop has been divided into dark and light halves. Notice that in Fig. 1-2B the dark half is moving parallel to the lines of force. Consequently, it is not interrupting or cutting these lines. The same is true of the light half, moving in the opposite direction. Since the conductors are cutting no

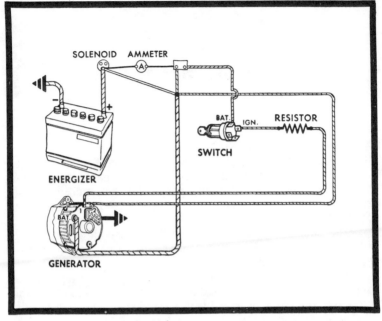

Fig. 1-1. Basic charging-system circuitry.

lines of force, no emf is induced. As the loop rotates toward the position shown in B, it cuts more and more lines of force per second, because it is cutting more directly across the field (lines of force) as it approaches the position shown in B. At position B, the induced voltage is greatest, because one conductor is cutting directly across the field.

As the loop continues to be rotated toward the position shown in C, it cuts fewer and fewer lines of force per second. The induced voltage decreases from its peak value. Eventually, one loop is once again moving in a plane parallel to the magnetic field, and no voltage (zero voltage) is induced. The loop has now been rotated through one half of a circle (one alternation, or 180 degrees). The sine curve shown in the lower part of one figure is a graph of the induced voltage at every instant of rotation of the loop. Notice that this curve contains 360 degrees, or two alternations. Two alternations represent one complete circle of rotation, or one *cycle*.

The direction of current during the rotation from B to C, when a closed path is provided across the ends of the conductor loop, can be determined by using the *left-hand rule for generators*. The left-hand rule is applied as follows: Extend the left hand so that the *thumb* points in the direction of *conductor movement,* and the *forefinger* points in the direction of

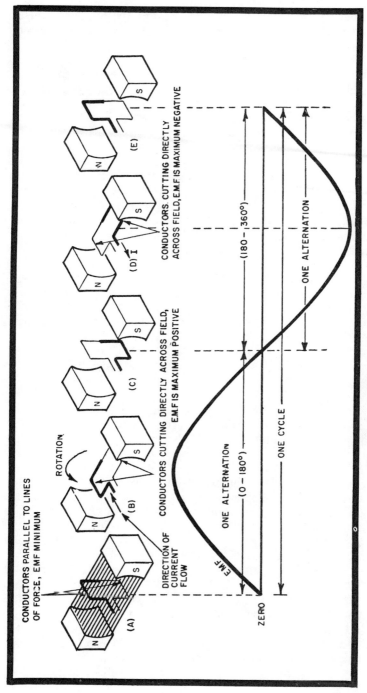

Fig. 1-3. Basic alternating-current generator.

11

magnetic flux, *north to south*. By pointing the middle finger 90 degrees from the forefinger, it will point in the direction of *current* within the conductor.

Applying the left-hand rule to the dark half of the loop in part B, the direction of current can be determined and is depicted by the heavy arrow. Similarly, the direction of current through the light half of the loop can be determined. The two induced voltages add together to form one total emf. When the loop is further rotated to the position shown in part D, the action is reversed. The dark half is moving up instead of down, and the light half is moving down instead of up. By applying the left-hand rule once again, it is readily apparent that the direction of the induced emf and its resulting current have reversed. The voltage builds up to maximum in this new direction, as shown by the sine-wave tracing. The loop finally returns to its original position (E), at which point voltage is again zero. The wave of induced voltage has gone through one complete cycle.

If the loop is rotated at a steady rate, and if the strength of the magnetic field is uniform, the peak voltage will remain fixed. Continuous rotation will produce a series of sine-wave voltage cycles or, in other words, an ac voltage. In this way mechanical energy is converted into electrical energy.

The rotating loop in Fig. 1-2 is called an *armature*. An armature may have any number of loops or coils.

THE ALTERNATOR

Automotive alternators were pioneered in the U.S. by the Chrysler Corporation. Other car makers soon recognized the advantages of alternators, however, and now all domestic manufacturers use this form of dynamo.

The alternator is the last important and useful development to be made standard equipment on all automobiles. (Probably the next such development will be the electronic ignition, also pioneered as standard equipment by Chrysler.) Compared to the dc generator, the alternator is lighter, more compact, and less trouble-prone. Also, it does a better job of charging the battery—especially at low engine speeds.

Alternators are made in many different sizes, depending on their intended use; one of the generators at Hoover Dam can produce *millions* of voltamperes, while generators used on cars produce only a few hundred volt-amperes.

Regardless of size, however, all generators operate on the same basic principle—a magnetic field cutting through conductors, or conductors passing through a magnetic field. Thus, all generators have at least two distinct sets of conductors. They are (1) a group of conductors in which the output voltage is generated, and (2) a second group of conductors through which direct current is passed to obtain an electromagnetic field of fixed polarity. The conductors in which the output voltage is generated are always referred to as the *armature* windings. The conductors in which the electromagnetic field originates are always referred to as the *field* windings.

In addition to the armature and field, there must also be motion between the two. To provide this, ac generators are built in two major assemblies—the *stator* and the *rotor*. The rotor rotates inside the stator.

TYPES OF ALTERNATORS

There are various types of alternators in use today. However, they all perform the same basic function. The types discussed in the following paragraphs are typical of those encountered in electrical equipment.

Revolving Armature Alternator

In the revolving-armature alternator, the stator provides a *stationary* electromagnetic *field*. The rotor, acting as the armature, revolves in the field, cutting the lines of force and producing the desired output voltage. In this generator, the armature output is taken through slip rings, and thus retains its alternating characteristic.

For a number of reasons, the revolving-armature generator is seldom used. Its primary limitation is that its output power is conducted through sliding contacts (slip rings and brushes) which are subject to frictional wear and sparking.

Revolving-Field Alternator

The revolving-*field* alternator (Fig. 1-3) is by far the most widely used type, and is the type used in cars. In this generator, direct current from a separate source (battery) is passed through windings on the rotor by means of slip rings and brushes. This maintains a rotating electromagnetic field of fixed polarity (similar to a rotating bar magnet). The rotating magnetic field, following the rotor, extends outward and cuts through the armature windings imbedded in the surrounding stator. As the rotor turns, alternating voltages are induced in the armature windings, since magnetic fields of first one polarity and then the other cut through them. Since the output power is taken from stationary windings, the output may be connected through fixed terminals T1 and T2 in Fig. 1-3. This is advantageous in that there are no sliding contacts, and the whole output circuit is continuously insulated.

Slip rings and brushes are adequate for the dc field supply, because the power produced in the field is much less than that in the armature circuit.

Rating of Alternators

The "rating" of an alternator pertains to the load it is capable of supplying. The *normal load* rating is the load it can carry continuously. Its *overload* rating is the above-normal load that it can carry for specified lengths of time only. The load rating of a particular generator is determined by the internal heat it can withstand. Since heating is caused mainly by current, the generator's rating is identified very closely with its current capacity.

In addition to a standard alternator, all auto manufacturers offer an optional heavy-duty alternator for cars with heavily laden electrical systems. A heavy-duty alternator is generally supplied to meet the current demands of air conditioning, for example. Chrysler offers 26 and 40A units; General Motors, 37, 42, and 62A units; and Ford, 40, 42, 60, and 65A units. In each case, the lowest rated alternator is standard equipment.

BASIC FUNCTIONS OF ALTERNATOR PARTS

A typical alternator is shown in Fig. 1-4A. Figure 1-4B is a simplified schematic.

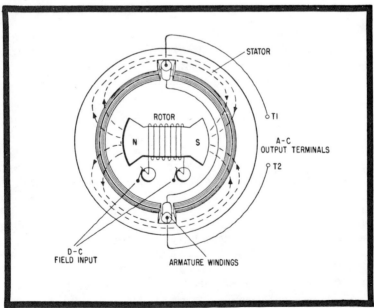

Fig. 1-3. Essential parts of a rotating-field ac generator.

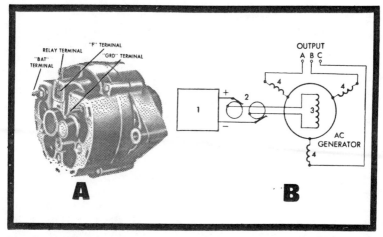

Fig. 1-4. General Motors Delcotron generator (in A) and alternator schematic (in B).

Any rotary generator requires a prime moving force to rotate the ac field and exciter (current supply) armature. This rotary force is transmitted to the generator through the rotor drive shaft by the car's engine. The voltage regulator (1, Fig. 1-4B) connects the battery output to the ac generator field input slip rings and brushes (2). Since these slip rings, rather than a commutator, are used to supply current through the ac generator field (3), current always flows in *one* direction through these windings. Thus, a fixed-polarity magnetic field is maintained at all times in the ac generator field windings. When the ac generator field is rotated, its magnetic flux is passed through and across the ac generator armature stator windings (4). Remember, a voltage is induced in a conductor if it is stationary and a magnetic field is passed through it, the same as if the field is stationary and the conductor is moved. The alternating voltage induced in the armature windings is connected through fixed terminals to a rectifier and load.

GENERATOR PHASE

A *single-phase* ac generator has a stator made up of a number of windings in series, which form a single circuit in which an output voltage is generated.

Figure 1-5 illustrates a schematic diagram of a single-phase ac generator having four poles. The stator has four polar groups evenly spaced around the stator frame. The rotor has four poles, with adjacent poles of opposite polarity. As the rotor revolves, ac voltages are induced in the stator windings. Since one rotor pole is in the same position relative to a stator winding as any other rotor pole, all stator polar groups are cut by equal amounts of magnetic lines of force at any given time. As a result, the voltages induced in all the windings have the same amplitude or value at any given instant. The four stator windings are connected to each other so that the voltages are in phase, or "series aiding." Assume that rotor pole 1, a south pole, induced a voltage in the direction indicated by the arrow, in stator winding 1. Since rotor pole 2 is a north pole, it will induce a voltage in the opposite direction in stator coil 2 with respect to that in coil 1.

In order that the two induced voltages be in series addition, the two coils are connected as shown. Applying the same reasoning, the voltage induced in stator coil 3 (clockwise rotation of the field) is in the same direction (counterclockwise as the voltage induced in coil 1. Similarly, the direction of the voltage induced in winding 4 is opposite to the direction of the voltage induced in coil 1. All four stator coil groups are connected in series so that the voltages induced in each winding add to give a total voltage that is four times the voltage in any one winding.

Three-Phase Generators

The *3-phase* ac generator, as the name implies, has three single-phase windings spaced so that the voltage induced in each winding is 120 degrees out of phase with the voltages in the other two windings. (Remember that 1 cycle is 360 degrees.) A schematic diagram of a 3-phase stator showing all the coils becomes complex, and it is difficult to see what is actually happening. A simplified schematic diagram, showing all the windings of a single phase, lumped together as one winding, is illustrated in Fig. 1-6A. The rotor is omitted for simplicity.

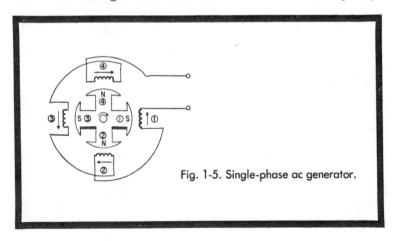

Fig. 1-5. Single-phase ac generator.

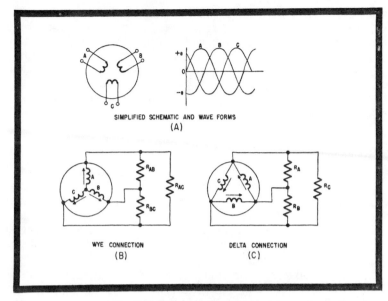

Fig. 1-6. Three-phase ac generator.

Voltage waveforms are shown to the right of the schematic. The three voltages are 120 degrees apart and are similar to the voltages that would be generated by three single-phase ac generators whose voltages are out of phase by angles of 120 degrees (1/3 cycle). The three phases are independent of each other.

The Wye Connection

Rather than have six leads come out of the 3-phase ac generator, one of the leads from each phase may be connected to form a common junction. The stator is then wye (or Y) connected. The common lead may or may not be brought out of the machine. If it is brought out, it is called *neutral*. The simplified schematic (Fig. 1-6B) shows a Y-connected stator with the common lead not brought out. In a Y-connected ac generator, the three start ends of each single-phase winding are connected together to a common neutral point, and the opposite, or finish, ends are connected to the line terminals A, B, and C (see Fig. 1-4).

The Delta Connection

A 3-phase stator may also be connected as shown in Fig. 1-6C. In a delta-connected ac generator, the start end of one phase winding is connected to the finish end of the third; and the start of the third phase winding is connected to the finish of the second phase winding; and the start of the second phase winding is connected to the finish of the first phase winding. The three junction points are connected to the line wires leading to the load. When the generator phases are properly delta connected, no appreciable current flows within the delta loop when there is no external load connected to the generator. If any one of the phases is reversed with respect to its correct connection, a short-circuit current exists within the unloaded windings, causing damage to the windings.

Frequency

The frequency of the ac generator voltage depends upon the speed of rotation of the rotor and the number of poles. The faster the speed, the higher the frequency will be; the lower the speed, the lower the frequency. The more poles there are on the rotor, the higher the frequency will be for a given speed. When a rotor has rotated through an angle such that two adjacent rotor poles (a north and a south pole) have passed one winding, the voltage induced in that winding will have varied through one complete cycle. A 2-pole generator rotates at twice the speed of a 4-pole generator to produce the same frequency of generated voltage. The frequency of the generator in hertz (cycles per second) is related to the number of poles and the speed, as expressed by the equation

$$f = \frac{PN}{120}$$

where P is the number of poles and N the speed in rpm.

Automotive alternators often have 14 poles (General Motors). Hence, if the alternator is turning at 1200 rpm, the frequency of its output is 14×1200 divided by 120, or 1400 hertz (cycles per second). The alternating current supplied to your house, in contrast, has a frequency of only 60 Hz (hertz). The much greater number of positive and negative impulses supplied by the automotive alternator means smoother power, just as eight cylinders means smoother power than six or four cylinders in an engine. Furthermore, the voltage peaks occur at different times in all three phases (stator windings) of a car's alternator. This means an additional multiplication of electrical impulses by a factor of 3, and still smoother electrical power. Figure 1-6A shows how the voltages overlap for a smoother output from a 3-phase alternator.

PRACTICAL ALTERNATOR

An exploded view of an automotive alternator is shown in Fig. 1-7. The rotor of the alternator consists of many turns of

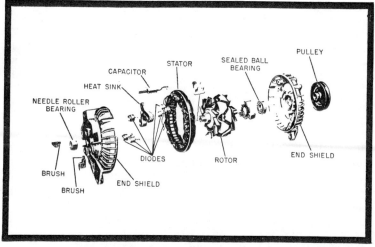

Fig. 1-7. Exploded view of alternator. (Courtesy Chrysler Corp.)

wire (the field coil) located inside two interlocking pole pieces (Fig. 1-8). In Fig. 1-8, each of the two pole pieces has 7 poles, providing a total of 14 for the complete rotor assembly.

The automotive alternator has three sets of windings (phases) in the stator, as shown in Fig. 1-9A. One end from each winding is connected to a single junction in a Y-connected alternator, as shown in Fig. 1-9B. In the Y-connected alternator, the output of the alternator is taken off the other end of each of the three windings. This connection is used by Ford, GM, and Chrysler. Ford also uses the delta connection in some of its alternators.

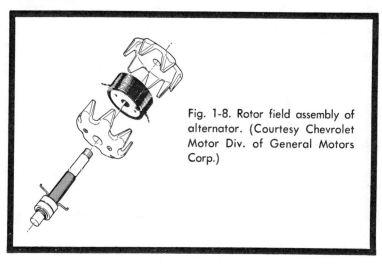

Fig. 1-8. Rotor field assembly of alternator. (Courtesy Chevrolet Motor Div. of General Motors Corp.)

The overlapping of the outputs of the three phases smooths out the total flow of current from the stator windings, as shown in Fig. 1-6A; however, half of the total output is still in one direction and the other half is in the opposite direction. This alternating current is not suitable for the dc system of the car. Therefore, it is necessary to change the alternating current flowing from the stator windings of the alternator to direct current by a process called *electrical rectification* by means of a *diode* or *rectifier*. The diode is an electrical device that will allow current to flow in *only* one direction. In circuit or wiring diagrams, such as the accompanying full-wave rectification diagram (Fig. 1-10), the diode is commonly represented by an arrowhead. Current can flow through the diode only in the direction *opposite* that indicated by the arrow.

When diodes are connected to the stator as shown, the current output from the alternator to the battery will be in only one direction (direct current). Two of the several possible conditions for current output have been shown in the illustration. From this illustration it is seen that regardless of which direction current is flowing from one phase of the stator, current will always enter the positive terminal of the battery and return to the stator via the negative terminal of the battery. The output of the other stator phases is converted to direct current in an identical manner, resulting in full-wave rectification (in which the entire output is converted to direct current).

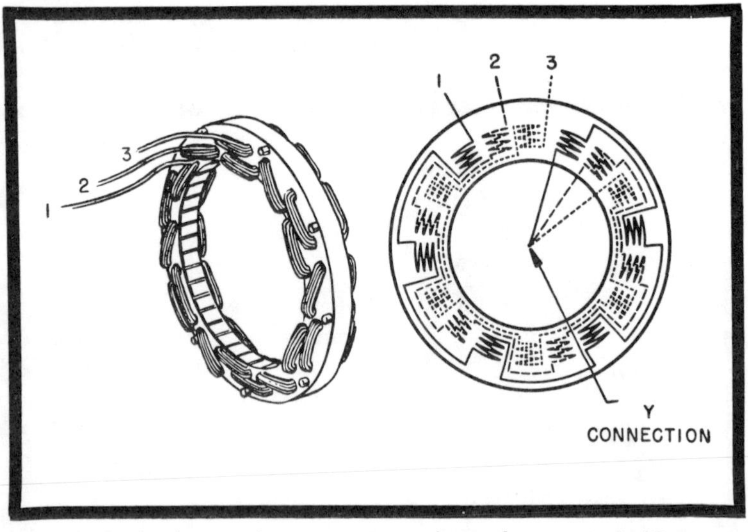

Fig. 1-9. External view of stator, in A; windings of stator, in B. (Courtesy Chrysler Corp.)

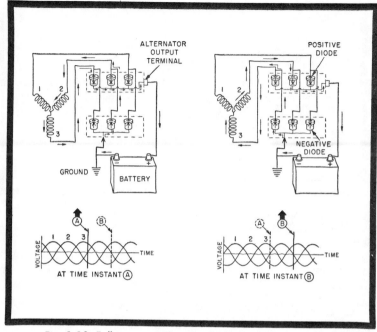

Fig. 1-10. Full-wave rectification. (Courtesy Chrysler Corp.)

A cross-sectional view of the diode is shown in Fig. 1-11 with the thin silicon wafer called a *die* at the bottom of the diode case. The heavy case walls protect the delicate silicon wafer and remove the heat produced by current flow. The diode is tightly sealed to prevent entry of moisture. It is the electrical characteristic of the silicon die or wafer within the diode that makes it a unidirectional conductor.

Care should be taken in handling diodes. Sudden impacts may crack the silicon wafer. If the diode lead is bent too much, the glass insulator may crack, letting moisture enter the diode; moisture could cause it to short and fail to operate. Pulling the diode lead should also be avoided because the solder joint between the diode lead and the silicon die might break. Six diodes are mounted in the slip-ring end of the generator. Three diodes are mounted in the end frame, and three diodes are mounted in the heatsink (dissipater) and are insulated from the end frame. These diodes, when connected, serve as a rectifier assembly that changes the alternating voltages developed in the stator windings to a single one-direction voltage. Therefore, voltage in only one direction appears at the output terminal of the generator, supplying dc (direct current) to charge the battery.

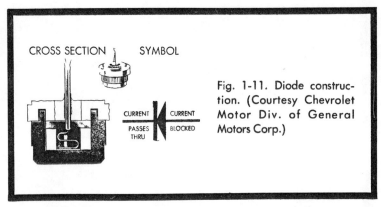

CROSS SECTION   SYMBOL

CURRENT   CURRENT
PASSES   BLOCKED
THRU

Fig. 1-11. Diode construction. (Courtesy Chevrolet Motor Div. of General Motors Corp.)

Since the blocking action of the diodes prevents battery discharge through the generator, the need for a cutout relay is eliminated.

A capacitor, connected between the BAT terminal of the generator and common ground, protects the diodes from voltage surges as they block current flow.

THE VOLTAGE REGULATOR

It has been shown how current through the field coil, located in the rotor, creates magnetic lines of force. These magnetic lines of force, cutting across the windings of the stator as the rotor turns, create an alternating voltage within the stator windings. This causes current to flow through the diode rectifier to the BAT terminal of the generator to charge the battery or supply power to the electrical accessories.

If the generator were connected to both the battery and the accessories, then either battery or generator voltage would be impressed upon the field coil whenever the ignition switch was closed. Battery voltage first provides the field current in the generator, but as the speed of the generator increases, the generator itself provides the voltage for field current. As generator voltage increases, then field current increases, which increases the magnetic lines of force in the rotor. This develops even more voltage in the generator and voltage rapidly increases as shown in Fig. 1-12.

The need to limit the voltage that is developed is very critical. Without voltage control, light bulbs, external wiring, relay coils, contact points, and all the other electrical parts of the vehicle would be damaged or greatly reduced in service life. A voltage regulator is used to limit the field current and magnetic field within the generator so that its voltage may be limited to a safe value. No *current* control of the generator is necessary since it can deliver only a given amount of current.

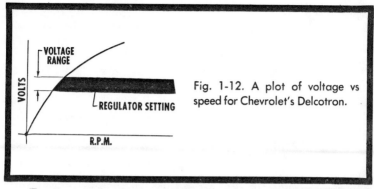

Fig. 1-12. A plot of voltage vs speed for Chevrolet's Delcotron.

Two types of voltage regulators are currently used—a solid state regulator that is usually mounted inside the generator, and a double-contact regulator that is mounted externally. Both regulators can be used in circuits containing either an indicator lamp or an ammeter; however, the external circuits on various cars may be quite different.

A COMPLETE CHARGING SYSTEM

A 2-unit double-contact regulator is shown in Fig. 1-13. The regulator has two units, the voltage regulator relay and the field relay. The voltage regulator relay in all types of regulators

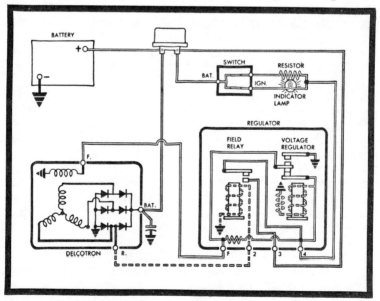

Fig. 1-13. Charging-circuit operation with key on and engine off. (Courtesy Chevrolet Motor Div. of General Motors Corp.)

23

limits the generator voltage to a preset value. The field relay disconnects the generator field coil and the voltage regulator winding from the battery when the relay contact points are opened and reconnects them when the points are closed.

The field relay of the 2-unit regulator may also act as an indicator lamp relay on some cars. The circuitry of regulators used with indicator lamps and indicator lamp relays is such that the indicator lamp lights when the ignition switch is first turned on.

When the generator builds voltage and begins to furnish power for the electrical system, the lamp goes out, indicating that the system is operating. Fig. 1-13 is a wiring diagram showing internal circuits of the 2-unit regulator and generator with an indicator light.

Voltage Regulator Operation

When the ignition switch is closed, and before the engine is started (Fig. 1-13), current flows from the battery through the indicator lamp (which is in parallel with the resistor), to terminal 4 of the regulator. From this terminal, current continues through the contact points of the voltage regulator to the field (F) terminal of the regulator. It continues through the external wiring to the generator F terminal and on through the field coil of the generator rotor. It returns to the battery through ground to complete the circuit; this energizes the field coil winding and lights the lamp, indicating that the generator is not operating.

When the engine starts and the generator rotor begins to rotate, the magnetism created in the field coil by the field current creates alternating voltage in the stator windings. Six diodes located in the end frame of the generator make up the rectifier which changes the alternating voltage to dc voltage. The dc voltage is then routed to the BAT terminal of the generator where it supplies the dc current to charge the battery and operate the vehicle's electrical accessories (Fig. 1-14).

The voltage which appears at the relay terminal of the generator causes a current flow to the terminal 2 of the regulator and from there it travels on through the shunt winding of the field relay. With current flow in the field relay shunt winding, a magnetic field is created about the winding which attracts the relay armature toward the core, causing the relay armature contacts to close. Closing the relay contacts permits the system voltage, which is impressed on terminal 3, to also be impressed on terminal 4. Since the indicator light now has system voltage on both sides of the bulb, there is no current flow and the light will go out. This indicates that the generator is producing system voltage.

If trouble should develop in the system, causing the voltage at the generator relay terminal to decrease to a low value, the field relay contacts will open, causing the light to indicate that there is trouble in the system.

As the generator speed increases, the voltage at the BATT terminal of the generator also increases. The higher voltage increases the current flow from the generator to terminal 3 of the regulator on through the field relay contacts and through the voltage regulator shunt winding. The increased magnetism created about this winding pulls the armature of the voltage regulator, causing the lower contact points to separate. The generator field coil current then must flow through a resistor which reduces the field coil current. This reduced field coil current causes the generator magnetic field and voltage to decrease, which in turn decreases the magnetic pull of the voltage regulator shunt winding. Spring tension on the armature of the voltage regulator then causes the contacts to reclose and shorts out the resistance in series with the field coils. This cycle is repeated many times per second to limit the generator voltage to a preset value.

As the generator speed increases more, the slightly higher voltage across the voltage regulator shunt winding causes the

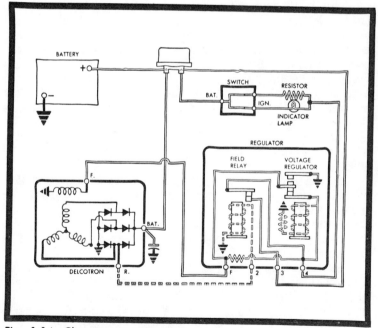

Fig. 1-14. Charging-circuit operation with engine running. (Courtesy Chevrolet Motor Div. of General Motors Corp.)

upper contacts to close. When this happens, both ends of the field coil are grounded and no current passes through the coil. With no current in the field coil, the generator voltage decreases, which also decreases the magnetic pull on the voltage regulator armature, and the upper contact points open. With these points open, field current again flows through the regulator resistor and the field coil. As the voltage again increases, the upper contacts close again. This cycle is repeated many times per second to limit the generator voltage to a preset value at higher operating speeds.

The voltage regulator unit limits the generator voltage throughout the entire generator speed range.

TRANSISTORS

Like a diode, a transistor is a semiconductor device that can pass or block current. *Unlike* a diode, a transistor can vary, or *regulate*, current. While a diode can be compared to a check valve in a fluid system (it permits a flow in one direction only), a transistor can be compared to a spigot. A transistor can allow electrons to flow freely, can reduce their flow, or can cut them off entirely.

While a diode has two terminals, a transistor has three: *base, collector,* and *emitter.* The addition of a third terminal gives the transistor an ability to control current. The base is the control element of a transistor. A small current flowing in the base terminal is able to control a much larger current flowing between the emitter and collector terminals, much as a moving gate or plunger inside a water valve controls the water flow between the inlet and outlet. Of course the water valve controls flow by mechanical action and the transistor controls flow by electrical action. (The exact nature of the transistor's electrical action is within the scope of solid-state physics, but beyond the scope of this book.)

Since a transistor is able to pass current freely or shut it off, and since it exercises its control electrically, a transistor may be used as an electrical switch. You are already familiar with another electrically operated switch—the relay. A transistor may be regarded as an all-electrical relay and is compared to a relay in Fig. 1-15.

The relay contacts in Fig. 1-15 are normally open, but when a small current is fed into the relay winding, the contacts are closed by electromagnetic action and a current flows in the main circuit. The winding is of very fine wire and carries but a very small current; however, the relay contacts are able to carry several amperes. Thus a small current in the relay winding is able to turn a relatively large current on or off.

Similarly, a small current in the base of a transistor is able to turn a relatively large current on or off. The base is analogous to the relay winding terminal in Fig. 1-15, and the emitter and collector are analogous to the contacts. When no current flows in the base terminal, no current flows between the emitter and collector. But if a small current is forced into the base, another *larger* current is allowed to pass between the emitter and collector. In effect, the transistor's collector—emitter terminals "close."

As switches, transistors have a number of advantages over relays. For one thing, they are much faster—in fact, they can operate millions of times per second. Their most important advantage in automotive applications is their reliability. They have no moving parts to wear out, no springs to lose tension, and no contacts to pit or corrode.

In some ways transistors are at a disadvantage compared to relays. A relay is practically an ideal switch; when its contacts are open, it has infinite resistance; when its contacts are closed, it has nearly zero resistance. On the other hand, even when there is no base current and the transistor is supposed to be *off*, a small current will flow between the emitter and collector; the transistor does not have infinite resistance. And when a base current is applied, and the transistor is turned on, there is always a significant resistance between the collector and emitter. In overcoming this resistance, the emitter—collector current generates heat—one of the main enemies of semiconductors.

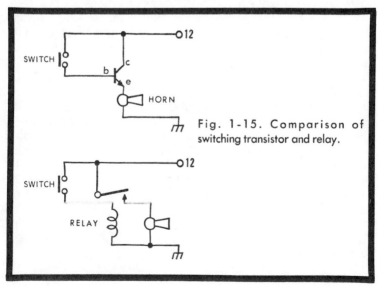

Fig. 1-15. Comparison of switching transistor and relay.

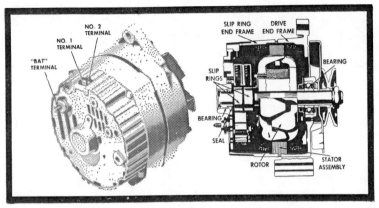

Fig. 1-16. The Delcotron generator. (Courtesy Chevrolet Motor Div. of General Motors Corp.)

Obviously, if a transistor is heated enough—whether by excessive current, careless soldering, or something else—it will be destroyed. To help prevent this, transistors intended to carry large currents (say, one ampere or more) are attached to *heatsinks*. A heatsink is a finned mounting device that works similar to a radiator to dissipate heat, preventing it from building up and destroying the transistor

The alternator in Fig. 1-16 uses transistors in its built in voltage regulator.

SOLID-STATE REGULATOR

A typical automotive wiring diagram of the charging system is shown in Fig. 1-17. The schematic diagram of the solid-state voltage regulator is a representative drawing used only to explain the circuit principles. Positive-to-negative current flow is assumed.

When the ignition switch is turned on, current flows from the battery through the indicator lamp, regulator terminal 1, resistor R1, transistor TR3 (collector to emitter) and transistor TR1 (base to emitter). Transistor TR3 is normally biased on by the small current that flows through resistor R5, transistor TR3 (base to emitter), and resistor R4. The current through TR3 (collector to emitter) is now sufficient to turn on TR1. When transistor TR1 turns on, most of the indicator lamp current flows through the low resistance of the field winding and through TR1 to ground. This causes the lamp to light, which indicates that the generator is not producing an output voltage.

When the engine is started, an ac voltage is produced by the stator windings and rectified by the diode trio and the rectifier bridge. The dc voltage from the rectifier bridge supplies the voltage to charge the battery, while the dc voltage from the diode trio supplies the operating voltage for the regulator and the field winding. Since the voltage on each side of the indicator lamp is now the same, the lamp goes out to indicate that the generator is charging the battery.

The battery voltage is applied across the voltage divider consisting of resistors R2 and R3. The values of these resistors are such that the current through them is negligible. As the generator speed and output voltage increases, the voltage at the junction of R2 and R3 increases to a point where zener diode D1 conducts. This turns on transistor TR2 which in turn turns off transistor TR1. With TR1 off, the field current and output voltage decrease to a level that causes diode D1 to turn off. When this happens, transistor TR2 also turns off, and TR1 turns back on. Current again flows through the field winding and the output voltage increases to a point where the cycle starts over again. This cycling action limits the generator voltage to its preset level.

Resistor R2 is a thermistor that causes the charging voltage to vary with temperature to insure the optimum voltage for charging the battery. Capacitor C1 smooths out the voltage applied to the base of transistor TR2.

Transistor TR3 prevents the generator from producing an output when the battery and the generator are disconnected

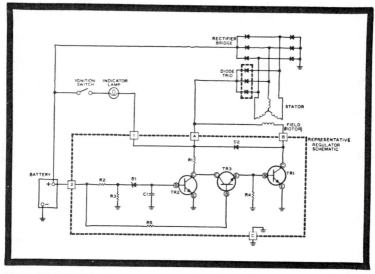

Fig. 1-17. Typical charging system with solid-state regulator. (Courtesy Heath Co.)

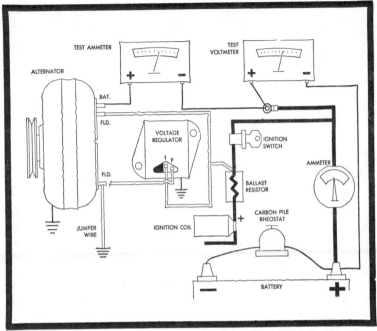

Fig. 1-18. Charging-circuit resistance test. (Courtesy Chrysler Corp.)

from terminal 2. When the voltage is removed from regulator terminal 2, transistor TR3 turns off. This prevents TR1 from turning on.

Diode D2 prevents high induced voltages in the field winding when transistor TR1 turns off.

Diode D1 and transistor TR2 form the voltage level sensor. This circuit monitors the battery voltage and then controls the generator field current switch circuit (B), which, in turn, controls the generator output (charging) voltage.

Transistor TR1 forms the field current switch. This circuit controls the current flow through the field winding, which controls the generator output voltage.

CHARGING CIRCUIT RESISTANCE TEST

The charging circuit resistance test will show the amount of voltage drop between the alternator output terminal wire and battery. For the charging circuit resistance test:

1. Disconnect the battery ground cable.
2. Disconnect the BAT lead at the alternator output terminal.
3. Connect a 0–75A scale dc ammeter in series between the alternator BAT terminal and the disconnected battery lead (Fig. 1-18).

4. Connect the positive lead of a test voltmeter to the disconnected BAT lead. Connect the negative lead of the test voltmeter to battery positive post.
5. Disconnect the green (regulator) field lead wire from the alternator.
6. Connect a jumper lead from the alternator field terminal to ground.
7. Connect an engine tachometer and reconnect the battery ground cable.
8. Connect a variable carbon pile (a special, heavy-duty) rheostat to the battery terminals. Be sure the carbon pile is in the off position before connecting the leads.
9. Start and operate the engine at idle. Immediately after starting, reduce engine speed to idle.
10. Adjust the engine speed and carbon pile to maintain 20A in the circuit. Observe the volemeter reading. The voltmeter reading should not exceed 0.7V. If a higher voltage drop is indicated, inspect, clean, and tighten all connections in the charging circuits. A voltage drop test may be performed at each connection to locate the connection with excessive resistance. If the charging circuit resistance tested satisfactorily, reduce engine speed, turn off carbon pile and turn off ignition switch.
11. Disconnect battery ground cable.
12. Remove test ammeter, voltmeter, and carbon pile.
13. Remove jumper wire between alternator filed terminal and ground. Connect the green field wire to the alternator field terminal.
14. Reconnect the battery ground cable.

CURRENT OUTPUT TEST

The current output test determines whether or not the alternator is capable of delivering its rated current output.

1. Disconnect the battery ground cable (Fig. 1-19).
2. Disconnect the BAT lead wire at the alternator output terminal.
3. Connect an ammeter (range 0−75A minimum) in series between the alternator BAT terminal and the disconnected BAT lead.
4. Connect the positive lead of a voltmeter (range 0−15V minimum) to the BAT terminal of the alternator.
5. Connect the negative lead of the voltmeter to a good ground.
6. Disconnect the field wire (to voltage regulator) at the alternator.
7. Connect a jumper wire from the alternator field terminal to ground.

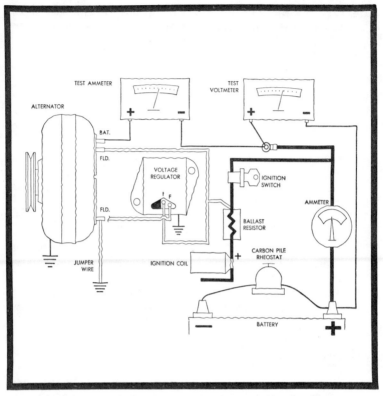

Fig. 1-19. Current output test. (Courtesy Chrysler Corp.)

8. Connect an engine tachometer and reconnect the battery ground cable.
9. Connect a variable carbon pile rheostat between the battery terminals. (Be sure the carbon pile is in the *open* or *off* position before connecting leads).
10. Start the engine and operate at idle. *Immediately* after starting, reduce engine speed to idle.
11. Adjust the carbon pile and engine speed in increments until a speed of 1250 rpm and voltmeter reading of 15 volts is obtained. Do not allow voltage meter to read above 16V.
12. The ammeter reading must be within the limits shown in the alternator specification chart for that size of alternator being tested.
13. If the reading is less than specified, the alternator should be removed from vehicle and bench tested.
14. After the current output test is completed, reduce engine speed, turn off carbon pile, and turn off ignition switch.
16. Remove test ammeter, voltmeter, and carbon pile.

17. Remove jumper wire between alternator field terminal and ground. Connect the field wire to the alternator field terminal.
18. Reconnect the battery ground cable.

VOLTAGE REGULATOR TEST

1. Clean the battery terminals and check the specific gravity. It should be avoe 1.200 to allow a proper regulated voltage check. If the specific gavity is below 1.200, charge or use another battery and do not leave the uncharged battery in the circuit.
2. Connect the positive lead from a voltmeter to the ignition No. 1 terminal of the ballast resistor (Fig. 1-20).
3. Connect the negative lead from the voltmeter to a good vehicle body ground.
4. Start and operate engine at 1250 rpm with all lights and accessories turned off. The regulator is working properly if the voltage readings are in accordance with the following chart.

Voltage Regulator Settings

Chrysler	14.3—14.6V
General Motors	13.8—14.8V
Ford	14.8—15.6V

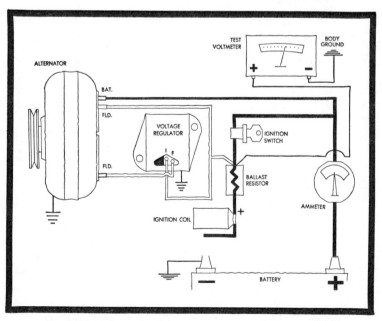

Fig. 1-20. Voltage regulator test. (Courtesy Chrysler Corp.)

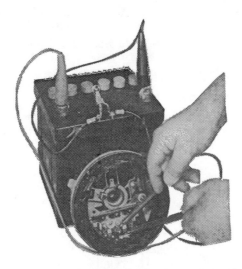

Fig. 1-21. Testing rectifiers with test lamp. (Courtesy Chrysler Corp.)

It is normal for the car ammeter to show an immediate charge and then gradually return to normal position. The amount of time the ammeter hand remains to the right will be dependent of the length of cranking time of charge.

5. If the voltage is below limits or is fluctuating, proceed as follows:

   (a) Check for a good voltage regulator ground.
   (b) Turn off ignition switch and disconnect voltage regulator connector. Be sure terminals of connector have not spread open to cause an open or intermittent connection.
   (c) *Do not* start engine *or* distort terminals with voltmeter probe; turn on ignition switch and check for battery voltage at the wiring of the voltage regulator terminals of the harness. Turn off ignition switch.
   (d) If the previous steps, 5(a) through 5(c), tested satisfactory, replace the regulator and repeat step 4.

6. If the voltage is above the limits shown in the chart, proceed as follows:

   (a) Turn off the ignition switch and disconnect voltage regulator. Be sure terminals on the connector have not spread open.
   (b) *Do not* start engine *or* distort terminals with voltmeter probe; turn on ignition switch, check for battery voltage at the wiring harness terminal. Both leads should read battery voltage. Turn off ignition switch.

7. Remove the test voltmeter.

TESTING RECTIFIERS, STATOR, AND ROTOR

1. Test rectifiers with a 12V battery and a test lamp equipped with a No. 67 bulb (½ candlepower). Connect one side of the test lamp to the positive battery post and the other side to a test probe. Another test probe should be connected to the negative battery post (Fig. 1-21).
2. Contact the rectifier heatsink with one test probe; and touch the other to the strap on the top of the rectifier.
3. Reverse the probes.

    If test lamp lights in one mode but does not light in the other, the rectifier is satisfactory. If the lamp lights in both modes, the rectifier is shorted. If test lamp does not light in either mode, the rectifier is open.
4. Repeat the above procedure for all rectifiers in both assemblies; change rectifier and heatsink assemblies which have shorted or open rectifiers. The lamp should light in the same manner for all rectifiers on each assembly.

Testing the Stator

1. Separate the stator assembly from both alternator end shields.
2. Press test probe firmly onto any pin on the stator frame. Be sure the varnish has been removed so that the pin is bare (Fig. 1-22).
3. Press test probe firmly to each of the three phase (stator) lead terminals one at a time. If the lamp lights, the stator lead is grounded.

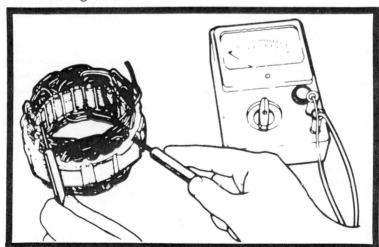

Fig. 1-22. Testing stator for ground. (Courtesy Chrysler Corp.)

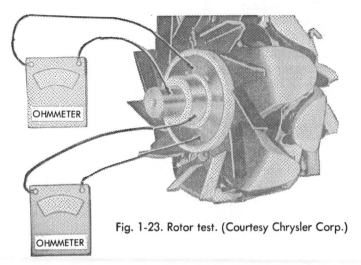

Fig. 1-23. Rotor test. (Courtesy Chrysler Corp.)

4. Press test probe firmly on one phase terminal lead and contact firmly each of the other two stator leads. The lamp should light when the probe contacts each of the terminals. If the lamp does not light, the stator winding is open.
5. Install new stator if stator tested is grounded or open.

Rotor Test

The rotor assembly may be checked electrically for grounded, open, or shorted field coils (Fig. 1-23).

To check for a grounded field coil, connect an ohmmeter from each slip ring to the rotor shaft. (Note: the ohmmeter should be set for infinite reading when probes are apart and zero when probes are shorted.) The ohmmeter should read infinite. If the reading is zero or higher, the rotor is grounded.

To check for an open field coil, connect an ohmmeter to the slip rings. The ohmmeter reading should be between 3 and 4 ohms on rotor coils at room ambient conditions. Resistance between 4 and 6 ohms would result from alternator rotors that have been operated at high engine compartment temperatures. Readings above 6.5 ohms would indicate high resistance rotor coils; further testing or replacement may be required.

To check for a shorted field coil, connect an ohmmeter to the two slip rings. If the reading is below 3 ohms, the field coil is shorted.

TRANSISTORIZED REGULATOR PROBLEMS

Although decidedly superior from an engineering standpoint, transistorized regulators have by no means overtaken the electromechanical regulator. In fact, some people in the automotive industry feel that it may be necessary to take a step backwards in time and convert from the transistorized regulators back to the old ones. Part of the reason is that the older regulators are more durable.

There have been a large number of regulator failures associated with booster battery starting of cars. When a booster battery is hooked up to a car with a dead battery, the regulator adjusts to the booster battery. Then, when the booster battery is disconnected, there is nothing to restrain the generator, since it's only connected to a dead battery. The generator voltage rises drastically for a very brief fraction of a second. In the case of an electrical regulator, there is no harm done. In the case of an electronic regulator, the transistor is destroyed.

One way around this is to turn on all the lights and accessories before unhooking the booster battery. These can safely absorb a momentary high voltage output (called a transient). Unfortunately, few tow-truck drivers know this. So there is still the other way around the problem—the old-style regulator.

The problem just discussed illustrates one reason why auto makers are notoriously slow in adopting technological advances such as electronic devices. The reason is that there is a scarcity of service personnel with enough knowledge to understand and deal with new devices. That is the reason why such detailed theory has been presented thus far; it is important for electrical servicemen to learn all they can about electrical and electronic theory to stay a jump ahead of the people who get all of their information out of shop manuals.

2 Electronic Ignition Systems

The ignition system in most cars consists of a battery, a coil, breaker points, and spark plugs. This system, invented by Kettering, has served long (since 1914) and well, with few changes over the years. One of the greatest inventions of all times, the Kettering ignition sparked a transportation and commercial revolution that transformed the automobile from a rich man's plaything into the No. 1 manufactured item of the nation.

Now, however, the time has come for this venerable system to be retired. Using transistors and other miracles of modern electronics, engineers have designed electronic ignition systems that can meet the demands the engine speeds, compression ratios, and horsepower in today's cars, and can operate at the peak of performance for many thousands of miles with little or no maintenance. This development came not a moment too soon; the demand for an ignition that would insure greater gas mileage and lower emissions, despite neglected maintenance, was as sudden as it was urgent.

To insure an easy and thorough understanding of electronic ignitions, a brief review of some basic engine theory and the Kettering circuit is in order.

ENGINE OPERATION

The actions that take place within the engine cylinder may be divided into four basic operations, or *strokes*. The first stroke in the sequence is called the intake stroke (Fig. 2-1).

Intake Stroke

During this stroke, the piston is moving downward and the intake valve is open. This downward movement of the piston produces a partial vacuum in the cylinder, causing air to rush into the cylinder past the opened intake valve. This is somewhat the same effect produced when drinking through a straw, in which the partial vacuum produced in the mouth is filled by the liquid moving up through the straw (Fig. 2-2). In the engine, the inrushing air passes through the carburetor before it enters the cylinder. The carburetor charges the air with gasoline vapor to produce a combustible mixture.

Compression Stroke

When the piston reaches bottom dead center (bdc) at the end of the intake stroke and is therefore at the bottom of the cylinder, the intake valve closes. This seals the upper end of the cylinder. As the crankshaft continues to rotate, it pushes up, through the connecting rod, on the piston. The piston is therefore pushed upward and compresses the combustible

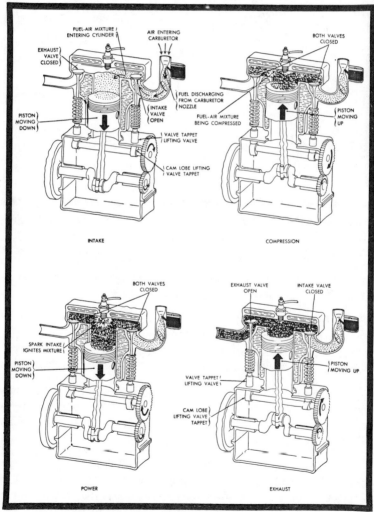

Fig. 2-1. The strokes in the 4-stroke-cycle gasoline engine.

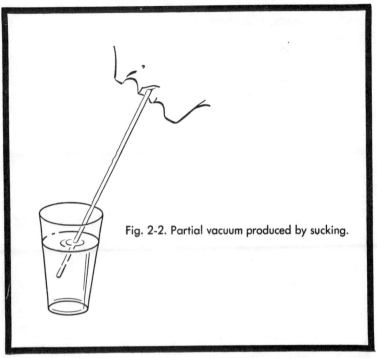

Fig. 2-2. Partial vacuum produced by sucking.

mixture in the cylinder; this is called the *compression* stroke. The mixture is compressed to a sixth or less of its original volume. This is the same as taking a gallon of air and compressing it until a pint or less of air is left. Compressing the mixture in this way makes it still more combustible; the energy in the fuel is concentrated into a smaller space.

Power Stroke

As the piston reaches top dead center (tdc) at the end of the compression stroke and therefore has moved to the top of the cylinder, the compressed fuel—air mixture is ignited. This ignition is produced by the ignition system. The ignition system causes an electric spark to occur suddenly in the cylinder. The spark sets fire to the fuel—air mixture. The mixture burns rapidly and the pressure in the cylinder goes up to as much as 400 psi. This means that the force pushing on the end of a 3-inch piston would be more than 2500 pounds. This force, or thrust, pushes the piston down. The thrust is carried through the connecting rod to the crankpin on the crankshaft. The crankshaft is given a powerful twist. This is called the *power* stroke. This turning effort, rapidly repeated in the engine and carried through gears and shafts, turns the wheels of a vehicle.

Exhaust Stroke

After the fuel—air mixture has burned, it must be cleared from the cylinder. This is done by opening the exhaust valve just as the power stroke is finished and the piston starts back up on the *exhaust* stroke. The piston forces the burned gases out of the cylinder past the opened exhaust valve. The four strokes (intake, compression, power, and exhaust) are continuously repeated as the engine runs.

KETTERING IGNITION SYSTEM

The basic ignition system (Fig. 2-3) consists of the ignition coil, condenser, ignition distributor, ignition switch, low and

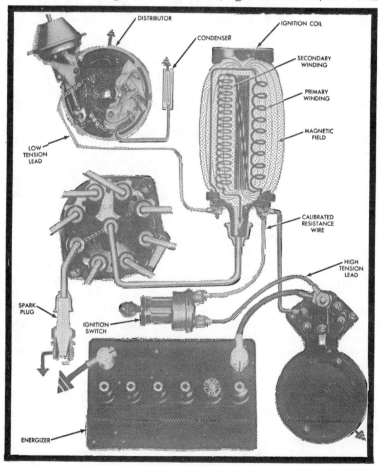

Fig. 2-3. Typical ignition system. (Courtesy Chevrolet Motor Div. of General Motors Corp.)

high tension wiring, spark plugs, and a source of electrical energy (battery or generator). The ignition system has the function of producing high voltage surges and directing them to the spark plugs in the engine cylinders. The sparks must be timed to appear at the plugs at the correct instant near the end of the compression stroke with relation to piston position. The spark ignites the fuel—air mixture under compression so that the power stroke follows in the engine.

There are two separate circuits through the ignition system. One of these is the primary circuit which includes the ignition switch, primary winding of the ignition coil, distributor contact points and condenser. The other is the secondary or high tension (voltage) circuit, which includes the secondary winding of the ignition coil, the high tension lead, distributor cap, rotor, and spark plugs.

With the switch closed, current flows through the primary circuit; that is, from the battery through the primary winding of the ignition coil and closed distributor contacts to ground, and then back to the battery. A cam mounted on the rotating distributor shaft causes the distributor contacts to open and close. When the contacts open, the current decreases very rapidly in the ignition coil primary winding, and a high voltage is induced in the coil secondary winding.

This high voltage is impressed through the distributor cap and rotor across one of the spark plugs. As the voltage establishes an arc across the spark plug electrodes, the air—fuel mixture in the cylinder is ignited to provide the power stroke.

The secondary current flows from the coil secondary winding, across the distributor rotor gap and spark plug gap, and then back to the secondary winding through ground, the battery, and switch. The distributor contacts then reclose, and the cycle repeats. The next-firing spark plug then will be the one connected to the distributor cap insert that is aligned with the rotor when the contacts separate. With the engine running, current flows through the coil primary calibrated resistance wire; the other lead connected between the coil and solenoid terminal is a bypass feature that will be covered in the section entitled "Ignition Coils."

When the contacts separate, a high voltage is induced in the coil primary winding. This voltage may be as high as 250V, which causes an arc to form across the distributor contacts. To bring the primary current to a quick, controlled stop, and in order to greatly reduce the size of the arc and thereby insure prolonged contact point life, a capacitor (condenser) is connected across the distributor contacts.

Distributor

The distributor has three jobs. First, it opens and closes the low tension circuit between the source of electrical energy and the ignition coil so that the primary winding is supplied with intermittent surges of current. Each surge of current builds up a magnetic field in the coil. The distributor then opens its circuit so that the magnetic field will collapse and cause the coil to produce a high voltage surge. The second job that the distributor has is to time these surges with regard to the engine requirements. This is accomplished by the centrifugal and vacuum advance mechanisms. Third, the distributor directs the high voltage surge through the distributor rotor, cap, and high tension wiring to a spark plug which is ready to fire.

The typical contact-point type ignition distributor (Fig. 2-4), consists of a housing, shaft, centrifugal advance assembly, vacuum advance assembly, breaker plate assembly, capacitor or condenser, and rotor.

The cap, rotor, and high voltage leads in a distributor form a distribution system that conveys the high voltage surges to the spark plugs in correct sequence.

The breaker plate contains the breaker lever, contact support, and capacitor. When the breaker cam rotates, each cam lobe passes by and contacts the breaker lever rubbing block, separating the contact points and producing a high voltage surge in the ignition system. With every breaker cam

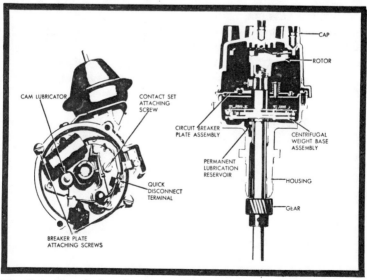

Fig. 2-4. Six-cylinder distributor. (Courtesy Chevrolet Motor Div. of General Motors Corp.)

revolution, one spark will be produced for each engine cylinder. Since each cylinder fires every other revolution in a four-cycle engine, the distributor rotates at one-half engine speed.

The shaft-and-weight base assembly is fitted in suitable bearings made of such materials as cast iron, bronze, or iron. Centrifugal advance weights are pivoted on studs in the weight base, and are free to move against calibrated weight springs which connect them to the breaker cam assembly. The breaker cam assembly fits on the top of the shaft (slip fit) and rotates with the shaft, being driven by the weight springs actuated by the advance weights.

Outward movement of the weights advances the cam assembly in relation to the shaft as engine speed is increased, providing an earlier spark. Each engine model requires an individual spark advance curve to insure delivery of the spark at the right instant for maximum power at all speeds. Because of this, very little standardization of complete distributors can be made.

It is possible to improve fuel economy on engines operating under part-throttle conditions by supplying additional spark advance. Vacuum advance mechanisms are provided on some distributors for this purpose. The mechanism used rotates either the complete distributor or the breaker plate in order to time the spark earlier when the engine is operating at part throttle.

Centrifugal Advance

The centrifugal advance mechanism times the high voltage surge produced by the ignition coil so that it is delivered to the engine at the correct instant, as determined by engine speed.

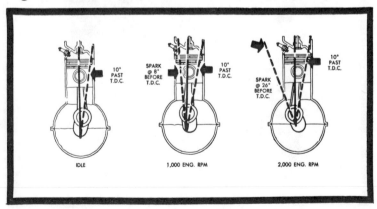

Fig. 2-5. Ignition spark vs engine speed. (Courtesy Chevrolet Motor Div. of General Motors Corp.)

When the engine is idling, the spark is timed to occur in the cylinder just before the piston reaches top dead center. At higher engine speeds, however, there is a shorter interval of time available for the fuel—air mixture to ignite, burn, and give up its power to the piston. Consequently, in order to obtain the maximum amount of power from the mixture, it is necessary at higher engine speeds for the ignition system to deliver the high voltage surge to the cylinder earlier in the cycle.

To illustrate this principle, assume that the burning time of a given gas mixture in an automotive engine is 0.003 second (3 milliseconds). To obtain full power from combustion, maximum pressure must be reached while the piston is between 10 degrees and 20 degrees past top dead center. At 1000 rpm, the crankshaft travels through 18 degrees in 3 milliseconds (ms); at 2000 rpm, the crankshaft travels through 36 degrees. (See Fig. 2-5.) Since the maximum pressure point is fixed, it is easy to see why the spark must be delivered into the cylinder earlier in the cycle in order to deliver full power as engine speed increases.

As previously mentioned, the timing of the spark to engine speed is accomplished by the centrifugal advance mechanism, which is assembled on the distributor shaft. The mechanism consists primarily of two weights and a cam assembly. The weights are thrown out against spring tension as engine speed increases. This motion of the weights turns the cam assembly so that the breaker cam is rotated in the direction of shaft rotation to an advanced position with respect to the distributor drive shaft. The higher the engine speed, the more the weights throw out and the further the breaker cam is advanced. (See Fig. 2-6.)

The centrifugal advance required varies considerably between various engine models. In order to determine the advance for a given engine, the engine is operated on a dynamometer at various speeds with a wide-open throttle. Spark advance is varied at each speed until the range of advance that gives maximum power is found. The cam assembly, weights, and springs are then selected to give this advance. Timing, consequently, varies from no advance at idle to full advance at high engine speed where the weights reach the outer limits of their travel.

Vacuum Advance

Under part-throttle operation a high vacuum develops in the intake manifold and a smaller amount of air and gasoline enters the cylinder. Under these conditions, additional spark advance (over and above advance provided by the centrifugal advance

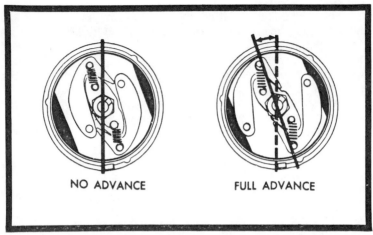

NO ADVANCE   FULL ADVANCE

Fig. 2-6. Centrifugal advance mechanism. (Courtesy Chevrolet Motor Div. of General Motors Corp.)

mechanism) will increase fuel economy. In order to realize maximum power, ignition must take place still earlier in the cycle.

To provide a spark advance based on intake manifold vacuum conditions, many distributors are equipped with a vacuum advance mechanism. The mechanism has a spring-loaded diaphragm connected by linkage to the distributor. The spring-loaded side of the diaphragm is air-tight, and is connected in many cases by a vacuum passage to an opening in the carburetor. (See Fig. 2-7.) This opening is on the atmospheric side of the throttle when the throttle is in the idling position. In this position, there is no vacuum in the passage.

When the throttle is partly opened, it swings past the opening of the vacuum passage. Intake manifold vacuum then can draw air from the air-tight chamber in the vacuum advance mechanism and this causes the diaphragm to be moved against the spring. This motion is transmitted by linkage to the distributor breaker assembly; rotation is governed by the amount of vacuum in the intake manifold up to the limit imposed by the design of the vacuum advance mechanism.

When the distributor breaker plate assembly is rotated, the contact points are carried around the breaker cam to an advanced position; the breaker cam contacts the rubbing block and closes and opens the points earlier in the cycle. This provides a spark advance based on the amount of vacuum in the intake manifold. Thus, for varying compressions in the cylinder the spark advance will vary, permitting greater economy of engine operation. It should be recognized that the additional advance provided by vacuum control is effective in providing additional economy only on *part-throttle* operation.

At any particular engine speed there will be a certain definite advance resulting from operation of the centrifugal advance mechanism, plus a possible additional advance resulting from operation of the vacuum advance mechanism. For example, an initial timing advance of 5 degrees, plus a centrifugal advance of 10 degrees, makes a total of 15 degrees advance at 40 miles an hour. If the throttle is only partly opened, an additional vacuum advance of up to 15 degrees more may be obtained, making a total of 30 degrees. When the throttle is wide open there is no appreciable vacuum in the intake manifold, so this additional advance will not be obtained. All advance then is based on engine speed alone and is supplied by the centrifugal advance mechanism.

The vacuum advance mechanism is a device which will increase fuel economy when properly used. The driver who drives with wide-open throttle whether in low or high gear will not obtain this increased fuel economy.

Cam Angle

The cam angle, often referred to as contact angle or dwell angle, is the number of degrees of cam rotation during which the distributor contact points remain closed. (See Fig. 2-8.) It is during this period of cam rotation that the current in the primary winding increases. Although the cam angle may not change, the length of time the contacts remain closed becomes less and less as the engine speed increases. At higher engine

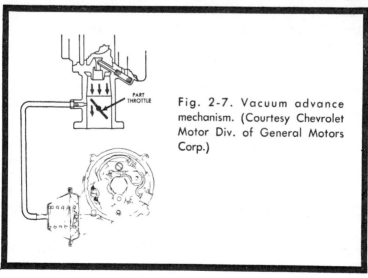

Fig. 2-7. Vacuum advance mechanism. (Courtesy Chevrolet Motor Div. of General Motors Corp.)

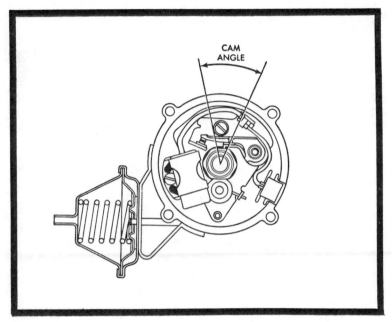

Fig. 2-8. Cam angle. (Courtesy Chevrolet Motor Div. of General Motors Corp.)

speeds, the ignition coil primary current does not reach its maximum value in the short length of time the contacts are closed. In order to store the maximum amount of energy obtainable from the coil, and consequently obtain sufficient energy to fire the plug, a breaker lever assembly is necessary that will operate properly at high speeds. The distributor is equipped with a special high-rate-of-break cam and a special high-speed breaker lever which is capable of following the cam shape at high speeds without bouncing. The high-rate-of-break cam separates the contact points faster for each degree of rotation and permits closing earlier, thus increasing cam angle. With the special cam and breaker lever combination it is possible to obtain the maximum cam angle and consequently optimum ignition performance at high speeds.

The point opening is the maximum distance that occurs between the separated contacts as the cam rotates. If the cam angle is properly set, the points will most likely also open according to specifications. In some cases, it may be necessary to measure point opening in addition to cam angle to insure that the contacts are properly set. A feeler gage for new contacts, or a dial indicator for used contacts, may be used to measure point opening.

Ignition Condenser (Capacitor)

The capacitor consists of a roll of two layers of thin metal foil separated by a thin sheet or sheets of insulating material (Fig. 2-9). This assembly is sealed in a metal can with a flat spring washer providing a tight seal.

The high voltage induced in the coil primary causes the capacitor plates to charge when the contacts first separate; the capacitor acts initially like a short circuit and current flows into the capacitor to minimize arcing at the contacts.

Ignition Coil

An ignition coil is a pulse transformer that steps up the low voltage from the battery or generator to a voltage high enough to ionize the spark plug gap and ignite the air—fuel mixture in the cylinder. A typical coil is made up of a primary winding, consisting of a few hundred turns of relatively large wire, and a secondary winding, consisting of many thousands of turns of very small wire (Fig. 2-10). These windings are assembled over a soft iron core and are enclosed by a soft iron shell. This assembly is inserted into a one-piece steel or diecast aluminum coil case, which is filled with oil and hermetically sealed by a coil cap made of molded insulating material. The cap contains the primary and secondary high voltage terminals.

Ignition coils are hermetically sealed to prevent the entrance of moisture, which would cause coil failure. During manufacture, the coil case also is filled with oil at a high temperature. As the oil temperature decreases to more nearly match the temperature of the surrounding air, the oil contracts to occupy less volume thus allowing room for expansion when the coil heats up during normal operation. The oil acts as an insulator to prevent high voltage arc-over within the coil.

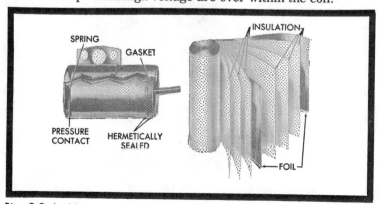

Fig. 2-9. Ignition capacitor. (Courtesy Chevrolet Motor Div. of General Motors Corp.)

In the design of an ignition system, sufficient primary circuit resistance must be present to protect the distributor contacts from excessive arcing or burning. In some ignition systems, part of this resistance may take the form of a separate resistor or a calibrated resistance wire connected between the ignition switch and the coil primary terminal.

During cranking, most external resistances are bypassed to provide full battery voltage to the coil for improved performance and easier starting. The higher currents developed during cranking are not sufficient to cause distributor contact deterioration because of the short periods of time spent during cranking. Also, the lowered battery voltage during cranking causes a lower primary current, so the resistor bypass feature is an offsetting factor. Bypassing the resistor with the engine

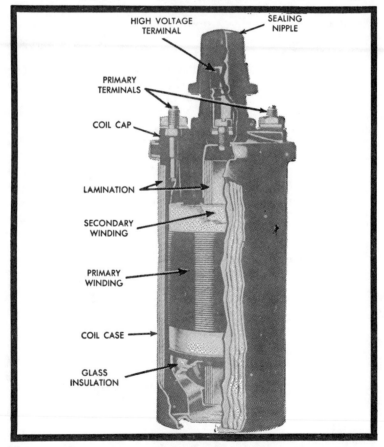

Fig. 2-10. Ignition coil. (Courtesy Chevrolet Motor Div. of General Motors Corp.)

operating will cause very rapid failure of the distributor contacts.

ADVANTAGES OF THE SOLID-STATE IGNITION

Listed below are the performance characteristics of the solid-state ignition as compared to the conventional ignition system. Take a moment to study the figures.

Ignition Systems	Spark Plug Voltage	
	Start (10V) at 200 rpm	Run (14V) at 800 rpm
Solid-State Ignition	32,000	26,000
Conventional Ignition	26,000	25,000

As you have noticed, there is considerably higher spark plug voltage for improved cold weather starting with the solid-state ignition system than with the conventional type of ignition. And there are other major advantages:

1. Parts replacement on a scheduled maintenance basis is not required...except for the spark plugs. Breaker points used in conventional ignition systems are generally replaced on a scheduled basis.
2. With solid-state ignition, the timing *does not* change (once set correctly) with mileage. Unless a malfunction occurs or the distributor is removed and replaced, the initial ignition timing remains constant.

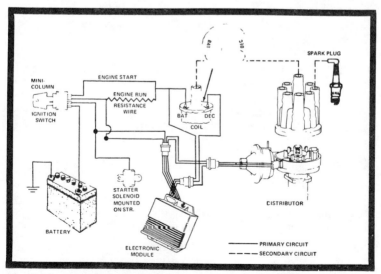

Fig. 2-11. A solid-state ignition system. (Courtesy Ford Customer Service Div.)

In a conventional ignition system, the rubbing block of the movable contact breaker point gradually wears (the gap decreases), regardless of the high polish of the cam lobes. Thus, ignition timing retards as dwell increases.

SOLID-STATE IGNITION SYSTEMS

In this system (Fig. 2-11), two components have been removed; namely, the capacitor and the distributor point set. Yet, both the solid-state and the breaker-type ignition systems retain the distributor rotor, a conventional-type ignition coil, the distributor. The stoppage of current flow in the ignition coil primary windings causes its magnetic field to collapse. This electrical action induces a surge of high-voltage current in the coil's secondary windings, which in turn is delivered to the spark plugs in the correct order and at the precise time needed for firing the mixture in the combustion chamber most efficiently. Timing circuitry in the electronic module senses when the coil has fired and then redirects electric current to the primary circuit of the coil. The dwell varies with engine speed. This is *normal* and cannot be altered, thus any measurement is meaningless.

Inside the module there are electronic components and circuitry which sense when the coil has fired and then redirect electric current to the primary circuit of the coil in order to repeat the firing process.

In other words, this action is similar to what happens when the points close and open in the conventional breaker-point type of distributor.

Although the ignition coil for a solid-state system is similar to that of the conventional system, there are two items worth mentioning: The tower terminal is labeled BAT for battery and the other is labeled BAT for distributor electronic control; the use of any other ignition coil with the Ford solid-state ignition system will cause the ignition system to malfunction, and possibly damage the electronic devices.

Solid-State Ignition Parts

Having discussed the basics of the solid-state ignition system and how it works, let's take a closer look at the parts that make up this new system and compare them with a conventional distributor. Note the exploded view in Fig. 2-12.

- Both the solid-state distributor and the breaker-point distributor are mounted and driven in the same way.
- The magnetic pickup (stator) assembly which provides the signal to the control module contains a permanent magnet.

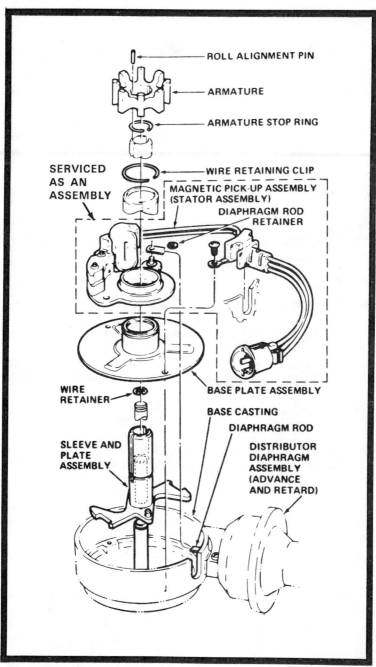

ROLL ALIGNMENT PIN

ARMATURE

ARMATURE STOP RING

WIRE RETAINING CLIP

SERVICED AS AN ASSEMBLY

MAGNETIC PICK-UP ASSEMBLY (STATOR ASSEMBLY)

DIAPHRAGM ROD RETAINER

WIRE RETAINER

BASE PLATE ASSEMBLY

BASE CASTING

DIAPHRAGM ROD

SLEEVE AND PLATE ASSEMBLY

DISTRIBUTOR DIAPHRAGM ASSEMBLY (ADVANCE AND RETARD)

Fig. 2-12. The distributor used in a solid-state ignition system. (Courtesy Ford Customer Service Div.)

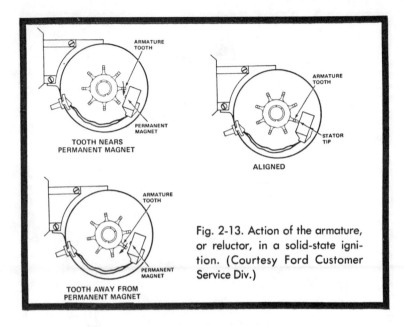

Fig. 2-13. Action of the armature, or reluctor, in a solid-state ignition. (Courtesy Ford Customer Service Div.)

Also, part of the stator assembly is a pickup coil with many windings of fine wire.

- The armature is mounted on the sleeve and plate assembly. It has the same number of teeth as there are cylinders in the engine.
- High voltage from the coil to the spark plugs is directed through the distributor in the same way as in a conventional ignition system. Also, automatic advance or retard of the spark is controlled in the same way as in a conventional system. However, instead of moving the breaker-point plate, the plate for the magnetic pickup coil is moved.

Note that there has been no change in the shaft, gear, weights, springs, cap, and rotor. They are the same design for both solid-state and conventional ignition systems.

How the Solid State Distributor Works

The breaker cam has been replaced with an armature resembling a rimless wheel with spokes or "teeth." As each tooth of the armature nears the permanent magnet, an electrical signal is generated in the pickup coil. Note Fig. 2-13A, which shows a top view of a solid-state distributor for a V-8 engine.

As each tooth of the armature moves away from the permanent magnet, an electrical signal of opposite polarity is generated in the pickup coil. Note in B that the armature tooth has rotated past the permanent magnet. As the armature tooth nears the permanent magnet and moves away (as the distributor shaft rotates), the signals generated go from positive to negative; however, when the armature tooth and the stator tip are in alignment, the signal is zero—between positive and negative. (See Fig. 2-13C.)

Whenever the armature tooth and the stator tip are in alignment, this zero signal tells the control module to turn off, producing the same effect in the coil primary circuit as the opening and closing of contacts in a conventional ignition system; it "breaks" the primary circuit.

The sudden stoppage of current in the ignition coil primary windings causes the magnetic field to collapse, thus inducing a high voltage in the coil secondary windings.

This high voltage surge is delivered to the correct spark plug (the one ready to fire) by the distributor rotor, cap, and high-tension wiring (exactly as it happens in a distributor using contact points).

Inside the electronic module is a timing circuit that turns the primary circuit on again to engage the coil for the next spark cycle. This can be compared to "dwell" in a conventional ignition system.

Note that there is no change in the operation of the secondary or high-tension portion of the ignition system.

Electronic Amplifier Module

In order to fire the spark plug, it is necessary to induce a high voltage in the igntion coil secondary winding by opening the circuit to the coil primary winding. In conventional systems, this is accomplished by opening the distributor contact points. In a typical electronic ignition system, this is accomplished in a different way.

When the switch is closed, and the engine not running, current flows through a part of the circuit as shown in Fig. 2-14A.

The current can be traced from the battery through the switch and resistor R7 to the amplifier. Current then flows through transistors TR1 and TR2, resistors R1, R2, and R5, and the coil primary winding and resistor R8 to ground, thus completing the circuit back to the battery. It is important to note that under this condition, full current flows through the coil primary winding, and capacitor C1 is charged with the positive voltage towards transistor TR2.

When the engine is running, the vanes on the rotating iron core in the distributor line up with the internal teeth on the pole

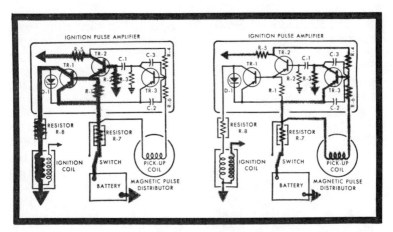

Fig. 2-14. Operation of an ignition pulse amplifier. In A, the switch is on but the engine is not running; in B, the engine is running. (Courtesy Chevrolet Motor Div. of General Motors Corp.)

piece. This establishes a magnetic path through the center of the pickup coil, causing a voltage to be induced in the pickup coil. This voltage causes transistor TR3 to conduct, resulting in current flow in the circuit as shown in Fig. 2-14B.

The charge on capacitor C1 causes transistor TR2 to turn off, which in turn causes transistor TR1 to turn off. This interrupts the circuit to the ignition coil primary winding, and the high voltage needed to fire the spark plug is induced in the coil secondary winding. These current flow conditions are shown in Fig. 2-14B.

The current flow conditions shown exist until the charge on capacitor C1 has been dissipated through resistor R2. When this happens, the system reverts back to the current flow conditions shown in Fig. 2-14A. The system is then ready to fire the next spark plug.

Resistor R1 is a biasing resistor that allows transistor TR1 to operate. Resistor R4 is called a *feedback* resistor, and its purpose is to turn TR3 off when TR2 returns to the *on* condition. Zener diode D1 protects transistor TR1 from high voltages which may be induced in the coil primary winding. Capacitors C2 and C3 protect transistor TR3 from high voltages which appear in the system. Resistor R6 protects transistor TR3 from excessive current in case the pickup coil circuit is grounded.

Chevrolet High-Energy Ignition

Beginning January 1974, a new high-energy ignition (HEI) system was introduced on certain high-powered Chevrolet models.

The HEI system consists of a completely different distributor assembly that combines all the ignition components into one solid-state electronic unit (Fig. 2-15). The distributor housing encloses the vacuum and centrifugal advance mechanisms, electronic module, pickup coil and pole piece, timer core, capacitor, rotor, and distributor shaft (Fig. 2-16). The distributor cap houses the ignition coil and distributes secondary voltage to the spark plugs Fig. 2-16).

A convenient tachometer connection is incorporated in the wiring connector on the side of the distributor. However, due to its transistorized design, the HEI system will not activate some models of engine tachometers.

The tachometer terminal on the distributor cap must never be grounded (Fig. 2-15). This could damage the electronic circuitry of the module. When making compression checks, disconnect the ignition switch connector from the HEI system.

The spark plug wiring used with the HEI system is a carbon impregnated fiber-glass conductor encased in an 8 mm diameter silicone rubber jacket. The silicone wiring is capable of withstanding very high temperatures and also provides an excellent insulator for the higher voltage produced by the HEI system. The silicone spark plug boots form a tight seal on the plug and should be twisted ½ turn before removing. Care should also be exercised when connecting a timing light or other test

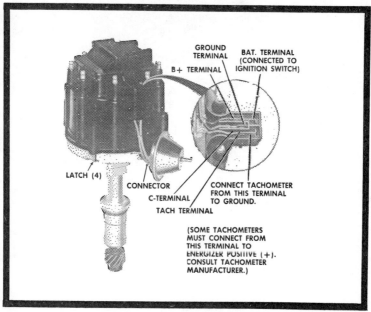

Fig. 2-15. Chevrolet HEI distributor.

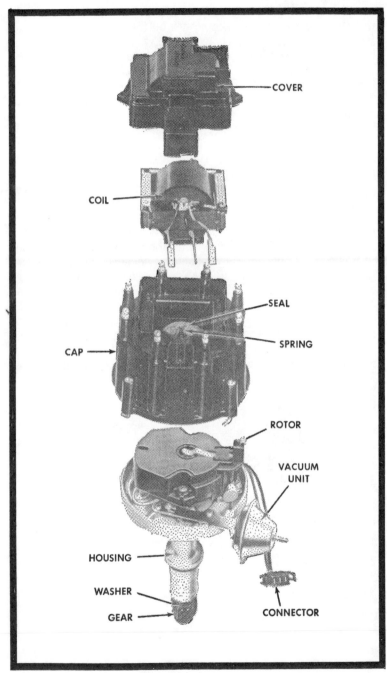

COVER

COIL

SEAL

SPRING

CAP

ROTOR

VACUUM UNIT

HOUSING

WASHER

GEAR

CONNECTOR

Fig. 2-16. Exploded view of Chevrolet's HEI distributor.

equipment. Do not force contacts between the boot and wiring, or through the silicone jacket. Connections should be made in parallel using an adapter. Spark plug changes, plug gapping, and maintenance intervals remain the same as with the standard breaker-point ignition system.

Like the Ford system, the HEI ignition is magnetically controlled; its theory of operation, therefore, is the same.

CONVERSION KIT

Hays Ignition Systems of Irvine, California, offers a transistorized magnetic-pulse kit, called the S-6, that is used to convert stock distributors to breakerless operation. The kit is designed to provide a precisely timed spark at engine speeds up to 10,000 rpm. At startup, the unit delivers an impulse of up to 40,000V, with a spark duration that is about 40 times as long as that of the average CD (capacitive discharge) system. This longer spark insures complete combustion for lower emissions and more power.

Hays' S-6 kit can be installed in a stock distributor in less than 30 minutes. On some cars, it's not even necessary to remove the distributor. To make the conversion, the stock points and capacitor are removed and discarded (Fig. 2-17). An adapter mounting plate and a precisely machined iron pole piece is slipped over the stock distributor cam. The pole piece provides 45 degrees of spacing between the firing impulses, with an accuracy unobtainable with the stock distributor cam. Next the pickup is adjusted to a 0.008—0.010 in. clearance between it and the pole piece. This about completes the conversion. None of the vacuum or centrifugal advance mechanisms is altered. All that's left is to slip the rotor and cap back in place and mount the transistorized switching module on the firewall. The module is only slightly bigger than a pack of cigarettes.

Versatility is an important feature of these kits. For example, there are only two basic kits for all Ford distributors and only one kit for all Delco (General Motors) units. Therefore, the owner can keep the kit for his new car when he trades the old one in, if it's the same make.

CAPACITIVE DISCHARGE IGNITION

Capacitive discharge (CD) ignitions are somewhat different in theory, and produce different results than magnetically controlled electronic ignitions. Magnetically controlled ignitions produce a long-lasting spark that produces relatively complete combustion and low emissions. The CD ignitions produce a short-lived high voltage (40,000V or more) impulse capable of firing spark plugs under difficult conditions—even when plugs

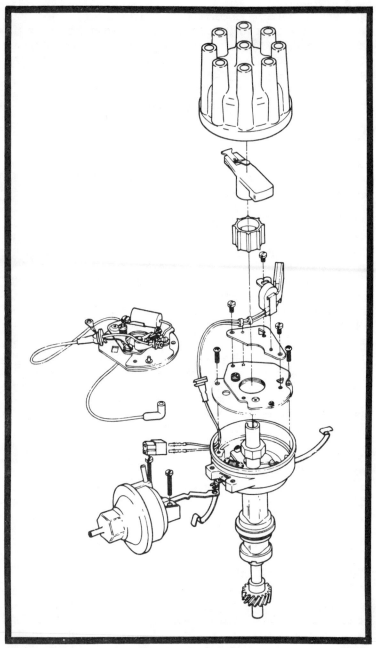

Fig. 2-17. Hays solid-state ignition conversion kit. (Courtesy Hays Ignitions Systems.)

are fouled. Most kit-type electronic ignitions are CD units. An important characteristic of a CD system is that the distributor points are retained to control the ignition. However, since the points carry less current in CD systems, they encounter fewer problems.

These ignitions often employ a kind of electronic switch not discussed so far—the SCR.

The SCR

The SCR, like the transistor, is a solid-state device. It provides a current path that consists of a solid material—silicon. In fact, the full name of this device is *silicon controlled rectifier*. Its schematic symbol is shown in Fig. 2-18A.

SCRs are similar to transistors in that they have three terminals and can act as switches.

The SCR as an element in a simple circuit is shown schematically in Fig. 2-18B. What we have here is actually two circuits in one. There is a high-power circuit consisting of the source battery and load, plus the anode and cathode of the SCR. There is a low-power control circuit consisting of the switch, gate battery, and the gate and cathode parts of the SCR.

The source battery in Fig. 2-18 is connected in the proper polarity to cause electrons to flow from the cathode to the anode of the SCR and through the complete high-power circuit. (A load is any useful device that consumes power.) However, the battery voltage would have to exceed a certain value—the

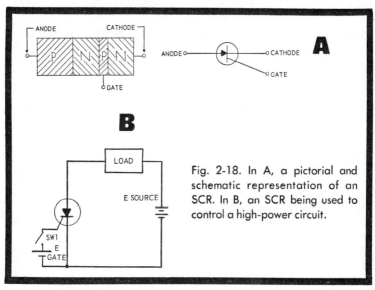

Fig. 2-18. In A, a pictorial and schematic representation of an SCR. In B, an SCR being used to control a high-power circuit.

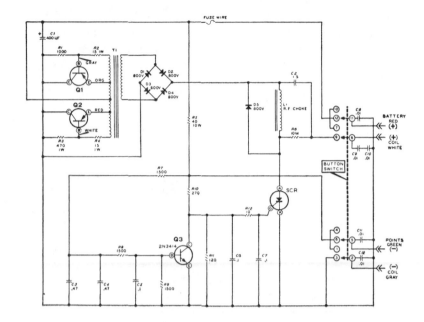

Fig. 2-19. Schematic of a CD ignition system. (Courtesy Heath Co.)

breakdown voltage of the SCR—for conduction to take place. A battery is chosen with a voltage *below* this value, and conduction would never exceed a small value except for the action of the SCR gate. When the switch is closed and the gate voltage is applied to the SCR gate, the breakdown voltage of the SCR is lowered. Now the source voltage is large enough for the SCR to conduct, completing the high-power circuit. Since the gate circuit consumes little power, the SCR permits a low-power circuit to switch on a high-power circuit.

The SCR, once turned on, is hard to turn off. The gate loses control, so that merely opening the switch is not enough to turn off the SCR. The SCR can be turned off if the polarity (direction) of the *source* voltage is reversed; that is what happens in a CD ignition system.

CD Ignition Kit

The schematic of a Heath CP1060 kit-type ignition system is shown in Fig. 2-19. This circuit exemplifies CD ignitions. When the ignition switch is turned on and the points are closed, the nominal 12V dc supplied from the vehicle battery is applied to the converter circuit. This circuit consists of the primary winding of transformer T1 and transistors Q1 and Q2. The battery voltage causes a current flow through two paths resistance. One path consists of resistors R1 and R2, and the other path consists of resistors R3 and R4. Because the combined resistance of R3 and R4 is less than the combined resistance of R1 and R2, a slightly larger current flows in the lower half of the primary winding of T1 than in its upper half.

Since the lower half of the primary winding carries a slightly higher current than does its upper half, voltages are developed that tend to increase the conduction of transistor Q2, while at the same time decrease the conduction of transistor Q1. This action tends to reinforce the original current imbalance, and results in voltages that further drive Q2 into conduction and Q1 into cutoff.

Transistor Q2 remains in conduction, with transistor Q1 cut off, until current through the power half of the primary winding can no longer increase. This reduces the voltage supplied to transistor Q2 and causes it to reduce conduction. At the same time, the collapsing magnetic field of the transformer develops voltages that are of opposite polarity to the original voltages. These opposite polarity voltages bring transistor Q1 into conduction and, at the same time, drive transistor Q2 into cutoff. Capacitor C1 is used to filter out noise transients before they reach the converter circuit.

The alternate conduction of transistors Q1 and Q2 convert the 12V dc to an alternating signal of approximately 400V at the secondary of transformer T1. The diode bridge (diodes D1 through D4) changes the alternating signal to a dc potential of about 400V, which causes capacitor D2 to charge through the engine's ignition coil. During this same time, battery voltage is applied through resistor R5 to the points. Capacitors C6 and C7, along with resistor R12, serve as a filter to prevent false triggering of the SCR by any random voltage variations.

As the first cylinder comes up on compression and reaches the position where its spark plug should fire, the points open. At this time, the voltage through R10 and R12 turns the SCR on and short-circuits the power supply. The effect of this short circuit is reflected to the primary of T1, where it removes the drive from transistors Q1 and Q2 and stops the converter operation. The SCR also connects the positive side of capacitor C2 to the negative ignition coil connection and thus forms a closed circuit consisting of C2, the SCR, and the primary winding of the ignition coil. This connection allows capacitor C2 to deliver its stored charge to the ignition coil and causes the voltage in its primary winding to rise from zero to some 400V in approximately 2 microseconds.

In the closed circuit made up of capacitor C2, the SCR, and the primary winding of the ignition coil, a resonant tank circuit

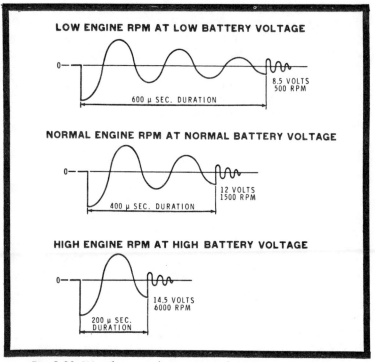

Fig. 2-20. Waveforms at the ignition coil. (Courtesy Heath Co.)

is formed between the primary winding and the capacitor. As capacitor C2 delivers its stored charge through the SCR to winding of the ingition coil, it creates a magnetic field within the coil. This field, representing stored energy, collapses when C2 reaches a zero charge, thus maintaining current through the primary winding of the ignition coil in the same direction is before. This current continues to flow in the circuit until C2 is charged in a reverse direction to approximately 300V. At this point, the current attempts to reverse and causes the SCR to turn off. The reverse voltage causes the diode bridge to conduct as a short circuit and discharges capacitor C2 back to zero from its reverse charge, and continues charging it to near its original voltage. This transfer of energy between the primary winding of the ignition coil and capacitor C2 continues until transistor Q3 is caused to turn on. Diode D5 and the rf choke are used to control the turn-on characteristics of the SCR.

The turn-on characteristics of transistor Q3 are determined by capacitors C3 and C4. Resistors R7, R8, and R9 form a voltage divider that allow C3 and C4 to charge to about 6V. At low engine speed, or low battery voltage, these capacitors must charge for a longer period of time before they can reach the voltage necessary to turn on Q3. Under these conditions, Q3 remains cut off to allow capacitor C2 to deliver its full energy to the ignition coil. At high engine speeds, or high battery voltage, these capacitors retain some residual charge that enables them to reach the turn-on voltage of Q3 sooner, thus lowering the overall amount of energy delivered to the ignition coil. Figure 2-20 shows a comparison of waveforms at the positive (+) side of the coil for different engine speeds and battery voltages. Capacitor C5 serves to prevent any erratic triggering of transistor Q3.

TROUBLESHOOTING THE SOLID-STATE SYSTEM

Before beginning any elaborate test procedures, make sure there are no loose, corroded, or disconnected terminals at the ignition coil, and make repairs as necessary. If you find that the engine is still not operating properly, look for loose electrical connections at the distributor.

If the engine is still not operating properly, loose, damaged or corroded connectors at the electronic control module may be the problem. The location of this module varies depending on the car model and engine. Make certain that all connectors are snug and tight; repair or replace as necessary.

If the engine still does not perform as it should, check the spark intensity at the coil by disconnecting the coil high-tension wire from the center of the distributor tower and holding it ¼ inch away from a good ground at the engine while it's cranking. You should get a good fat spark jumping the gap regularly.

If you've had no success thus far, make the following secondary ignition tests:

- Check spark intensity at each spark plug.
- Check resistance of spark plug wires where the real spark appears.
- If the spark is weak or intermittent, check the ignition coil. Commonly used test equipment will do the job.
- Check the distributor cap for cracks, hairline fractures, moisture, or any signs of damage.

Caution: When making the spark intensity test on Ford ignitions, never pull the 1st or 5th spark plug wires on six-cylinder engines. On eight-cylinder engines, never pull the 1st or 8th spark plug wires. Doing so may cause arcing within the distributor.

The secondary circuit in a solid-state ignition system is exactly the same as that in a conventional ignition system. Thus, all secondary tests are performed exactly the same way.

If you find any faulty secondary ignition system parts or bad high-tension wiring, make the necessary repairs or

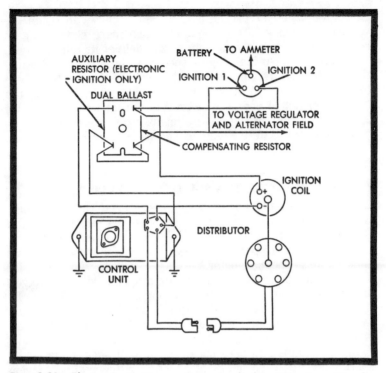

Fig. 2-21. Electronic ignition system—6-cylinder. (Courtesy Chrysler Corp.)

replacements. If the secondary circuit checks out properly, then the engine condition is not the fault of the ignition system.

If at this point the engine still fails to function properly, proceed to pinpoint the suspected difficulty in the ignition system using the tests recommended by the auto manufacturer. Chrysler Corp. specifies the use of a special tester for checking their electronic ignitions. The electronic ignition systems of Ford and Chevrolet, however, may be checked using an ordinary voltmeter or ohmmeter.

Chrysler Electronic Ignition Tester

Figure 2-21 presents the circuit diagram of the Chrysler electronic ignition system. The 6-cylinder model is shown. The diagram of the 8-cylinder model is identical except, of course, for the fact that it has more distributor terminals.

The Chrysler electronic ignition tester is shown in Fig. 2-22. Looking at the tester, you see two rows of lights, a circuit breaker, and a high-voltage *test* switch. The top row of lights are red and the lower row are green.

When the tester is used (for bench or vehicle tests) the green light indicating "ignition input voltage" must light as soon as the connections are complete. This light must be on before any other light can be red, because it indicates that system input voltage is high enough for the system to operate. Using the tester, one may check the overall system or its specific components.

To check the electronic ignition system, the vehicle must mave a good battery (12V minimum). This is necessary for the tester to give reliable results.

With the ignition switch off, remove the screw from the harness lead on the electronic control unit and disconnect the lead. Connect the female tester lead to the control unit and the male tester lead to the system control unit lead. This puts the tester in the vehicle ignition circuit.

Turn the ignition switch on. If the green *ignition input voltage* light does not come on, check the light with a battery known to be good. Then check the vehicle battery, ignition switch, and the associated wiring until the fault is found and corrected. If the green lights are both on and all red lights are off, this indicates a good system.

Disconnect the ignition coil secondary wire from the distributor cap tower and, while holding the end of the wire and ¼ inch from the engine, actuate the high voltage coil *test* switch. A good spark should be observed between the wire and the engine. While still holding the coil *test* switch, pull the wire away from the engine until the spark stops. Closely observe the coil tower to be sure that no arcing occurs at this time. This

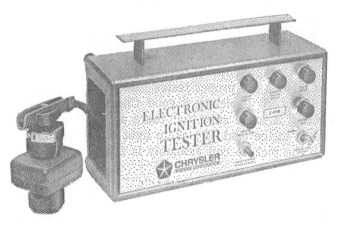

Fig. 2-22. Electronic ignition tester with adapter. (Courtesy Chrysler Corp.)

completes the testing of a good system. Proceed further only if the following trouble indications are obtained.

If the *ignition input voltage* and *pickup circuit* lights are both on, check the pickup connectors and wiring. If the *pickup circuit* light remains on, replace the pickup coil. The tester checks the resistance of the pickup coil circuit, and under these circumstances, indicates that the coil is shorted or open.

If the *ignition input voltage* and *primary circuit* lights are both on, check the coil primary for an open circuit, the suppression capacitor for a short, the dual ballast resistor for an open, and the wiring harness for an open or incorrect connection. The tester checks the voltage at the negative side of the coil.

If the *ignition input voltage* light is on and the *control unit* light is off, check the control unit for a good ground. If the light remains off, check the wiring and, if need be, replace the control unit. If the control unit is shorted, the circuit breaker will pop to protect the tester. Wait 30 seconds before attempting to reset an open circuit breaker.

A number of component tests may be made with the tester. Connect the tester clips to a fully charged battery (red clip to positive terminal) and the *ignition input, voltage* light will come on if the battery is okay.

With the ignition control unit removed from the vehicle, it may be tested with the tester as explained below. Only the *ignition input voltage* and *control unit* lights apply to this test—disregard any red lights that may appear. Connect the control unit test lead to the control unit; a *control unit* light on at this time indicates a good control unit. If the *control unit* light remains off, check all connector pins for corrosion and security, and check all plug holes to be sure they are clean. If the *control unit* light is still off, the control unit is bad.

The pickup coil may be tested while assembled in a distributor, or as a separate unit. Disregard all other lights on the tester except the *ignition input circuit* and *pickup circuit* lights. Connect the clip leads to the battery and connect the pickup lead to the proper tester lead. The red *pickup* light will be off if the pickup is good. Check the pickup lead by flexing it to be sure that there are no intermittent faults in the lead. If the *pickup* light blinks or stays on during the flexing, the pickup coil assembly is faulty and must be rejected.

Testing the Ford Solid-State Ignition

Ford's solid-state ignition system can be checked using a voltmeter and ohmmeter. Other requirements are a well charged vehicle battery and three jumper wires: two jumper

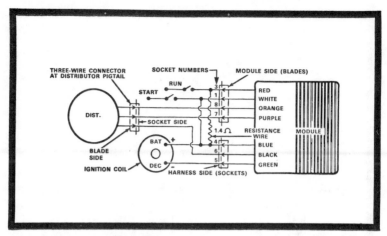

Fig. 2-23. Parts and wiring of the Motorcraft solid-state ignition. (Courtesy Ford Customer Service Div.)

	TEST VOLTAGE BETWEEN	SHOULD BE "HARNESS SIDE"	TEST BEING MADE
KEY ON	Socket #3 and Engine Ground	Battery Voltage ± 0.1V	Module Bias Test (Power to Operate)
	Socket #5 and Engine Ground	Battery Voltage ± 0.1V	Battery Source Test
CRANKING	Socket #1 and Engine Ground	8 to 12 volts	Cranking Test
	Socket #5 and Engine Ground	8 to 12 volts	Starting Circuit Test
	Socket #7 and Socket #8	Any D.C. volt wiggle or ½ volt A.C. min.	Distributor Hardware Test

	TEST RESISTANCE BETWEEN	SHOULD BE	TEST BEING MADE
KEY OFF	Socket #7 and Socket #8 Socket #6 and Engine Ground Socket #7 and Engine Ground Socket #8 and Engine Ground	400 to 800 ohms 0 ohms more than 70,000 ohms more than 70,000 ohms	Magnetic Pick-up (Stator) Test
	Socket #3 and Coil Tower Socket #5 and Socket #4	7000 to 13000 ohms 1.0 to 2.0 ohms	Coil Test
	Socket #5 and Engine Ground	more than 4.0 ohms	Short Test
	Socket #3 and Socket #4	1.0 to 2.0 ohms	Resistance Wire Test

Fig. 2-24. Testing the Motorcraft ignition. (Courtesy Ford Customer Service Div.)

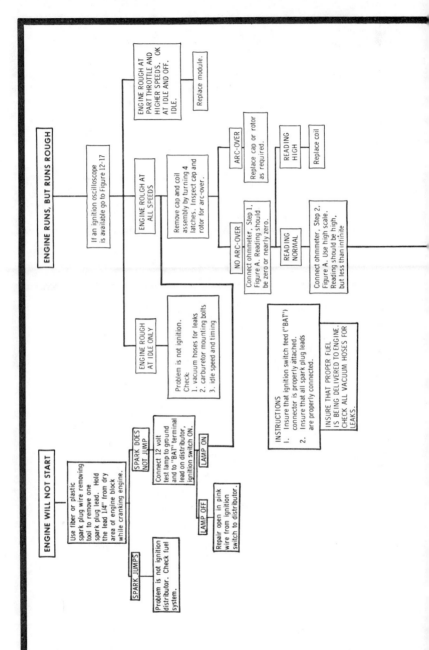

ENGINE RUNS, BUT RUNS ROUGH

If an ignition oscilloscope is available go to Figure 12-17

ENGINE ROUGH AT PART THROTTLE AND HIGHER SPEEDS. OK AT IDLE AND OFF. IDLE.

Replace module.

ENGINE ROUGH AT ALL SPEEDS

Remove cap and coil assembly by turning 4 latches. Inspect cap and rotor for arc-over.

NO ARC-OVER

Connect ohmmeter, Step 1, Figure A. Reading should be zero or nearly zero.

READING NORMAL

Connect ohmmeter, Step 2, Figure A. Reading should be high, but less than infinite

READING HIGH

Replace coil

ARC-OVER

Replace cap or rotor as required.

ENGINE ROUGH AT IDLE ONLY

Problem is not ignition. Check:
1. vacuum hoses for leaks
2. carburetor mounting bolts
3. Idle speed and timing

INSTRUCTIONS
1. Insure that ignition switch feed ("BAT") connector is properly attached.
2. Insure that all spark plug leads are properly connected.

INSURE THAT PROPER FUEL IS BEING DELIVERED TO ENGINE. CHECK ALL VACUUM HOSES FOR LEAKS.

ENGINE WILL NOT START

Use fiber or plastic spark plug wire removing tool to remove one spark plug lead. Hold the lead 1/4" from dry area of engine block while cranking engine.

SPARK DOES NOT JUMP

Connect 12 volt test lamp to ground and to "BAT" terminal lead on distributor, ignition switch ON.

LAMP ON

LAMP OFF

Repair open in pink wire from ignition switch to distributor.

SPARK JUMPS

Problem is not ignition distributor. Check fuel system.

Fig. 2-25. Diagnosing the HEI system with an ohmmeter. (Courtesy Chevrolet Motor Div. of General Motors Corp.)

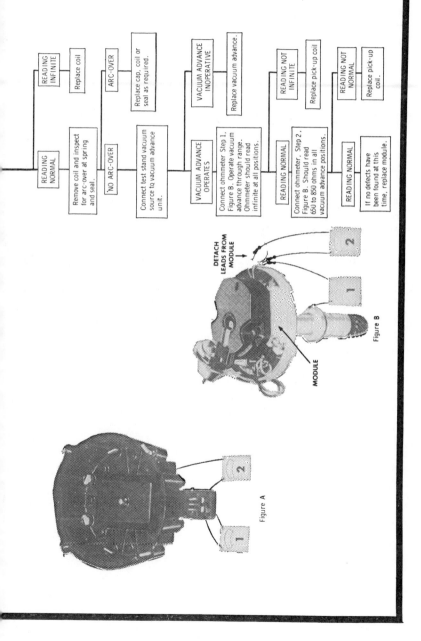

Figure A

Figure B

wires approximately 6 in. long with blade ends (to match the ignition system wiring harness) and one jumper approximately 12 in. long with alligator clips.

The Ford solid-state ignition module and its connectors are shown in Fig. 2-23. The tests are made on the harness side of the 3-wire and 4-wire connectors coming from the module—the socket side. Tests of the distributor are made on the distributor side of the 3-wire pigtail connector, which is the blade side (Fig. 2-23).

Figure 2-24 shows the voltage and resistance tests to be made on the Ford ignition. In the drawing, the color codes next to each socket number indicate the color of the wires coming from the module to the *blade* side of the connectors, although the harness side is illustrated.

Testing the Chevrolet HEI System

The Chevrolet HEI system described earlier may be tested with an ohmmeter as shown in Fig. 2-25. The programed troubleshooting chart is designed to help you find any defect in the HEI system with a minimum of time and effort, provided that you follow the chart carefully. Note that there are two starting points on the chart, one for an engine that won't start and one for an engine that runs rough.

Before using the chart, there are a few preliminary checks to make. Insure that the ignition switch feed connector (labeled BAT) is properly attached. Be sure that all spark plug leads are properly connected, and check to see that proper fuel is being delivered to the engine.

Safety Group

Although auto makers have been slow in applying electronics technology to their cars, state and federal laws are forcing them to consider many new uses for electronics. Safety is an area in which new demands are being made of auto makers. Aside from the electronic charging system, the only electronic system offered as standard equipment on all domestic cars is the seat-belt interlock system; this system makes it virtually impossible to start a car without first fastening the seat belts.

IMPROVED BELT SYSTEM

All 1974 cars are equipped with a passenger restraint system which includes an improved belt system with automatic locking retractors and a starter interlock system. This system was developed to comply with federal Motor Vehicle Safety Standard 208 (MVSS 208).

Starter Interlock: Function and Components

The starter interlock system, a federal requirement, is standard equipment on all 1974 automobiles. The interlock allows the driver to start the engine only after all front seat occupants are seated with their restraint harnesses fastened.*

The operation of the starter interlock depends upon input to an *interlock control unit* from the ignition switch, the gear selector, and other switches located in the front door pillars, in the seats, and in the seat-belt buckles.

The interlock control unit, heart of the interlock system, is mounted under the instrument panel (Fig. 3-1), fully enclosed in a plastic case.

Inside the plastic case is a circuit board capable of receiving and interpreting signals from eleven different sensing switches. An electronic circuit, located on the circuit board, is responsible for the actual "interpretation" of switch input. It is made up of numerous *logic gates* fabricated inside a tiny plastic

*Cars built after January 31, 1975, will not have seat-belt interlocks. It is legal to disconnect the interlocks in 1974 and early 1975 models.

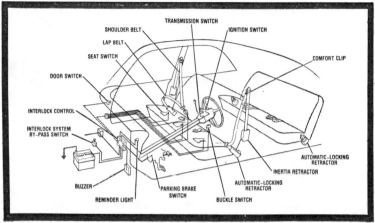

Fig. 3-1. Restraint system with interlock. (Courtesy Chrysler Corp.)

package; it is this integrated circuit, with its "minicomputer" characteristics, that governs the operation of the control unit.

To start any car equipped with this system, a specific starting sequence must be followed:

1. Assume a seated position in the car.
2. Buckle the seat belt and shoulder harness.
3. Turn the ignition key and start the engine.

The starting sequence must be followed because the various switches in the car each signal the control unit which allows or prevents starting. When passengers sit down, seat switches close to start the interlock sequence (Fig. 3-2). The seat switches are of two types because of their particular application. The left and right front slider-type switches are attached to the seat springs. The center front seat switch is a *pressure* type made up of two contact strips separated by a foam pad. This switch is mounted just beneath the upholstery covering.

The slider-type switches are sensitive to deflection over a wide area to be sure that they close when someone sits anywhere in the outboard positions; the center switch senses deflection in a more restricted area. This switch helps to prevent false signals to the interlock control due to seat deflection in the outboard seating positions.

Switches in the front seat belt buckles close when the buckle connectors are inserted, sending signals to the interlock control. If the buckle connector is not inserted, or if it is inserted before the passenger sits down, the interlock will not allow the starter to operate. The belt switches no longer directly control the warning system as they did in the past.

Once the sit and buckle sequence has been completed and the doors closed, the domelight ground circuit provides an "antisquirm" feature. While the doors remain closed, and the driver and passengers remain buckled, they may lift off the seat or move around as in reaching for brief cases or into the glove compartment without causing a "no-start" condition.

If the engine should stall, it is possible to restart so long as the driver remains seated, with belts fastened or unfastened, provided the ignition is not turned off.

Reminder System

A warning buzzer and FASTEN SEAT BELTS reminder light operate in conjuction with the restraint and interlock system.

The reminder system will operate if the ignition key is turned to the START position when any or all of the belts in the occupied front seat positions have not been fastened.

When the engine is running, the reminder system will operate if any front seat occupant unfastens his seat belt after the transmission is shifted into any forward or reverse gear (automatic transmission), or after the parking brake is released in cars with manual transmission.

The "antisquirm" feature mentioned above also prevents operation of the reminder system as long as the driver and front passengers remain buckled.

Under certain circumstances, the reminder system also operates for a short period of time when a front seat passenger leaves the car. Suppose, for example, the car is stopped at the curb and the transmission is in gear and the engine is running. When the right front passenger leaves the car, the warning system will operate for about two seconds. In earlier cars the warning system ceased to operate as soon as the passenger left the seat cushion.

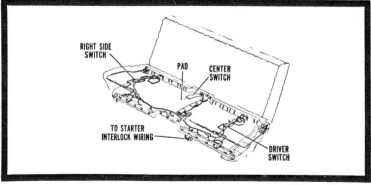

Fig. 3-2. Starter interlock system seat switches. (Courtesy Chrysler Corp.)

The Interlock Bypass Switch

In the event the interlock system should malfunction, the car may still be started and moved. An interlock bypass switch is located inside the engine compartment. This switch, in intermediate and full size cars, contains two sets of contacts for two separate circuits, both of which are normally held open by a mechanical blocker. Pushing and releasing the red button on the switch brings the bypass circuitry into play by moving the blocker and allowing both circuits to be completed. One set of contacts completes the starter relay circuit and the other set completes a circuit to a small heating element coiled around a bimetal spring strip. The heating coil is connected into the ignition-on circuit.

After the bypass button is pushed and released, the circuit for the starter relay is complete up to the neutral safety switch, (or to the clutch switch, on cars with manual transmission). At this point, starting can be accomplished in the normal manner, without recycling the bypass switch.

When the ignition is on, the heating element warms the bimetal spring, causing it to bend and hold the bypass and heater contacts closed. When the ignition is turned off, the circuit to the heating element is interrupted. As a result, the bimetal strip cools, the contacts open, and the blocker moves in the hold the contacts open. When the switch is cooling, it is often possible to restart the engine if the ignition switch is turned off for a short time. But if the switch has cooled, the button will have to be pressed again to reactivate the bypass system.

In some cars, the bypass switch is different. To use it, the ignition switch must be on before the bypass button is pushed. Depressing the button on the switch requires the use of a pencil, pen, or other small-diameter object because the button is encircled by a metal tube. Once the switch is pushed, the car may be started, driven, and stopped in the normal manner—with one important exception: the bypass switch deactivates immediately when the ignition is turned off.

This typical interlock system, used by Chrysler Corp., is convenient to use and unobtrusive in appearance. It fulfills the requirements of MVSS 208 and it includes engineered extras, such as the "antisquirm" feature and the emergency bypass switch.

LOGIC CIRCUITS

This section contains a detailed description of logic circuits. A good understanding of basic logic circuitry adds to one's understanding of the seat-belt interlock control as well as several other automotive units.

Gating Circuits

Formal logic requires that a statement be either true or false; no other condition can exist for the statement. A logic circuit is basically a switch or gate that is either closed or open; no other condition can exist for the circuit. By logical arrangement of these gating circuits, electrical functions can be performed in a predetermined sequence by opening or closing the gates at the proper time.

A single-pole, single-throw switch is equivalent to a binary device with only two possible operating conditions: either opened or closed. If point "C" of Fig. 3-3 is to be made equal to potential V, switches A and B must be closed. It can then be said that A and B = C.

If switches A and B are considered as gates, then potential V is said to be gated to "C" when both gates are closed. By representing the closed state of a switch or gate as "1" and the open state of a switch or gate as "0" then all possible conditions for the AND gate are shown in the truth table in Fig. 3-3.

In Fig. 3-4, if point "C" is made equal to potential V, either switch A or B (or both) may be closed. It can then be said A or B = C. All possible conditions for the OR gate are shown in the truth table in Fig. 3-4.

In gating circuits, the desired state of the gate may be represented by either *1* OR *0*. In this section, 1 will be used to represent a positive potential (approximately +6 volts) and 0 will be used to represent a low potential (near zero volts).

OR Gate

A simple diode OR gate is shown in Fig. 3-5. The same conditions exist in this circuit as the switch gate of Fig. 3-3. Application of a positive potential at *any* of the inputs will result in an output of the same polarity, representing the 1 state.

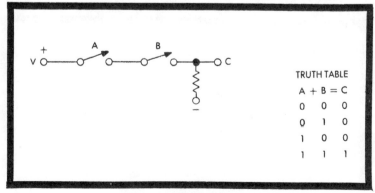

Fig. 3-3. Simple AND gate.

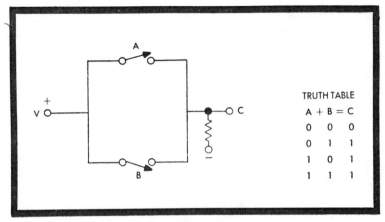

Fig. 3-4. Simple OR gate.

AND Gate

A simple diode AND gate is shown in Fig. 3-6. The same conditions exist in this circuit as in the switch gate of Fig. 3-3. Application of a positive potential to the diodes at *all* inputs will result in a positive potential at the output. This represents the 1 state of the gate.

Application of a positive potential to one or two terminals will result in no potential developed, representing the 0 state of the gate.

NAND Gate

A NAND gate is simply an AND gate with a transistor inverter stage added (see Fig. 3-7). Applying a positive potential to inputs A and B back-biases diodes CR1 and CR2, permitting inverter Q1 to conduct. When conducting, the collector of Q1 drops to near ground potential.

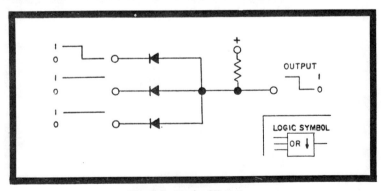

Fig. 3-5. Diode OR gate.

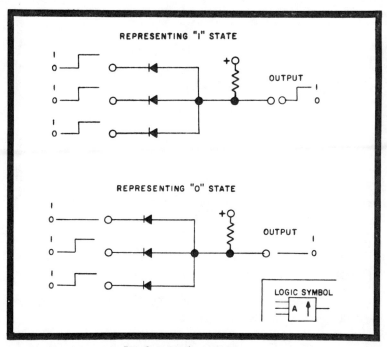

Fig. 3-6. Diode AND gate.

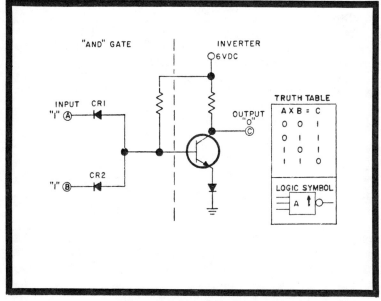

Fig. 3-7. Simplified NAND gate.

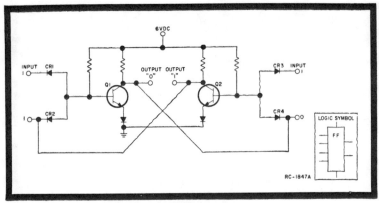

Fig. 3-8. A NAND gate flip-flop.

Flip-Flop

Two NAND gates connected as shown in Fig. 3-8 form a flip-flop (bistable multivibrator).

Assume that a positive potential is applied to all inputs. Momentarily grounding the cathode of CR4 turns off Q2, causing its collector voltage to rise to approximately +6 volts. This turns on Q1, causing its collector voltage to drop near ground potential, keeping Q2 turned off. The flip-flop will remain in this state until CR1 is grounded.

Integrated Circuits

Integrated circuits (ICs) are normally used to perform logic functions. Symbols of ICs are used in wiring diagrams instead of showing each diode, resistor, and transistor in the circuit. The symbols in the wiring diagram are labeled to indicate how each gate is connected and the logic function performed. Circles are used at the input or output of the IC symbol to indicate the circuit functions as an inverter.

INTERLOCK SYSTEM OPERATION

Refer to Fig. 3-9, a diagram of the seat-belt interlock system used by Ford. Let's trace the circuitry starting with the battery circuit (54) that powers the actuator assembly at all times, even when the ignition key is off and no one is in the car.

Note that circuits 32 and 33 to the actuator assembly have been disconnected. On 1974 vehicles, this connection provides the starter interlock circuit through a set of relay contacts inside the actuator. For 1973½, this path was bypassed to have no effect on the ability to start the car.

The seat sensor switch circuits (86 and 150) are normally open When the driver or front outboard passenger sits down, the switch at that position becomes closed. This completes a circuit to ground and signals the actuator of the presence of an occupant.

The next circuit required to be activated is the lap belt retractor switch, circuits 42 and 85. When the occupant extends the belt (14 in. or more) the retractor switch is opened, breaking the circuit to ground and signaling the actuator.

The transmission switch circuit (520) functions as a shutoff switch for the buzzer and warning light circuit (640 and 469) when the transmission shift lever is placed in PARK or NEUTRAL. If the proper sequence has not been followed, the warning light and buzzer will come on when the selector is moved from PARK (or NEUTRAL).

The actuator assembly employs logic circuits to detect the sequence in which seat sensor switches and lap belt retractor switches are activated.

The actuator turns off the warning light and buzzer when the offending condition has been corrected. For example, when the driver or front outboard passenger is seated after the lap belt is extended, the warning will be turned off if the lap belt is returned to a fully retracted position and reextended.

The actuator also incorporates a time delay feature which postpones warnings (for about ten seconds) if weight is lifted

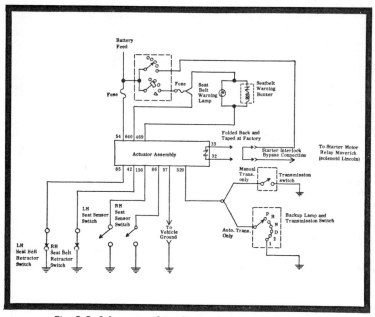

Fig. 3-9. Schematic of Ford's seat-belt interlock system.

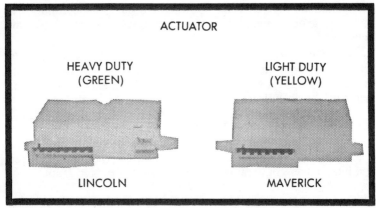

ACTUATOR

HEAVY DUTY (GREEN)

LIGHT DUTY (YELLOW)

LINCOLN

MAVERICK

Fig. 3-10. Actuator assemblies used in interlock systems of Ford Motor Co.

from the seat temporarily (after the proper sequence has been followed).

Seat Sensor Servicing

Seat sensor switches in 1974 models are essentially the same as in 1973, except that to detect the occupancy of all seating locations, the number has been increased on some models. Because of the various designs of seat and cushion thicknesses, both beam- and pressure-type seat sensor switches are used.

Like previous seat sensor installation, beam-type switches are attached to the seat springs. Weight of an occupant on the seat forces the switch to bend. This bending motion causes the top metal band to move laterally and make electrical contact, completing the circuit.

Under certain conditions, the buzzer may continue to operate with no weight on an outboard seating position. When this occurs, it is necessary to reset the seat sensor switch. To do so, apply 50 lb or more weight to the seat cushion (near the center of the passenger seat) to reset the sensor switch.

Pressure-type switches are located in the seat cushion. The weight of an occupant compresses the switch, causing two metal blades to come into contact.

Access to seat sensors requires disconnecting the sensors at the lead-in connector and removal of the front seat.

Actuator Servicing

Two types of actuator assemblies are used on Ford Motor Company passenger cars (Fig. 3-10).

In function and operation, the two types of actuators are identical. The only differences are in load current tolerences and connector construction. For purpose of simplification, one type is called the heavy-duty actuator and the other type the light-duty unit.

The light-duty unit is bright yellow and connects to the wiring assembly with a 14-terminal printed circuit connector and also has a 2-terminal blade connector.

The heavy-duty unit is used with the solenoid-actuator starter, when installed without a starter relay in the Lincoln; the light-duty unit is used in all other installations. The two units must not be interchanged.

Access to the Maverick actuator assembly is obtained by removing the metal bracket which is attached to the bottom of the lower instrument panel just below the radio. The actuator assembly is attached to this bracket with two screws.

Access to the Lincoln actuator assembly necessitates removing the glove box. The actuator is attached to the right-hand side of the glove box with two screws. (see Fig. 3-11).

AUTOMATIC HEADLIGHT BEAM CHANGER

The automatic beam changer is a control unit which senses the light intensity from approaching vehicles and automatically adjusts the headlights to a high or low beam. Chrysler's *Sentinal* system is illustrated in Fig. 3-12.

A driver-operated sensitivity control is coaxial with the headlamp switch (see Fig. 3-12). Rotating the knob clockwise increases sensitivity and headlights will switch to low beam when an approaching car is relatively far away. Rotating the knob counterclockwise toward the word OFF produces the opposite effect. The extreme counterclockwise position of the

Fig. 3-11. Location of the actuator in Lincoln models.

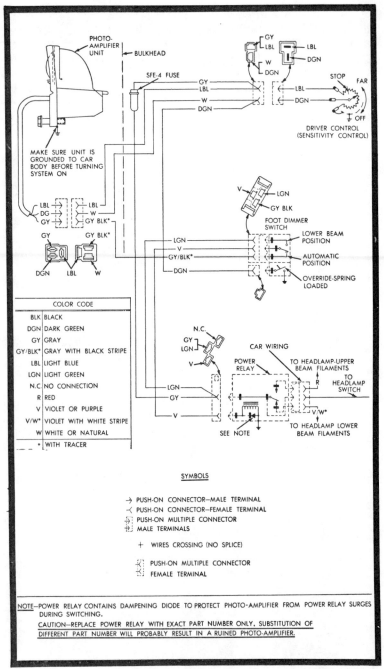

Fig. 3-12. Headlamp beam changer schematic. (Courtesy Chrysler Corp.)

control is an off position and gives manual control of the headlight beams by means of the foot switch.

The photoamplifier unit contains a light sensing optical device and a transistorized amplifier with sufficient power to operate a relay for switching headlight beams. The unit is mounted under the hood just ahead of the radiator cradle assembly. A leveling assembly for use in setting correct vertical aim is part of the unit. (Do not disturb the factory calibration of level).

The power relay is a single-pole, double-throw 12-volt unit which switches the headlight beams. The upper beam position is the *normally closed* position. The power relay is mounted on the front floor pan just above the combination dimmer—override type foot switch mounted on the conventional dimmer switch location.

The override foot switch replaces the standard foot dimmer switch. One position of the override foot switch provides automatic control of the headlight beams. The other position provides low beam only.

In the automatic position, partially depressing the foot switch provides an overriding high beam as long as the switch is held in this position. Automatic operation is restored when the driver releases the foot switch.

An in-line 4A fuse is also incorporated into the wire harness. If this fuse should blow, the circuit will revert to manual control of the headlight beams by means of the foot switch.

Servicing the Beam Changer

Place the vehicle in a well lighted area. Start the engine and operate at fast idle (Note: this transistorized unit does not require a warmup). Troubleshoot the wiring, foot switch, driver sensitivity control, and power relay with a 12V battery and test lamp equipped with a No. 53 bulb (one candlepower). The test procedures must be performed in the sequence as outlined below:

(1) Set the sensitivity control knob to approximate center of its rotation.

(2) Turn the headlight switch on; headlights should remain on lower beam in both positions of the foot dimmer switch. If not, see step 1.

(3) Depress foot switch slightly. If high beams come on, the switch is in the AUTOMATIC position. If high beams do not come on, completely depress and release foot switch to put it in AUTOMATIC position. Depressing foot switch slightly should cause lights to switch to high beam. If not, see step 2.

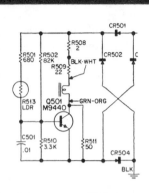

Fig. 3-13. Photoamplifier using an LDR.

(4) With the foot switch in the AUTOMATIC position, cover the photoamplifier with a black cloth; headlights should switch to high beam. If not, see step 3.

(5) Remove the black cloth from the photoamplifier; headlights should return to low beam. If not, see step 4.

(6) With headlights on AUTOMATIC lower beam, rotate driver control counterclockwise to off; headlights should switch to high beam. If not, see step 5.

(7) Fully depress foot switch to the manual position; headlights should switch to low beam. If not, see step 6.

Photoamplifier Circuit

An example of a photoamplifier circuit is given in Fig. 3-13. This circuit uses a kind of photocell called an *LDR*. The LDR, or light dependent resistor (R513), is mounted behind a lens in the hooded photoamplifier unit, which is aimed so the light from the headlights of an oncoming car impinges on the LDR. The unit is aimed so that the light acts on the LDR at the proper time for the headlights to be switched from high to low beam.

When the headlight switch is on, transistor Q501 conducts. Its collector current flows through the relay coil. The LDR, which is part of the base-biasing circuit for Q501, controls the base current flowing into the transistor. Consequently, the current passing through the relay coil is inversely related to the resistance of the LDR (less LDR resistance means more coil current).

The resistance of the LDR is controlled by the amount of light striking it. The resistance of the LDR decreases as the light intensity increases. When the light from an oncoming car strikes the LDR and causes its resistance to drop, the collector current of Q501 is increased to a high level, and the relay is actuated by the heavy current through its coil. This completes the circuit of headlamp lower beam filaments. After the car passes, the LDR resistance increases, the base and collector currents of Q501 decrease, and the relay is released. This "makes" the circuit of the headlamp high-beam filaments.

AUTOMATIC LIGHTING SYSTEM—CHRYSLER CORP.

The Safeguard Sentinel Lighting System is a light-sensing device that automatically controls the use of the driving lights after the ignition key is turned on. The system automatically activates the taillights and the headlights when the light intensity outside the car requires road illumination. If light intensity reaches a point (selected by the driver with the sensitivity control located on the photocell), when the lights are no longer needed, the Sentinel turns them off. In periods of darkness, the headlights and taillights will remain on and the backup lights will come on for a period of from one to three minutes after the ignition key is turned off, depending on the desired setting of the time delay control switch. The system can be disconnected at any time by turning the knob to OFF. Use of the driving lights is then controlled by the headlight switch.

Three units control the system. The time control switch is coaxial with the headlamp switch. Turning the knob on activates the system. The headlight switch remains turned off. Rotating the control knob clockwise increases the period of time the driving lights remain on after the ignition key is turned off.

A photocell, mounted on the top left side of the instrument panel pad, may be adjusted by the driver to automatically determine when the light outside the car makes it necessary to use the driving lights. Turning the control clockwise decreases the light sensitivity of the cell. Rotating the knob counterclockwise increases the sensitivity and will turn the lights on earlier.

The amplifier is mounted under the right side of the instrument panel on the heater plenum chamber flange. This unit receives the signals from the photocell and control knob and activates the headlight circuit accordingly. The entire Safeguard circuit is grounded through the time control switch. When the switch is off, a malfunction of any of the Sentinel components cannot interfere with normal operation of headlight switch.

The backup lights will light regardless of the position of the time control switch when the headlight switch is turned on with the ignition key off. They will go out when the ignition key is turned on.

The circuit breaker in the headlight switch protects the headlight circuit during normal manual operation. When the Safeguard time control switch is turned on, the headlight switch is bypassed. Therefore, a second circuit breaker, mounted in the amplifier, protects the headlight circuit.

SEQUENTIAL TURN SIGNAL SYSTEM

The sequential turn signal system of Ford Motor Company's *Cougar* model provides a moving light display to signal the driver's intention to turn.

The sequential turn signal system consists of:

20A fuse in fuse panel.
Turn signal flasher.
Turn signal and hazard indicator switch assembly.
Transistorized sequencer assembly in the luggage compartment.
Two indicator bulbs.
Eight outside lights—two front, six rear.

The electrical feed source originates through the ignition switch, and is routed through a set of contacts on each of the following units:

1. Turn signal flasher—contacts normally closed.
2. Hazard indicator switch—contacts open with switch in OFF position.
3. Turning the ignition switch on energizes the system up to the turn signal switch as described above. When the turn signal switch lever is moved into a turn position, electrical feed is directed to two separate circuits.

Circuit 1 is directed to the transistorized sequencer (Fig. 3-14) and also energizes the front turn signal bulb, and the indicator bulb for the turn selected.

Circuit 2 is directed to the transistorized sequencer, and also energizes the inboard bulb of the three rear lights on the side selected.

With these components energized simultaneously, the sequencer begins to control the electrical feed to the rear lights and thus creates the sequential effect.

The four outside lights on the side selected illuminate in the following order.

The front light and inboard rear light always illuminate first and remain on; the center light of the three rear lights then illuminates and also stays on; then the outboard rear light illuminates. At this point (when the current load routed through the turn signal flasher reaches the four light stage) the contacts on the turn signal flasher open, extinguishing the four outside lights and the turn indicator bulb. The turn signal flasher contacts then close again the cycle repeats itself until the turn signal switch is returned to the neutral position.

The opening and closing of the turn signal flasher contacts causes the flashing effect of the front light and the indicator bulb.

Brake application during a turn will illuminate only the three lights.

During the turn, the sequencer switch electrically separates the affected stoplight circuit from the sequential turn signal cycle.

When one of the eight exterior light bulbs burns out, the three are lighted. They will remain lighted until the turn signal switch is returned to the neutral position. The indicator bulb also remains lighted until the turn signal switch is returned to the neutral position. The indicator bulb also remains lighted until the opening of the turn signal switch.

INTERMITTENT WINDSHIELD WIPER

The continuous operation of the windshield wipers during a long drive in the rain can be monotonous and annoying. An improved system using electronic control is offered on Nissan Motor Company's **Datsun**.

The windshield wiper and washer system consists of a wiper motor, wiper link and arm, washer nozzle, washer tank, washer motor, intermittent amplifier, and wiper switch.

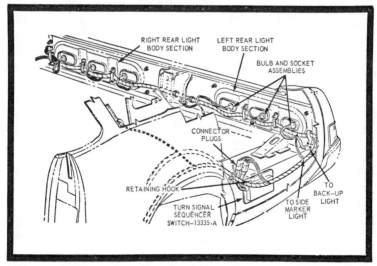

Fig. 3-14. Wiring of Cougar's sequential turn signals. (Courtesy Ford Customer Service Div.)

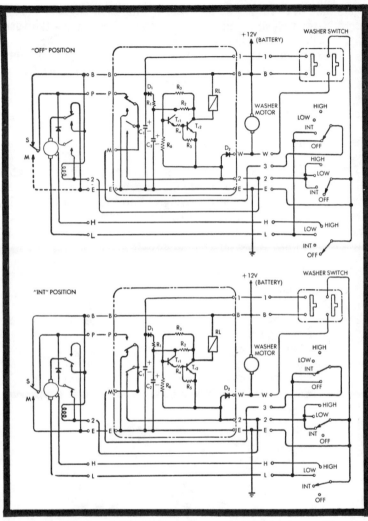

Fig. 3-15. Circuit of Datsun intermittent windshield wipers. (Courtesy Nissan Motor Co.)

This system incorporates a rise-up features; the wiper motor counterrevolves for one turn after switchoff with the aid of a relay, and sequentially, the wiper linkage varies in length to stop the wiper blades at a position below the normal wiping area.

Both the wiper motor and the intermittent amplifier have control contacts (see Fig. 3-15. The motor contacts are closed by the wiper switch, while the amplifier is switched by a self-contained integrated circuit; electric current flowing through the coil (RL) is not powerful enough to switch the contacts in the amplifier.

When capacitor C2 is charged with current flowing through coil RL, the current flowing through coil RL, transistors TR1 and TR2 switch on and current increases. The contacts are then changed.

The amplifier contacts are for bypassing the auto-stop mechanism in the wiper motor; when the amplifier contacts change, the motor begins to rotate. The capacitor discharges as the wiper link rotates one turn and the contacts revert to their original position. The wiper motor then stops with the aid of the auto-stop mechanism.

When the capacitor is recharged, the motor starts again. The wiper motor contacts are for changing rotation direction; i.e., from normal to reverse rotation. When the wiper switch is turned off, the motor counterrevolves and stops. If the washer is in use, capacitors C1 and C2 (charged through the washer motor circuit), change the contacts in the amplifier; the wiper motor thus rotates without stopping automatically.

When the washer motor is stopped, capacitors C1 and C2 begin to discharge; the amplifier contacts revert back to their original positions and the wiper motor is automatically stopped.

HEATED REAR WINDOW SYSTEM

The heated rear window system consists of a series of electrically conductive grid lines baked on the inside of glass, a control switch, and a delay relay (see Fig. 3-16).

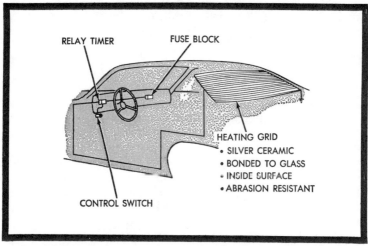

Fig. 3-16. Heated-rear-window system. (Courtesy Chrysler Corp.)

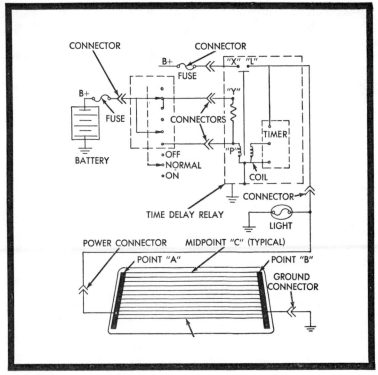

Fig. 3-17. Circuit of heated-rear-window system. (Courtesy Chrysler Corp.)

When the switch is turned on, current is directed to the rear window grid lines. The heated grid lines in turn heat the rear window to clear the surface of the glass.

Time Delay System

The time delay system has an electronic timing circuit in the relay. The timer allows current to flow through the grid system for a specified time and then shuts off. The timer system permits current flow for 3 to 7 minutes.

Control Switch

The rear window heater control is a 3-position switch which is spring-loaded to return from on or off to its center or normal position. The switch connects power from the ignition switch to the internal holding resistor in series with the relay coil (see Fig. 3-17).

When the switch is moved to on, it energizes the relay coil, thereby causing the normally open relay contacts to close and

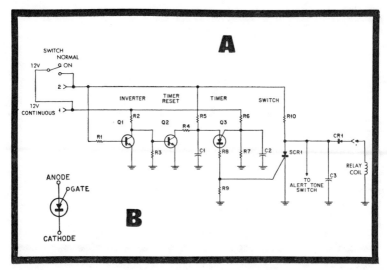

Fig. 3-18. In A, an electronic timer; in B, the symbol for a programmable unijunction transistor.

provide power to the rear window grid and the warning indicator light on the instrument panel. When the switch returns to its normal position, the current provided to the relay through the holding resistor is sufficient to maintain the relay coil energized.

The relay coil will remain energized for 3 to 7 minutes (governed by the timer circuit), or until the switch is turned off.

Electronic Timer

An electronic timer is illustrated in Fig. 3-18. When the switch is closed, forward bias is applied to the base of inverter transistor Q1, turning it on. The collector voltage of Q1 consequently decreases, and the timer reset transistor, Q2, turns off. This allows C1 to begin charging through R5, increasing the anode voltage of programmable unijunction transistor Q3.

A programmable unijunction transistor is actually a diode (Fig. 3-18B), but it will not conduct in the forward direction until ohe voltage on the anode exceeds the voltage applied to the gate by 0.6V. When that point is reached, the programmable unijunction transistor conducts until capacitor C1 is completely discharged. The time it takes for the charge on C1 to exceed the gate voltage by 0.6V is determined by the size of C1 and resistor R5, through which it charges. Component values are selected to provide the 3−7 minute interval. The gate voltage is determined by the divider resistors, R6 and R7.

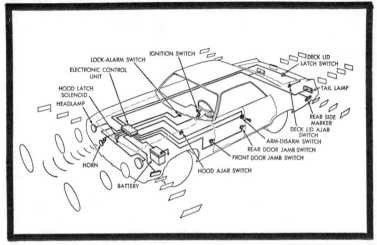

Fig. 3-19. Electronic security alarm system. (Courtesy Chrysler Corp.)

The conduction of Q3 fires SCR1, causing it to conduct and ground the + terminal of the relay coil through CR1. With the coil thus deenergized, the relay contacts open, interrupting current to the rear window grid lines.

Other timing circuits are used in automotive electronics, but the use of a timing capacitor to control the switching of a solid-state device is typical.

SECURITY ALARM SYSTEM

A security alarm system available on Chrysler Corp. cars equipped with power door locks, courtesy lamp switches at all doors, and a power tailgate lock when applicable. An alarm signals intrusion by making the headlamps, taillamps, and side markers flash, and the horn sound, at a cycle rate of approximately 90 times per minute for a 3 to 5 minute duration when the system is armed (Fig. 3-19).

When either front door is locked with the key, the system is armed; unlocking deactivates the system.

Arming the system will lock all doors, the hood, and tailgate. Once the system is armed, forced entry of any door, hood, trunk, or tailgate will set off the system.

The alarm will continue to operate for 3 minutes or until the system is turned off using the door key. The trunk can be opened with the key without activating the armed system.

Operation of Security System

The system is armed and unarmed by normal use of the key in lock cylinders of either front door. The system is not affected by operation of the inside door buttons or door latches. The internal door switches or wiring are not readily accessible from the outside of the vehicle if the lock cylinders are forcibly removed from the doors.

System arming will cause all doors to lock (including tailgate) and power-locking of the hood. Disarming will cause the power hood lock to release and only the door in which the key was inserted will unlock (normal for current power door lock vehicles).

An instrument-panel-mounted switch is provided, which when pushed will cause all doors to lock with power locking of the hood and will cause the alarm to operate for 3 minutes. The panel switch will not arm the control system. After the alarm has operated for the prescribed time, reapplication of the switch will cause the alarm to repeat another 3-minute cycle. The time sequence will start after removal of the input which caused the system to trigger. If the alarm triggering input is not removed, the alarm will continue to operate. The system, when armed, will set off the alarm with forced entry of the doors, hood, trunk, tailgate, or application of voltage to the accessory circuit of the ignition switch. When the alarm is sounding, including excitation initiated by the instrument panel switch, it will stop if the key-operated door switch is turned to the DISARM position.

FORD ANTITHEFT ALARM SYSTEM

The antitheft alarm system (Fig. 3-20) is designed to sound vehicle horns intermittently when a door or trunk is opened, after the system has been armed with the door key. If a door or the trunk lid is opened with the system armed, the horns will blow for approximately 5 minutes.

Once the alarm is activated (horns blowing), closing the door(s) or the trunk lid will not deactivate the system. The horns can only be turned off by inserting the key in the ignition switch and turning it to the accessory or run position. The system can once again be armed by locking either front door with the key and then removing the key from the lock cylinder. The switch in that door is temporarily moved to ON, and the alarm system remains armed even after the switch is returned to its normal position. Care must be taken not to overtravel when rotating the key back to the center position in the lock cylinder. Overtravel (going over the center position) may disarm the system. To disarm the alarm system (before the horns blow), one of the doors must be unlocked with the key.

The hood latch release with this system can only be opened from inside the vehicle, using the trunk key and pulling on the

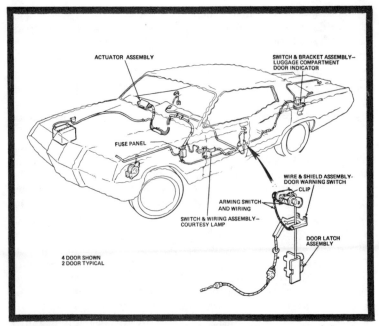

Fig. 3-20. Cable routing of an antitheft system. (Courtesy Ford Customer Service Div.)

hood release handle. A metal shield over the hood latch assembly prevents the hood from being opened from outside the vehicle.

The alarm system has a sensor (warning actuator) mounted to a bracket and is located under the instrument panel pad and above the glove box door (Fig. 3-20). To gain access to the sensor (warning actuator), the instrument panel must be removed. The sensor (actuator) receives its power from the battery and is electrically connected to an arming switch attached to each front door lock cylinder. The switch and retaining clip assembly is serviced separately from the door lock cylinder. The spring clip retainer holds the switch to the lock cylinder; removing the clip separates the switch and lock cylinder assembly. If the switch is separated from the lock cylinder (for any reason) a new switch must be installed.

A trunk lid warning switch and bracket is attached to the left hinge support assembly and senses an open trunk lid. This switch is also programed through the actuator; it operates in conjunction with the right and left side door courtesy lamp switches, and signals the actuator to trigger the alarm system when an intrusion has been made. The system must not be armed while the dome lamp circuit is energized—the horns will blow. The system must be disarmed by unlocking a door with the key before opening the trunk lid.

Diagnosis and Testing

To determine if the alarm system is functioning properly, close all doors (leaving one with the window rolled down). Then, lock that door with the key. Next; unlock the door by lifting up on the door lock button, and open the door. The horns should blow, indicating the alarm system is functioning properly. To disengage the alarm system insert the key in the ignition switch and turn it to the ACCESSORY position.

The actuator is located under the instrument panel pad and above the glove box compartment. Being transistorized, it cannot be tested or repaired.

ANTISKID SYSTEM

Modern brake systems are a vast improvement over those available just a few decades ago. Today all cars are equipped with dual master cylinders. Most have self-adjusting brakes. Many can now be purchased with front wheel disc brakes; four-wheel disc brakes, with their improved performance, may soon become an option or standard equipment. Power brakes are installed on an ever-growing number of automobiles.

With all these advances, there is still the need for driver skill in the application of his brakes. This is especially true in bad weather or in emergency situations. The solution for this problem has been beyond the capability of engineering until very recently.

The new knowledge that engineers have gained in electronics miniaturization and computerization has made a new and exciting advances in braking-safety possible. A new system, popularly known as antiskid (in reality antilock), prevents the wheel lockup that often causes uncontrollable skids.

An optimum antiskid system can be defined as individual, automatic control of each wheel in a manner that produces maximum braking effort under any and all braking and road surface conditions as initiated by the driver. The result will be shorter stopping distances (than the driver could obtain unaided) with retained vehicle lateral stability and steerability.

In essence, an antiskid system takes over command of the vehicle's braking to produce straight, smooth stops in the minimum distance that the vehicle's brake torque can provide. It does this under any and all circumstances, at any time the driver demands maximum deceleration. He need not pump the pedal, or in any other way assist the system.

That is, of course, the optimum. Initially, antiskid systems may fall short of reaching that goal. But as the systems are installed and operated, and more data and experience are gained, the engineers will come closer and closer to achieving it.

Bendix Corp. engineers are now testing an antiskid system that is said to provide the following advantages:

1. Reduce stopping distance by as much as 40% on slick or icy surfaces, and as much as 8% on surfaces affording good traction.
2. Match or reduce stopping distances over locked wheel conditions on normal road surfaces.
3. Maintain steering control ability to enable the driver to manuever during panic stops or on slippery surfaces.
4. Adapt to changes in road/tire friction due to surface or weather conditions.
5. Revert to normal system braking in the event of system failure, and provide suitable warning to the driver that it is out of operation.
6. Cut out automatically at a predetermined low speed to allow normal traffic braking operation.
7. Be completely automatic in operation, requiring no driver retraining or special driver skill.

This system, and ones already in use by Ford and Chrysler, involve three new types of automotive equipment: a speed sensor that measures wheel acceleration; a control center that computes inputs and actuates solenoid valves; and a pressure control circuit, containing a power unit.

Together these parts function to fully control the braking system any time the driver steps on the brake pedal for the maximum braking effort.

MECHANIZATION

The adaptive braking system is a vacuum—electronic system which uses an air—vacuum modulator to supply the information that translates directly into controlled brake-pressure application; an electronic circuit serves as the "brain." Wheel-speed information is supplied by an electromagnetic pickup mounted in the wheel. The pulses, generated by a toothed wheel passing through the magnetic field, are counted in an electronic speed counter. A voltage proportional to wheel speed is then generated and supplied to an amplifier which computes wheel acceleration. This signal is processed in the electronic logic module, and electric pulses are generated to activate solenoid valves in the modulator.

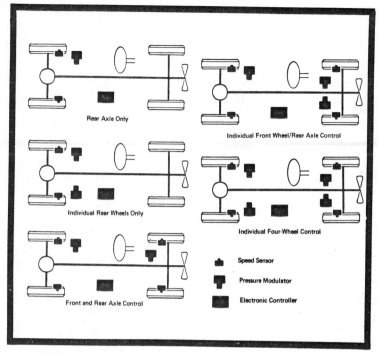

Fig. 3-21. Adaptive-braking configurations. (Courtesy Bendix Corp.)

Configuration

Five configurations for adaptive braking systems on passenger cars are illustrated in Fig. 3-21. Only two of these, rear-axle-only and rear-axle-individual-front-wheel, have been tested to any significant extent.

Rear-axle control is the least expensive method of implementation since only one modulator and one set of electronics are required. Wheel-speed information can be fed to the system from a prop shaft sensor or from individual sensors in each wheel. In the latter case, logic selects which wheel will control the modulator. Since maximum lateral stability is maintained by preventing either wheel from locking, a "select-low" system, with control from the slower-turning wheel, is preferable from the stability viewpoint. On the other hand, a system which selects the higher-speed wheel for control will provide slightly shorter stopping distances under most conditions. Because stability is considered the more important factor, a "select-low" system is favored.

Four-wheel control by rear axle plus individual front modulators results in shorter stopping distances under the

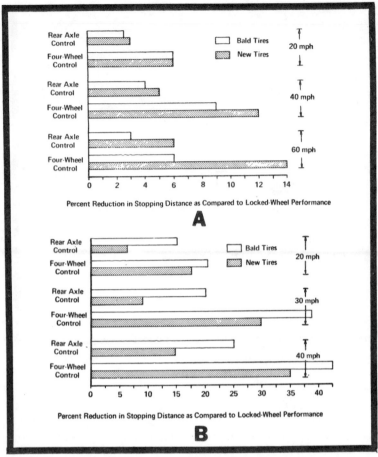

Fig. 3-22. In A, braking improvement on high-coefficient pavement; in B, improvement on low-coefficient (i.e., relatively slick) pavement. (Courtesy Bendix Corp.)

majority of road conditions and also permits steering control. This is used by Chrysler in its *Sure Brake* system.

Component Design

The choice of an air—vacuum modulator as the power source was advantageous in that concepts, materials, and technology could be used from previous vacuum-assisted power brake programs. It also afforded a cost advantage in that much production know-how was available for the manufacture of such devices. Although the design principle for the modulator was established early, a number of studies had to be conducted to determine specific design parameters. Requirements such as frequency response, average and peak power, and total travel (fluid displacement), for example, had to be established for a variety of extreme conditions.

Design of the wheel-speed sensor proved to be a particularly difficult problem because of environment extremes and limited space. An extensive laboratory program was required to establish a tradeoff in geometry that would yield a satisfactory electromagnetic pickup output. Road tests of vehicle installations were used for final evaluation.

Computer time-response studies indicated that acceptable modulator response could not be obtained using any standard-production solenoid valve. Calculations were made, therefore, to determine magnetic force requirements for different solenoid valve configurations. The force available from a solenoid is dependent upon the air gap in the magnetic path, the area of the metal in the conductive path, and the magnetic flux generated—the latter being a function of the number of turns of wire used and the current generated. The current generated is limited by the nominal 12-volt supply available in passenger cars as well as by the resistance of the wire used. As in the case of the speed sensor, a number of solenoid valve designs were fabricated and tested. Primary emphasis was placed on developing a valve with minimum opening and closing times over the voltage and temperature ranges associated with the extreme environmental conditions of an engine compartment.

VERIFICATION

Stopping-distance test data for a rear-axle system and for a four-wheel (rear-axle-plus-individual-front-wheel) system are presented in Fig. 3-22. The results shown are for bald tires and new tires at initial speeds of 20, 40, and 60 mph on the high-speed track and at initial speeds of 20, 30, and 40 mph on the special test surface. All data were taken under simulated panic-stop conditions, where the driver applied the brakes as fast and as hard as possible. At least five stops were made for each set of conditions and the results averaged. The data indicate that improvement is greatest at highest initial speeds; it is greater for new tires than for bald tires on high-traction surfaces but greater for bald tires than for new tires on slippery surfaces. In all cases, the four wheel system achieved a greater percent improvement than the two-wheel system. The four-wheel system also provides steering control and fares better in stops on a curve, on a crowned road, on surfaces with unequal side-to-side friction coefficients, and where avoidance maneuvers are required.

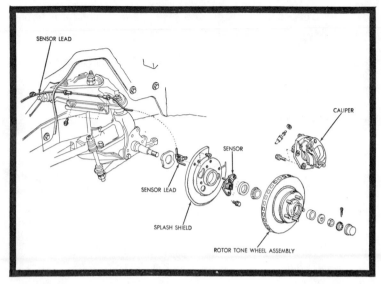

Fig. 3-23. Front-sensor mounting and sensor lead routing. (Courtesy Chrysler Corp.)

CHRYSLER SURE BRAKE

The Sure Brake system is designed to prevent any wheel from locking up during brake applications above a speed of approximately 5 mph. The system reduces the skid potential of a locked wheel and still maintains the brake pressure for maximum stopping effort. The end result is to improve the directional control and steerability of the vehicle, and in many cases, to reduce the distance required to bring the vehicle to a stop.

The major components of the Sure Brake system, shown in Figs. 3-23, 3-24 and 3-25 are:

(1) A mechanically driven speed sensor at each wheel.
(2) A logic controller (LC) located inside the right rear quarter panel.
(3) Three pressure modulators; one modulator is under each front fender ahead of the wheels and one is next to the radiator on the right side of the engine compartment.

Speed Sensors

The speed sensors are mechanically driven electromagnetic devices. Speed sensors used on the rear wheels are a friction-drive type.

The rear-wheel speed sensors consist of a stationary permanent magnet and coil in a case and a tone wheel attached

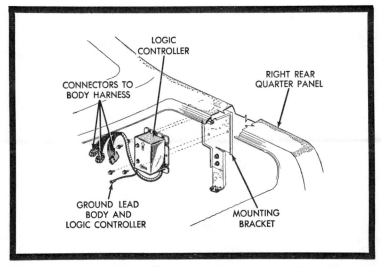

Fig. 3-24. Logic controller mounting. (Courtesy Chrysler Corp.)

to a mounting bracket. A part of the mounting bracket forms a spring to hold the shaft of the tone wheel in contact with a band that is pressed into a drive ring. The drive ring is secured between the axle flange and the drum (by the wheel studs), and rotates with the rear wheel. The clearance between the magnet and the tone wheel teeth is not adjustable.

The front wheel speed sensors are a frictionless-drive type as shown in Fig. 3-23. These sensors also include a stationary permanent magnet and coil in a case which is attached to a

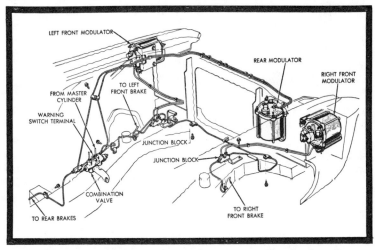

Fig. 3-25. Hydraulic tube routing. (Courtesy Chrysler Corp.)

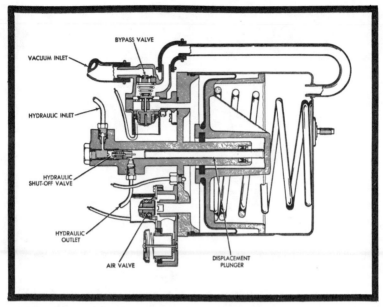

Fig. 3-26. Sure Brake pressure modulator. (Courtesy Chrysler Corp.)

mounting bracket. Instead of the small friction-driven tone wheel used on the rear sensors, however, a large tone wheel is pressed on the hub of the disc brake rotor. The tone wheel rotates with the front wheel. The clearance between the magnet and tone wheel teeth is adjustable.

Pressure Modulators

The Sure Brake system includes three pressure modulators as shown in Fig. 3-25. There is a pressure modulator for each front brake and one pressure modulator for the two rear brakes.

The hydraulic brake tubes are routed as follows (Fig. 3-25):

Front Wheels. From the combination metering proportioning valve outlet port to both front brake modulators; from each modulator to one of the disc brake calipers.

Rear Wheels. From the combination metering proportioning valve outlet port to the rear brake modulator; from the modulator to the wheel cylinders of both rear brakes.

Engine vacuum is made available to each pressure modulator. The intake manifold is connected to the pressure modulators by hoses.

Each pressure modulator (Fig. 3-26) consists of a vacuum chamber, bypass tube, end plate, air valve, bypass valve, and pressure modulator switch.

The pressure modulator vacuum chamber is divided into a front and a rear section by a diaphragm and diaphragm plate in the forward position (against and the end plate). The bypass tube connects the bypass valve to the rear of the vacuum chamber.

The modulator end plate includes a hydraulic cylinder as an integral part of the plate. The cylinder has a port which is connected to the master cylinder and a port connected to the wheel brake. A shutoff valve and a displacement plunger are assembled inside the hydraulic cylinder.

The bypass valve and air valve are attached to the end plate. Both of these valves are solenoid operated. An electrical circuit connects the bypass valve on the rear pressure modulator to an amber light located on the instrument panel.

The pressure modulator switch is a spring-loaded switch screwed into a threaded opening in the end plate. The switch is designed to provide a warning signal under certain abnormal conditions.

Logic Controller

The logic controller (LC) is essentially a small computer and contains various electronic components. The unit (Fig. 3-24) includes the necessary cables and connectors. Electronically, the LC contains three channels, one for each of the three pressure modulators.

Wiring System

The wiring system consists of three separate wiring harnesses plus the leads from the wheel sensors and the pressure modulators. The wiring diagram in Fig. 3-27 shows the harnesses and the other leads that make up the wiring system.

Operation

The wheel sensors do not generate any signals for transmission to the LC when the vehicle is not in motion. In the absence of signals from the wheel sensors, the LC does not send any commands to the pressure modulator.

Engine vacuum is available to the bypass valve on the end plate of the pressure modulator. The bypass valve is open in the absence of a command from the LC and vacuum is admitted to the front and rear sections of the vacuum chamber.

The air valve is closed in the absence of a command from the LC, and no atmospheric pressure is admitted to the front section of the vacuum chamber. Thus, the diaphragm return spring holds the diaphragm plate forward against the end plate.

If the brakes are applied under these conditions, the full hydraulic pressure from the master cylinder passes through the

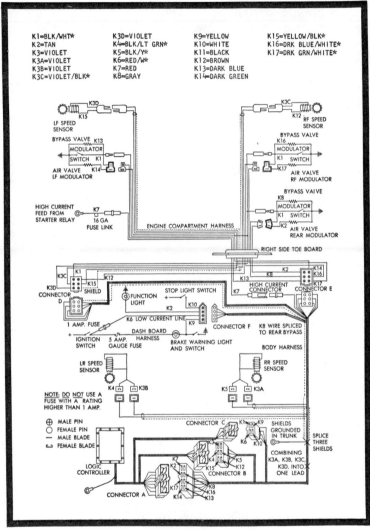

Fig. 3-27. Sure Brake wiring diagram. (Courtesy Chrysler Corp.)

modulator hydraulic cylinders to the calipers and wheel cylinders.

When the vehicle is in motion, an alternating voltage is generated at each wheel sensor and sent to the LC. The frequency of the voltage is directly proportional to the speed of the wheel.

The LC processes the signals received from the wheel sensors to sample the speed of each wheel. If the brakes are not applied or if they are applied lightly, the LC does not send any commands to the pressure modulator.

When the brakes are applied with greater force, the LC, based on the signals received from the wheel sensors, determines the rate at which each wheel is decelerating. If the rate of decelerations is great (at a point that might produce excessive wheel slippage (or wheel lockup), the LC sends a command to the modulator that controls the braking for the wheel or wheels concerned.

The command from the LC does two things at the pressure modulators:

(1) It closes the bypass valve. This shuts off the vacuum to the front section of the vacuum chamber.

(2) It opens the air valve. This permits atmospheric pressure to enter the front section of the vacuum chamber. In addition, the LC rear modulator air valve channel completes an electrical circuit to the amber light on the instrument panel, and the amber light comes on.

With vacuum in the rear section and atmospheric pressure in the front section, a pressure differential is created. The return spring is compressed and the diaphragm and diaphragm plate move slightly to the rear. This permits the displacement plunger to move slightly to the rear. Note: For descriptive purposes, any diaghragm plate movement that compresses the diaphragm return spring is described as *to the rear*, and any movement toward the end plate is described as *forward*.

A slight movement of the displacement plunger to the rear closes the shutoff valve in the hydraulic cylinder. Closing the shutoff valve isolates the calipers or wheel cylinders concerned from master cylinder hydraulic pressure.

The continued movement of the displacement plunger to the rear provides additional space for the brake fluid trapped between the hydraulic shutoff valve and the caliper or wheel cylinders. This permits a small amount of fluid to return from the caliper or wheel cylinders to the modulator, and thus reduces the hydraulic pressure at the caliper or wheel cylinders. With the pressure reduced, the brakes are released, and the wheel speed starts to increase.

The LC, which continuously analyzes the signals received from the wheel sensors, detects the increase in wheel speed. Depending upon the rate of increase in wheel speed, one or both commands (air valve and bypass valve) are removed from the modulator. This, in turn, may accomplish two things:

(1) Close the air valve. This prevents atmosphere from entering the front section of the vacuum chamber.

(2) Open the bypass valve. This makes engine vacuum available to both the front and rear sections of the vacuum chamber.

With vacuum in both the front and rear sections, the diaphragm is balanced in vacuum, and the return spring moves the diaphragm plate forward against the end plate.

The movement of the diaphragm also moves the displacement plunger forward. The forward movement of the plunger decreases the space for the brake fluid trapped between the hydraulic shutoff valve and the caliper or wheel cylinders. This forces fluid back to the caliper or wheel cylinders and thus increases the hydraulic pressure to reapply the brakes. The LC, by controlling the air valve and bypass valve, determines the rate at which the hydraulic pressure increases.

Under some conditions, the displacement plunger may move forward far enough to open the hydraulic shutoff valve. If this happens, the driver may notice a slight drop in the brake pedal.

Each time the rear modulator bypass valve is actuated (closed), the amber light on the instrument panel comes on momentarily to inform the driver that the Sure Brake system is in operation.

At the end of a brake stop, the diaphragm plate and displacement plunger should always move forward far enough to open the hydraulic shutoff valve in the pressure modulator.

Exercise Cycle

If the car engine is started with the brake pedal depressed (stop lights on), the pressure modulators go through two exercise cycles. When the ignition switch is turned to start, all three modulators cycle once, and when the switch returns to on, the modulators cycle again. These cycles are to insure that the system is functioning properly. The cycles can be heard under some conditions (in a garage or a quiet place), but should not be a cause for concern.

Warning System

The Sure Brake system includes a secondary system to warn the driver of certain types of failures in the system. The warning system uses the vehicle's brake warning light to warn the driver that a failure exists.

The warning system will cause the brake warning light to come on under the following conditions:

(1) If the pressure modulator is activated (diaphragm and plate displaced to rear) in the absence of a brake light signal.

(2) If the LC sends a signal to open the air valve on a modulator in the absence of a signal to close the bypass valve.

(3) If the electrical continuity of the air valve wire is broken.

(4) If all speed sensor signals are not received at the LC, or if the signals are not properly converted in the LC at speeds above 15 mph.

Emissions and Performance Group

Recent federal regulations setting limits on the exhaust gas emissions of auto engines have spurred auto makers to explore various means of reducing emissions. Some of them will be discussed in this chapter. There is a relationship between emission control measures and engine performance—unfortunately, it's usually an inverse one. But this chapter will present an electronically controlled system that promises *both* low emissions and good performance—EFI (electronic fuel injection).

VOLKSWAGEN OPEN-LOOP EFI

Volkswagen's electronic fuel injection system—standard in all the company's Type 3 and Type 4 vehicles now built for the U.S.—combines a number of sensors with a compact computer which meters just the right amount of gasoline into an engine at all times.

About the size of a cigar, each computer (Fig. 4-1) contains dozens of transistors, thermistors, resistors, and other electronic components—over 250 in all—to insure proper engine operation under all possible road and load conditions.

When the system was introduced by Volkswagen in 1968, it marked the first time that fuel injection was used as standard equipment on a mass-produced series of cars. Since then it has become standard on some models.

Functions of the Three Systems in EFI

The electronically controlled fuel injection system is made up of three interrelated systems—fuel, air, and electronic control system (Fig. 4-2). The fuel system (1) supplies a pressurized flow of gasoline in sufficient quantity to meet any engine requirement. Excess fuel flows back into the tank through the pressure regulator. The air system (2) controls the flow of air required for proper combustion, and the control system (3) monitors engine load, engine speed, and temperature. This insures injection of only the exact amount of fuel required by the engine at any given time.

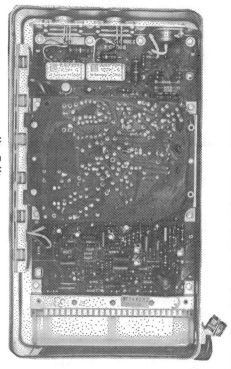

Fig. 4-1. The electronic "heart" of the Volkswagen fuel injection system. (Courtesy Volkswagen of America, Inc.)

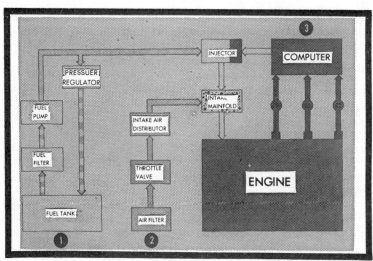

Fig. 4-2. Fuel, air, and electronic control sections of VW fuel injection system. (Courtesy Volkswagen of America, Inc.)

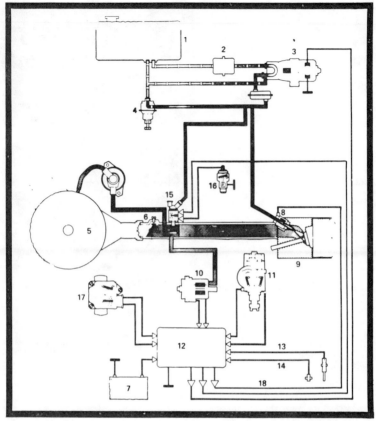

Fig. 4-3. Details of the Volkswagen EFI. (Courtesy Volkswagen of America, Inc.)

This is further illustrated by the more detailed diagram in Fig. 4-3. The fuel system includes the fuel tank, fuel filter, fuel pump, and pressure regulator, numbers 1, 2, 3, and 4 in Fig. 4-3. Main components in the air system are the air cleaner (5) and the intake air distributor (6).

Those two systems are "tied" together by the electronic computer (12) which, based on engine speed, engine load (intake manifold pressure), and engine temperature, controls the amount of fuel to be injected to the cylinders.

When the ignition is switched on, current flows to the computer from the battery (2), and opens the injector valves (8) electrically by a signal transmitted over a connecting wire (18). The amount of fuel injected into each combustion chamber (9) depends upon the length of time the injectors remain open. This, in turn, is determined by the control unit, which processes information fed to it be sensing devices mounted on the engine. "Readings" are transmitted to the computer through a cable harness.

Sensing Devices

Sensing devices used in the VW system include:

- Pressure sensor (10), which controls the basic fuel quantity by measuring intake manifold pressure; it also controls fuel enrichment.
- Temperature sensors (13 and 14), which monitor engine temperature. These control the mixture enrichment during engine warmup period. Cold starting is accomplished by the cold start injector and the cold start temperature sensor (15 and 16).
- Trigger contacts (11), which feed signals into the control unit. These determine when and into which cylinders fuel is to be injected.
- Throttle valve switch (17), which cuts off the fuel supply on deceleration.

Volkswagen EFI Components

The control unit used in Volkswagen's electronic fuel injection fystem constantly calculates the exact amount of fuel to be injected into the engine and transmits the information in the form of electrical impulses of varying length. The control system is illustrated in Fig. 4-4. Helping the computer do its job is the battery (A) which supplies electric power through the current-supply relay (B). Throttle valve switch (C) indicates whether the vehicle is accelerating or coasting. Pressure sensor (D) informs the control unit about engine load. Trigger contacts in the distributor (E) measure engine speed and determine ohe start of injection. Temperature sensors (G and F) control air—fuel mixture and measure engine temperature. All this information helps determine the length of time—varying from 2 to 10 milliseconds that the injectors are to be open each cycle.

The VW air supply system is depicted in Fig. 4-5. Air for Volkswagen's electronic fuel injection engine passes through the air cleaner (1), past the throttle valve (2), and through the intake air distributor (3) to individual cylinders. At idling speed, the fuel injection engine's throttle valve is fully closed and air passes through an idling circuit into the air distributor, as shown. At engine temperatures below 120°F, more air is required and comes through a line leading from the air cleaner to the intake air distributor. An auxiliary air regulator (4) in that line varies the amount of air, meeting requirements which change as engine temperature varies. An automatic choke

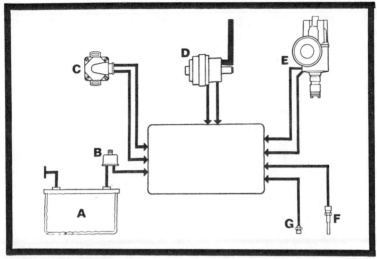

Fig. 4-4. Volkswagen EFI control system. (Courtesy Volkswagen of America, Inc.)

performs this function on engines not equipped with fuel injection.

The air system components are pictured in Fig. 4-6. The principal parts of the air system used in Volkswagen's electronic fuel injection engine are the air cleaner (1); intake

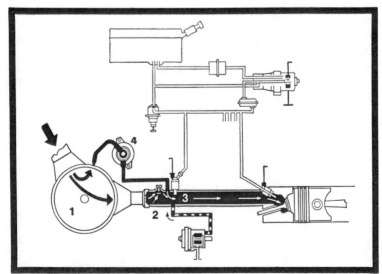

Fig. 4-5. The VW air supply system. (Courtesy Volkswagen of America, Inc.)

Fig. 4-6. Location of the air system components. (Courtesy Volkswagen of America, Inc.)

air distributor (2); intake manifolds (3); which supply air separately to each cylinder; and the auxiliary air regulator (4), which controls the amount of air while the engine is warming up. Engine idling speed is controlled by the idle adjusting screw (arrow).

The VW electronic fuel system injectors are shown in Fig. 4-7. Each of the four injectors in Volkswagen's electronic fuel

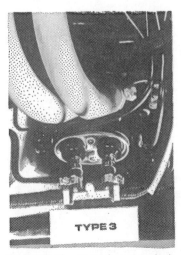
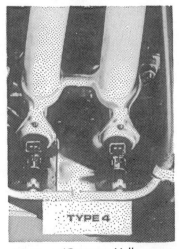

Fig. 4-7. The VW electronic fuel system injectors. (Courtesy Volkswagen of America, Inc.)

Fig. 4-8. Heathkit tachometer model MI-18.

injection system supplies a cylinder with just the right amount of fuel. The injectors open by electrical impulse; the length of the impulse is determined by the computer. Injectors are attached to the intake manifolds at the cylinder heads.

ELECTRONIC TACHOMETER

The Heathkit model MI-18 tachometer (Fig. 4-8) indicates engine speed in rpm (revolutions per minute) with full-scale values of 6000 and 9000 rpm. The model MI-18-1 tachometer is designed to be flush-mounted in a panel or dashboard; the MI-18-2 tachometer is the same, except that a mounting case and base mounting hardware have been added. These tachometers can be used with almost any type of 12V conventional, magneto, transistor, or capacitor-discharge ignition system. The accuracy of the tachometer remains within ±5% over a temperature range of 0°F to 120°F.

In most cases where a tachometer lead is available, you may obtain satisfactory operation by connecting the tachometer directly to this lead. However, a pickup coil and shielded cable are also provided, since not all engines are equipped with a tachometer lead. This pickup coil will give satisfactory results on any spark-type ignition system.

The tachometer is equipped with a built-in lamp which can be connected to the panel lamps of a vehicle. This will allow the tachometer lamp to be dimmed when the panel lamps are dimmed. A calibration circuit is also provided to insure that the tachometer will be accurately calibrated.

TACHOMETER OPERATION

As you read this circuit description, refer to the schematic diagram (Fig. 4-9) for a better understanding of the circuit.

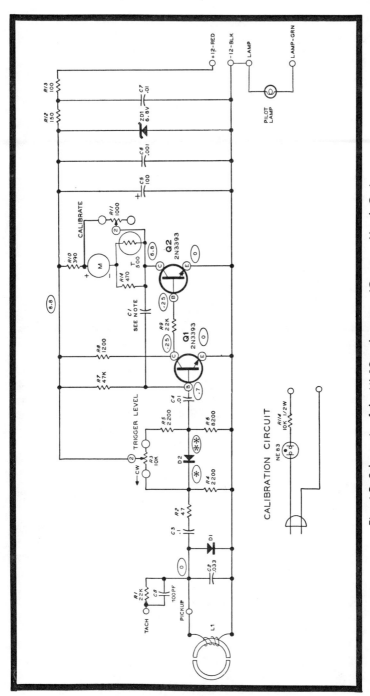

Fig. 4-9. Schematic of the MI-18 tachometer. (Courtesy Heath Co.)

117

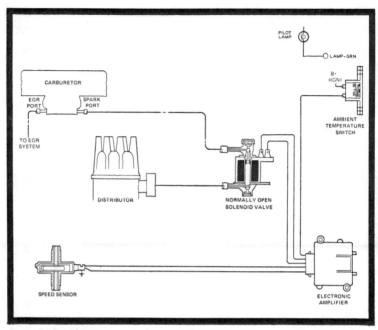

Fig. 4-10. Electronic spark control (ESC). (Courtesy Ford Customer Service Div.)

The tachometer circuit is basically a monostable multivibrator which is triggered by a spark pulse from the engine. The triggering pulse biases transistor Q1 into cutoff, which causes transistor Q2 to conduct. After a time determined by the value of capacitor C1, transistor Q1 again starts to conduct and transistor Q2 is turned off until the next triggering pulse arrives. A meter in the collector circuit of Q2 is calibrated to read collector current in rpm.

Pickup Circuit

Coil L1 forms the secondary of a transformer which wraps around an ignition lead; the ignition leads acts as the primary of the transformer. A pulse of current flowing through the ignition lead induces a voltage into the pickup coil, which is coupled through capacitor C3 and resistor R2 to the cathode of diode D2. The positive portion of the pulse is clamped by diode D1 and the negative pulse is used to trigger the multivibrator.

Triggering control R3; resistors R4, R5, R6; and diode D2 comprise a level-selecting network. As triggering control R3 is adjusted counterclockwise, the reverse bias on diode D2 is decreased until the pulse is strong enough to overcome the reverse bias. At this point, the pulse is coupled through diode D2 and capacitor C4 to the base of transistor Q1.

Multivibrator Circuit

Due to the positive base current supplied through resistor R7, transistor Q1 is normally conducting. This causes a low voltage on the collector of Q1, which prevents any base current from flowing through resistor R9; therefore, transistor Q2 is turned off.

A negative pulse from the engine's ignition momentarily turns transistor Q1 off; this causes the collector voltage of Q1 to increase, which causes transistor Q2 to conduct. At this point, the base of Q1 appears negative with respect to its emitter and Q1 remains cut off. The positive current supplied through resistor R7 begins to charge capacitor C1, which restores the positive voltage at the base of Q1. When this positive voltage is sufficient to cause transistor Q1 to conduct, the multivibrator returns to its normal state again until the next triggering pulse.

When transistor Q2 is conducting, collector current flows through resistor R10, *calibrate* control R11, and the meter circuit, causing the meter to deflect. As engine speed increases, the triggering pulses increase in frequency, causing a corresponding increase in the meter reading.

Calibration Circuit

A 60 Hz alternating current is supplied to the neon lamp. As this current increases on the negative half-cycle, the neon lamp fires and provides a triggering pulse to the multivibrator. The positive pulse from the calibrator circuit is clamped by diode D1.

Thermistor T in the meter circuit decreases in resistance as temperature increases, providing temperature stability for the meter circuit. Zener diode ZD1 provides a constant 6.8V dc supply voltage to the tachometer circuit, while the input supply voltage may vary from 10.5 to 17.5V dc.

ELECTRONIC SPARK CONTROL

The purpose of this system is to make it possible to use considerable spark retard at low vehicle speeds, when power requirements are low, without incurring unacceptable performance penalty at higher vehicle speeds with their higher power demands.

This system (Fig. 4-10) functions as follows: A sensor, which is installed in the speedometer cable, generates a signal that is proportional to vehicle speed. This signal is routed to the electronic module and solenoid vacuum switch assembly, which contains an electronic counting circuit and a solenoid vacuum switch. Part-throttle spark vacuum from the carburetor must pass through the solenoid vacuum switch in order to act upon the distributor diaphragm and advance the spark.

The electronic module is calibrated to switch the vacuum solenoid on and off in a manner which results in no spark vacuum reaching the distributor until the vehicle reaches a predetermined speed between 25 and 40 mph (depending on the vehicle—engine combination). Once the speed is reached, the distributor receives part-throttle spark advance vacuum until the vehicle speed falls below 18 mph, when spark vacuum is cut off again.

Because vehicles require part-throttle spark advance for proper operation at low ambient temperature, a thermal switch is added to the system to provide part-throttle spark advance regardless of vehicle speed.

Radios and Tape Players

The first widespread use of electronics in automobiles was in the form of car radios. Radios still bulk large in the automotive electronics market, but over the past several years they have undergone tremendous changes and have been joined in the passenger compartment by a large and varied array of other products—8-track tape players, digital clocks, solid-state two-way radios, siren—PA systems, etc.

It is impossible to discuss even briefly all of the various types of electronic equipment to be found in the passenger compartments of modern cars. Instead, this chapter will discuss a representative variety of entertainment and related equipment in sufficient detail to provide real help in the selection, use, and maintenance of almost any such equipment.

AM—FM RADIO

A typical factory-installed AM—FM radio is the Chrysler model pictured in Fig. 5-1. The pushbuttons in this model are adjusted in the same familar manner as in standard AM radios.

To operate the radio, the ignition must be on or the switch in the accessory position. The same knob that turns the radio on adjusts the volume. The ring behind the left knob provides tone adjustment. Either AM or FM can be selected by moving the slide switch above the pushbuttons. Station selection is accomplished by pressing the pushbuttons or by turning the

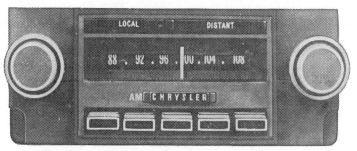

Fig. 5-1. An AM—FM radio. (Courtesy Chyrsler Corp.)

knob at the right. With the *search tune* radio, station selection is accomplished automatically by pressing the bars marked LOC (local) or DIST (distant), or by the foot-operated button located to the left of the brake pedal.

AM Reception

AM is an abbreviation for *amplitude modulation*. In this transmission mode the voice is superimposed upon a carrier signal in such a way as to vary the amplitude or strength of the signal. Due to the carrier frequencies used (550 to 1600 kHz), long range is easily achieved. At night, the signals travel farther than during the day, and station mixing becomes a problem. Many stations are required to go off the air or reduce their power at dusk. The AM radio waves are reflected by the atmosphere providing long-range reception.

AM transmission is subject to noise; absence of noise is only possible when listening to strong stations. Most electrical disturbances will enter an AM radio; weak stations will suffer the most interference.

An *automatic gain control* (agc) circuit, used on AM, responds very well to changes in signal strength and keeps the volume at a constant level. Although radio reception on AM is not generally good when passing under bridges, the agc tends to maintain the volume level.

FM Reception

FM is the abbreviation for *frequency modulation*, which is a method of varying the frequency of a carrier wave in such a manner as to represent the audio signal. The FM band includes the frequencies from 88 to 108 MHz, and each station is assigned a frequency in this band. With no audio signal present, the station is dead-centered on its assigned frequency. When audio information is applied it shifts the frequency slightly from one side to the other of the assigned frequency. The amplitude, or strength, remains constant and only the frequency changes.

Since the operating frequencies are high (88 to 108 MHz), the FM wave is not reflected by, but escapes through the atmosphere. Range is limited due to this fact, as it is with television broadcasts. This type of wave is often called *line of sight*, since the receiver antenna must "see" the transmitting antenna. This is particularly true in "fringe" areas, where the signals are very weak. A building or hill can very easily blank out the FM wave. In metropolitan areas, where the signal is very strong, the waves can bounce off buildings and reception is possible even though the transmitter is not in line-of-sight. In metropolitan areas, reception is possible in tunnels, due to the reflectability of the FM wave, whereas AM reception is impossible.

FM reception is usually noise-free due to the fact that the receiver responds to frequency changes rather than amplitude changes, which can contain noise. This factor alone makes FM reception very desirable. An FM radio will have more noise when not tuned to a station than AM, but this noise completely disappears when a station is tuned in. Under certain conditions (weak signals) the FM radio will pick up noise. The noise-canceling features of an FM radio require a certain signal strength before they can perform their function. An FM radio operated in a *fringe* area, where signals are weak, will pick up motor noise from cars and be subject to other electrical disturbances.

The household FM radio has a decided advantage over the FM automobile radio; once the radio is placed in motion, the problems multiply.

The factors governing FM automobile reception are listed below with a brief description of the design features which minimize reception difficulties. These reception difficulties are restricted primarily to fringe areas—usually, metropolitan reception is excellent.

Range

Normal range for an AM–FM radio is approximately 35 miles with, naturally, some exceptions. On flat terrain, and with powerful transmitters, the range could be considerably extended. Educational stations are generally weak and may be listenable only at a distance of from a few blocks to a few miles. If the automobile is not moving, reception can be very satisfactory at distances over 25 miles. Once the automobile is set into motion, it is possible to drive past hills or buildings in fringe areas and momentarily lose the station.

Reception under 25 miles is reliable on practically all commercial stations, and fluttering reception due to hills and buildings will seldom be troublesome.

For maximum range capability, the Chrysler AM–FM radio contains four stages of intermediate-frequency amplification.

Flutter

Flutter is produced in fringe areas when objects come between the station and the receiver. The signal will be lost momentarily; then it will return. The rate at which the flutter occurs is dependent upon the car's speed in passing objects. The effect is very similar to the way a television picture flutters when an airplane passes overhead.

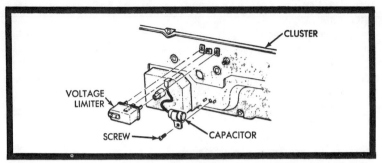

Fig. 5-2. Installation of radio interference capacitor. (Courtesy Chrysler Corp.)

Flutter is kept to a minimum in the Chrysler AM–FM radio due to its high-gain circuitry.

Automatic Frequency Control (AFC)

Because of the high frequencies used in FM transmission, it is imperative that the receiver does not drift off station. A home radio uses a stable voltage supply and is rarely subjected to wide variations in temperature. The car FM radio operates under less constant conditions. The temperatures may range from below freezing to well over 100°F. The voltage supply may go from 12V to as high as 14.5V with the alternator charging.

The easiest method of combating these variables is to build a strong afc system which can "draw the station back in," even though the receiver oscillator frequency has drifted off. But this can be an undesirable feature. With a strong afc circuit, station tuning becomes very broad, producing a bad *capture effect*. (See the section on capture effect.)

Rather than using an overpowering afc circuit, the Chrysler FM tuner is designed to operate with a zener-diode-controlled power supply. The zener diode maintains the same voltage on the FM tuner under all driving conditions. An afc circuit is used to provide excellent holding on frequency without the disadvantages of broad tuning and capture effect.

Capture Effect

A capture effect is noticed when driving in the downtown area of large cities when the radio tuned to a distant station. The afc circuit will attach itself to, or "capture," the strongest station located where the dial pointer is set. If you are listening to a station which is not located in the downtown area and you pass the transmitter of a station *close to* the one you are tuned to, the afc may possibly attach itself to, or "capture," the stronger signal.

FM receivers are unlike AM receivers in this respect, since they do not mix two stations but "decide" which of the stronger to shift to.

The capture effect is kept at a minimum in Chrysler AM−FM receivers by the use of a zener diode power supply and an afc system of sufficient strength to keep the receiver on frequency. Receivers with strong afc circuits (associated with unregulated power supplies) are plagued with capture effect problems.

Motor Noise

Noise in general is no problem in FM receivers—provided sufficient signal is available from the station. FM receivers, however, are only immune to noise under strong signal conditions. With no signal, or a very weak one, motor noise can be received from passing cars and trucks. This is particularly true of passing cars that do not use TVRS television−radio suppression spark plug wires. As the station signal strength increases, the FM circuit rejects the noise; noise will not be noticed in metropolitan areas or anywhere within approximately 25 miles of the station.

Radio Interference Elimination

Capacitors are used to keep engine interference from the Chrysler radio. The alternator is equipped with an internal capacitor integral with the output stud. A second capacitor is mounted on the back of the instrument cluster with a self-tapping screw. The lead wire of the capacitor is connected to the input terminal of the voltage limiter (Fig. 5-2 and 5-3). A third capacitor is installed on the ignition coil with the lead connected to the positive primary terminal of the coil (Fig. 5-4).

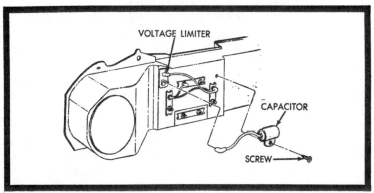

Fig. 5-3. Another capacitor installation for reducing interference. (Courtesy Chrysler Corp.)

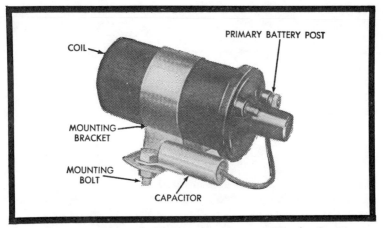

Fig. 5-4. Ignition coil and capacitor. (Courtesy Chrysler Corp.)

Radio resistance-type wires in the high-voltage circuit of the ignition system complete the interference-suppression system.

If radio noises are evident capacitor lead wires are not making good contact on their respective terminals or are not securely mounted. Faulty or deteriorated spark plug wires should be replaced.

Antenna Trimming

All radios are antenna-trimmed at the factory and ordinarily require no further adjustment. However, if a radio is being installed after repair, or if verification of trimmer adjustment is desired, proceed as follows:

1. Allow the radio to warm up for 5 minutes.
2. Extend the antenna to normal height.
3. Manually tune radio to a weak signal between 1400 and 1600 kHz.
4. Increase volume to full and set tone control to maximum treble.

Adjust the antenna trimmer back and forth until a position is found that gives peak volume response.

CAR RADIO DIAGNOSIS

The following radio trouble diagnosis guide is intended as an aid in locating minor faults which can be corrected without a specialized knowledge of radio and without special radio test equipment. If the suggestions given here do not effect correction, further testing should be done only by a trained radio technician with proper test equipment.

No Turn-On Thump Heard

Check fuse.

- Fuse blown: Check receiver and speaker connectors.
- Connectors loose or defective: Correct as required.
- Connectors okay: Check speaker by substituting a known good speaker.
- Radio does not play even with a known good substitute speaker: Defective receiver. Remove for servicing.

Thump Heard

Check antenna connection at back of radio and at base of windshield or antenna.

- Connections defective: Substitute a known good lead-in cable.
- Radio still won't play, even with good lead-in cables: Defective radio. Good radio still won't play: Defective antenna.

Radio Cuts On and Off

Check for defective or loose receiver or antenna connectors at the rear of radio or base of windshield or antenna and make necessary repairs.

- Connectors okay: Substitute a known good lead-in cable.
- Radio still cuts out with a good lead-in cable: Check speaker by substituting a known good speaker.
- Radio still plays intermittently, even with a good speaker: Defective receiver.

Radio Noisy

Start and rev engine several times, listening for speaker static.

- Static Heard: Trim antenna; check for spark plug wire breakdown, loose or improperly seated wire, or loose or missing engine ground strap. Check suppressors on voltage regulator, alternator, and resistor on timing control solenoid. Static still present: Defective receiver.

Weak Radio Signal

Test windshield antenna.

Distorted Tone

Turn on the radio and adjust for high volume and maximum bass; substitute a good speaker.

Distortion: Defective receiver—remove for servicing.

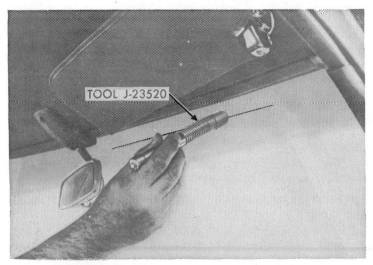

Fig. 5-5. Testing a windshield antenna. (Courtesy Chevrolet Motor Div. of General Motors Corp.)

Testing Windshield Antenna

Many new cars with factory-installed radios are equipped with windshield antennas. To positively identify antenna failure and eliminate the possibility of unnecessary windshield replacement, a windshield antenna tester should be used to determine the continuity of the thin antenna wire. An example is the Chevrolet device shown in Fig. 5-5.

When antenna failure is suspected, the following checks should be made before replacing the windshield.

1. Check the tester battery by applying the unit to an antenna that is operating normally.
2. Check all antenna connections to insure that the antenna is electrically coupled to the radio.
3. Turn ignition switch to the accessory position; turn the radio on and select the AM band. Tune to an off-station position.
4. Hold tester to antenna, beginning at the upper corner. Caution: The plastic shield must be on the tester at all times to avoid scratching the windshield.
   a. If a shrill sound is emitted through the speaker when both antenna wires are tested, the antenna is operational.
   b. If no sound is emitted through one or both antenna wires, move the tester along the wire toward the center of the windshield and down toward the radio.

c. If a shrill sound is picked up, find the exact location where the noise begins; this is the area of the defect.

d. If no noise is heard over the entire length of the antenna, unplug the antenna lead at the radio and touch the tester to the antenna socket in the radio.

e. If the radio now makes a shrill sound, check connectors and antenna lead for possible defect before replacing windshield.

f. If no noise is emitted, the radio, speaker, or fuse is defective.

NOISE REDUCTION TECHNIQUES

It has long been known by ignition engineers that the addition of a series resistance adjacent to a spark discharge will serve to damp out troublesome oscillation which causes interference. Spark plug noise suppression techniques, to be consistent with good engine performance, should always be in accordance with car manufacturer recommendations. If resistance wire is used, the length is critical and should add to the total permissible resistance. In addition to spark plug suppressors or resistance wire, an economical basic kit of noise reduction items can consist of special coaxial capacitors, combinations of resistor and capacitor assemblies, and hood wiper springs.

Noise reduction can only be achieved if components are properly grounded. Be sure that all capacitors and the generator field assembly are properly grounded. On some vehicles, standard bypass capacitors may already be installed at the locations referred to in these instructions. When these instructions call for coaxial capacitors, remove the standard bypass capacitor and mount the coaxial type.

Generator Interference

The generator is often the source of electrical interference frequently blamed on the ignition system. Current passing between the brushes and commutator creates many small arcs as the armature rotates. Generator noise is characterized by a high-pitched whine that varies with engine speed. A 0.5 μF coaxial capacitor should be placed in series with the armature to reduce interference.

Voltage Regulator Interference

The voltage regulator contains three separate control systems operating with breaker contacts that cause arcing, which may result in interference. This interference is usually noted in the form of erratic popping in the receiver which

Fig. 5-6. A method of reducing ignition coil interference.

changes only slightly in frequency with increase in engine speed.

Disconnect the ground terminal from the battery before attempting to add any components to the battery (BAT) terminal of the voltage regulator; failure to do so may result in blown fuses.

To reduce voltage regulator hash noise, use two 0.5 μF coaxial capacitors and a resistor—capacitor assembly. Install the 0.5 μF coaxial capacitors at the (BAT) terminal in series with the battery lead and at the generator (ARM) terminal in series with the armature lead. The capacitors are not required in alternator-equipped vehicles.

Install the RC filter, composed of a 3.3Ω resistor in series with a 0.002 μF capacitor, in series with the field (F) terminal of the voltage regulator to a common ground.

Ignition Coil Interference

At the ignition coil, mount a 0.1 μF coaxial capacitor as follows:

1. Ground the capacitor (Fig. 5-6) to a convenient ignition coil mounting bolt.
2. Disconnect the wire (or wires) from the *primary* (low voltage) terminal, battery side, of the ignition coil and reconnect it to one end of the 0.1 μF coaxial capacitor (Fig. 5-6).
3. Connect a 5-inch lead with identical lugs on each end between the other end of the capacitor and the primary (low voltage) terminal of the ignition coil.

Ordinary bypass capacitors should not be used in place of coaxial capacitors. The ordinary bypass capacitor displays a resonance effect with high rf noise attenuation, at about 2 MHz. The coaxial type is noninductive and provides a high attenuation of rf noise up into the UHF region.

Distributor Interference

Radio interference can be caused by the sparking that occurs between the rotor and the distributor cap inserts. Interference can be effectively reduced by connecting a length of coil to the distributor cap (if the vehicle is not already equipped with radio ignition wire).

1. Remove the ignition cable connecting the high-voltage (secondary) terminal of the ignition coil to the distributor cap.
2. Replace this lead with suppressor cable (Fig. 5-6). If necessary, take up the slack by tying an overhand knot in this cable.

Battery Connection

Connecting the radio's primary power lead directly to the battery instead of the starter relay can help to keep noise off the power lead. The battery acts as a large capacitor (about one farad for 50 ampere-hour batteries) bypassing noise to ground. This large capacitor serves as a very effective bypass. The battery ground return should also be bonded to the frame. Using the car frame as a common ground when practical tends to minimize the possibility of inducing undesirable parallel ground currents.

Hood Wipers

The ground return for electrical circuits is the body and frame of the automobile. Differences in conductivity, inadequate bonds between adjacent connectors, and unequal current distributions result in potential differences that cause miniature arcs. Using copper braid and brass contact wipers as hood bonds will minimize this interference.

To install the hood wipers, mount them on the surface where the hood closes at the firewall. Remove all paint from surfaces where electrical contact is to be made. Bend the wipers by hand so that they make firm contact with the paint-free surface when the hood is closed.

A *DO NOT REMOVE* tag should be used to alert mechanics or technicians not familiar with radio equipment that a certain noise reduction component is essential for proper operation of the equipment. Add the tag to the lead between the coaxial capacitor and ignition coil.

Additional Noise Reduction Techniques

Maximum noise reduction can be obtained by applying the following source remedies: (1) ammeter-to-battery lead (bypass with 0.5 μF capacitor); (2) oil signal, gasoline, and

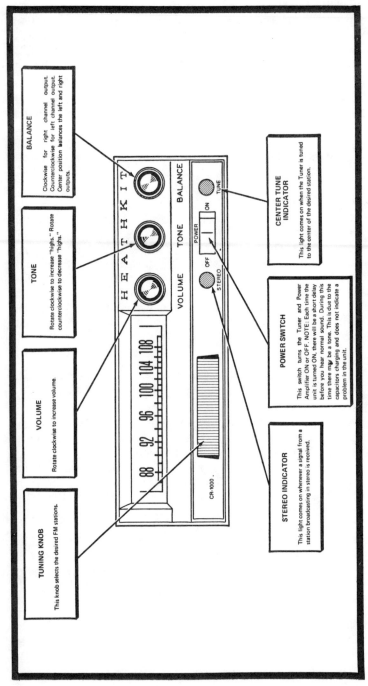

TUNING KNOB

This knob selects the desired FM stations.

VOLUME

Rotate clockwise to increase volume.

TONE

Rotate clockwise to increase "highs." Rotate counterclockwise to decrease "highs."

BALANCE

Clockwise for right channel output. Counterclockwise for left channel output. Center position balances the left and right outputs.

CENTER TUNE INDICATOR

This light comes on when the Tuner is tuned to the center of the desired station.

POWER SWITCH

This switch turns the Tuner and Power Amplifier ON or OFF. NOTE: Each time the unit is turned ON, there will be a short delay before you hear normal sound. During this time there may be a tone. This is due to the capacitors charging and does not indicate a problem in the unit.

STEREO INDICATOR

This light comes on whenever a signal from a station broadcasting in stereo is received.

Fig. 5-7. Heathkit model CR-1000 FM stereo tuner.

temperature gages (bypass with a 0.5 μF capacitor); (3) ignition switch (bypass with 0.5 μF capacitor); (4) headlight, taillight, or dome light leads (bypass with 0.5 μF capacitor); (5) accessory wiring, electrical windshield wipers, heat motor, window openers, and others (bypass with 0.5 μF capacitor); (6) wheel static (use wheel-static collector rings on both front wheels); and (7) acute cases of generator noise, in vehicles so equipped (install a 0.5 μF coaxial capacitor in series with the armature lead).

FM STEREO TUNER

The Heath CR-1000 high-fidelity FM stereo tuner (Fig. 5-7), along with a companion power amplifier, gives home-quality music entertainment in the automobile.

The all-solid-state stereo tuner provides high-quality reception with a preassembled, prealigned, ceramic-filtered tuning circuit. Also included is a muting circuit for noise quieting when tuning between stations and an automatic frequency control (afc) which locks on stations tuned in.

An antenna adapter cable and an extension cable, supplied with the kit, allow both FM and an already-installed AM car radio to use the same antenna.

FM Tuning Unit

Refer to the schematic diagram (Fig. 5-8) and the block diagram (Fig. 5-9) as you read the following information.

FM broadcast signals (88–108 MHz) are received by the FM tuning unit and converted to an intermediate frequency of 10.7 MHz. The unit contains an rf amplifier stage, a mixer stage, and an oscillator stage. FM signals are coupled from the automobile antenna to the primary winding of transformer T101 through capacitor C1. The secondary winding is part of a tuned circuit which is tuned to the frequency of the desired station by variable capacitor C101A.

The tuned signal is then coupled to the gate of transistor Q101, amplified, and tuned by coil L101 and variable capacitor C101B. From here, the signal is coupled to the base of mixer transistor Q102.

Transistor Q103 operates as a grounded-base oscillator. The oscillator frequency, which is 10.7 MHz above the incoming rf signal, is determined by the tuning action of coil L102 and variable capacitor C101C. A portion of the oscillator signal is then coupled to the base of mixer transistor Q102. The mixing of these two signals in Q102 produces the 10.7 MHz i-f signal which is then coupled through i-f transformer T102 to the i-f circuits.

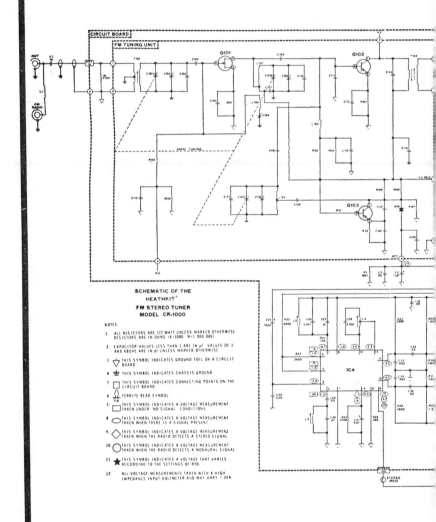

SCHEMATIC OF THE
HEATHKIT®
FM STEREO TUNER
MODEL CR-1000

NOTES

1. ALL RESISTORS ARE 1/2 WATT UNLESS MARKED OTHERWISE
   RESISTORS ARE IN OHMS (K=1000   M=1,000 000).

2. CAPACITOR VALUES LESS THAN 1 ARE IN µf   VALUES OF 1
   AND ABOVE ARE IN pf UNLESS MARKED OTHERWISE

3. ▽ THIS SYMBOL INDICATES GROUND FOIL ON A CIRCUIT
   BOARD

4. ⏚ THIS SYMBOL INDICATES CHASSIS GROUND

5. ☐ THIS SYMBOL INDICATES CONNECTING POINTS ON THE
   CIRCUIT BOARD

6. ⬥ FERRITE BEAD SYMBOL
   FB

7. ☐ THIS SYMBOL INDICATES A VOLTAGE MEASUREMENT
   TAKEN UNDER 'NO SIGNAL CONDITIONS

8. ◯ THIS SYMBOL INDICATES A VOLTAGE MEASUREMENT
   TAKEN WHEN THERE IS A SIGNAL PRESENT

9. ◇ THIS SYMBOL INDICATES A VOLTAGE MEASUREMENT
   TAKEN WHEN THE RADIO DETECTS A STEREO SIGNAL

10. ◯ THIS SYMBOL INDICATES A VOLTAGE MEASUREMENT
    TAKEN WHEN THE RADIO DETECTS A MONAURAL SIGNAL

11. ★ THIS SYMBOL INDICATES A VOLTAGE THAT VARIES
    ACCORDING TO THE SETTINGS OF R50.

12. ALL VOLTAGE MEASUREMENTS TAKEN WITH A HIGH
    IMPEDANCE INPUT VOLTMETER AND MAY VARY ± 20%

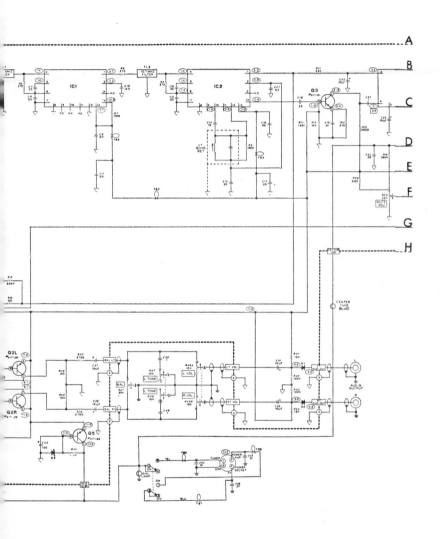

Fig. 5-8. Schematic of the CR-1000 FM tuner. (Courtesy Heath Co.)

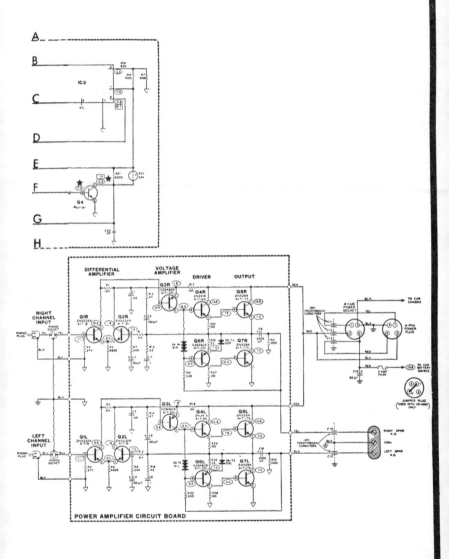

Fig. 5-8. Cont'd.

FM I-F Circuit

The signal is coupled from transformer T102 to ceramic filter FL1 through capacitor C4. Transformer T102 and capacitors C4 and C5 form a low-cmpedance circuit to match ceramic filter FL1. The signal goes through ceramic filter FL1 and is direct-coupled to pin 4 of integrated circuit IC1 which amplifies the signal and couples it through resistor R6 to ceramic filter FL2. The signal then goes through FL2 and is direct-coupled to pin 4 of integrated circuit IC2. The combination of ceramic filters FL1 and FL2 provide most of the selectivity for the signal, offers good alternate channel attenuation, and good phase linearity for best multiplex performance. Integrated circuit IC2 further amplifies the signal, limits its amplitude, and detects the audio. The limiting action by IC1 removes most noise pulses and any AM signal that may be part of the i-f signal. Integrated circuit IC1 also *limits* on strong signals. The signal at pin 1 of integrated circuit IC2 is the detected audio plus a dc voltage.

This dc voltage remains the same as long as the tuning unit is tuned to the exact center frequency of the FM station. When the tuning unit is tuned away from the center frequency, the voltage varies up or down depending on which direction the tuning unit shaft is turned. This voltage is coupled back to pin 4 of the tuning unit through resistor R4 and is used for afc. This afc is an aid to tuning and produces station-holding stability with temperature changes. Resistor R4 and capacitor C3 prevent any of the audio signal at pin 1 of integrated circuit IC2 from reaching pin 4 of the tuning unit. Resistors R2 and R3 establish the proper afc sensitivity.

Center-Tune and Mute Circuits

The dc voltage at pin 1 of integrated circuit IC2 is also coupled to pin 3 of center-tune integrated circuit IC3 through

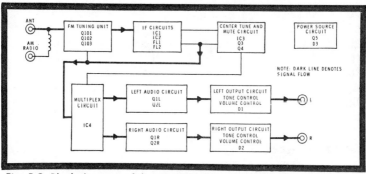

Fig. 5-9. Block diagram of the CR-1000 FM tuner. (Courtesy Heath Co.)

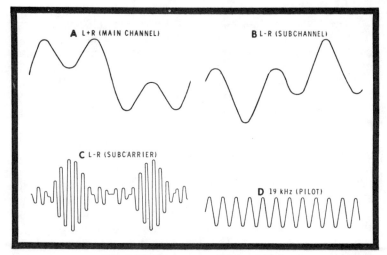

Fig. 5-10. FM stereo multiplex signals.

resistor R11. R11 and capacitor C20 prevent any audio signal from reaching pin 3 of integrated circuit IC3. The voltage at pin 3 must match the voltage at pin 2 of integrated circuit IC3 to turn the tune lamp on. This happens when the tuning unit is tuned to the center frequency of an FM station. The voltage at pin 2 is produced by voltage-divider resistors R17 and R18.

When the tuning unit is tuned between stations, a noise signal at pin 14 of integrated circuit IC2 is coupled through capacitor C18 to the base of transistor Q3. Transistor Q3 amplifies this signal and couples it through capacitor C21 to pin 4 of integrated circuit IC3. This signal at pin 4 prevents the integrated circuit from turning on the tune lamp. This is done in case the voltages at pins 2 and 3 should match due to an unwanted noise signal on pin 3.

When tuning between stations, transistor Q4 and the mute adjustment control keep multiplex integrated circuit IC4 turned off. When the tuning unit is tuned to the center frequency of a station, the tune lamp comes on. Then the bias voltage for the base of transistor Q4 is lowered and transistor Q4 turns off. As transistor Q4 turns off, a voltage determined by resistor R21 appears at its collector. This voltage is coupled to pin 5 of integrated circuit IC4 which unmutes IC4. Thermistor R51 keeps this voltage constant when there is a temperature variation.

Multiplex Circuit

Left- and right-channel signals are produced at a radio station that is broadcasting FM stereo. The transmitting circuits then combine these signals to produce the L+R (main channel) signal shown in Fig. 5-10A and the L−R (subchannel) signal shown in Fig. 5-10B. Note that the L−R signal is superimposed on a 38 kHz signal as shown in Fig. 5-10C. This amplitude modulated L−R signal is transmitted as the subcarrier channel.

The L+R (main channel) signal and the L−R (subcarrier) signal are combined with the 19 kHz pilot signal shown in Fig. 5-10D, and the whole complex signal then frequency modulates the transmitted rf carrier.

A second subcarrier signal is transmitted by some stations at a frequency of 67 kHz. This channel, which is modulated by a commercial music signal, is called the *SCA* (subcarrier authorization) channel.

Figure 5-11 shows where the different components are to be found in a stereo FM signal. The L+R signal, which is in the audio spectrum (50 Hz to 15 kHz), is called the "main channel." Monophonic FM receivers use only this part of the signal, and the remaining signal components are attenuated by a deemphasis network.

For simplification, the internal operation of integrated circuit IC4 will not be described in detail. However, its features and the associated circuits will be explained.

The integrated circuit separates the detected audio coming from the i-f circuits into the proper left- and right-channel audio signals. The detected audio signal is coupled from pin 1 of integrated circuit IC2 to pin 3 of integrated circuit IC4 through resistor R10 and capacitor C25. IC4 has the ability to cancel the SCA channel signal which would otherwise be present at the audio outputs. Normally, elaborate filters would have to be designed to do this, sacrificing high-frequency audio separation. The voltage, coupled from the collector of transistor Q4, controls the integrated circuit to attenuate (mute) noisy low-level rf signals and in-between-station noise.

When a stereo station is being received, pin 6 of integrated circuit IC4 is grounded. This turns the stereo lamp on. Coils L2

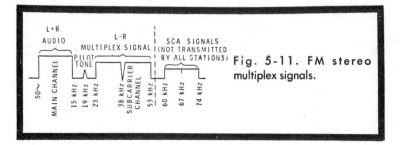

Fig. 5-11. FM stereo multiplex signals.

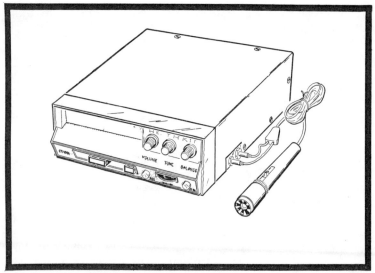

Fig. 5-12. Stereo cassette player, model CT-1001. (Courtesy Heath Co.)

and L3 prevent false triggering of integrated circuit IC4 on extraneous signals. Coil L4 provides proper tuning to the station subchannel for best multiplex operation. The left- and right-channel audio signals appear at pins 11 and 12 of integrated circuit IC4 respectively.

Audio and Supply Voltage Circuits

Since the operations of both audio channels are identical, only the right channel will be described here.

From pin 12 of integrated circuit IC4, the signal is coupled through capacitor C36 to the base of transistor Q1. Resistor R28 and capacitor C34 form a deemphasis network. Transistors Q1 and Q2 form a complementary amplifier circuit. Resistors R36 and R40 make up a voltage divider to provide the proper feedback voltage to the emitter of Q1.

From the collector of transistor Q2, the signal passes through resistor R38 and capacitor C38 to the balance, tone, and volume controls. The signal is coupled from the volume control to the output jack through capacitor C42 and diode D2. Diode D2 acts as a switch when the Heath CT-1001 stereo cassette player is part of the system and the player is on. The diode prevents the balance, tone, and volume controls from interfering with the controls on the player.

Transistor Q5 is a capacitance multiplier which multiplies the value of capacitor C43. Zener diode D3 provides regulation of the supply voltage.

TAPE PLAYER

The Heathkit model CT-1001 stereo cassette player, (Fig. 5-12), when used with the Heathkit CRA-1000-1 stereo power amplifier, provides high-fidelity music entertainment in a car, recreation vehicle, or boat.

The tape player turns on when you insert a cassette into the unit. An electronic shutoff circuit automatically rejects the cassette when the tape reaches the end of its travel, if the tape breaks or hangs up in the cassette, or power is removed from the player. An automatic *record interlock* protects prerecorded tapes from being accidentally erased.

Two pushbuttons and four knobs allow you to operate the player. A *power on* lamp and a *record level* lamp provide visual information at a glance.

Because of a built-in solid-state voltage regulator, a quality long-life motor (that insures a smooth playback operation with a minimum of wow and flutter), and solid-state components, the cassette player provides high performance and a long life.

Tape Cassettes

Cassettes operate on a reel-to-reel basis. The tape is first wound on reel A, and reel B is empty (see Fig. 5-13).

Since the two stereo tracks are side by side on the tape, a stereo-recorded tape can be replayed monophonically on a monophonic cassette player. Also a monophonic tape can be replayed on this cassette player, although is will replay as monophonic and not stereo.

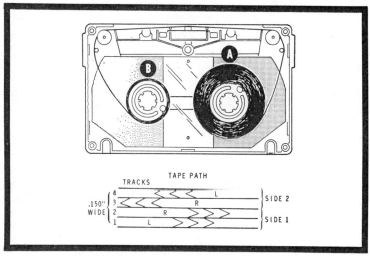

Fig. 5-13. Tape cassette. (Courtesy Heath Co.)

Playback

The magnetic coating on the surface of a prerecorded tape contains a varying magnetic field (signal) which corresponds to the recorded signal. When the tape is passed across the face of the record—play head, the magnetic field induces a voltage into the coil in the head. This induced signal voltage varies at the same amplitude and frequency as the signal on the tape.

The signal voltage from the record—play head coil is amplified by the preamplifier and coupled to the left- and right-channel output jacks.

Record

Because of the extreme nonlinear nature of the magnetic coating on the tape, a bias signal is used to preenergize the tape. This bias signal is required for recording only, and is not used in the playback process. The bias signal is produced by the oscillator circuit and is coupled to the recording head.

The recording signal is coupled from the microphone inputs to the left-channel preamplifier only (in the sample unit). There the signal is amplified and then mixed with the bias signal at the record—play head. As the tape passes the record—play head, the signal is recorded on the tape.

The individual circuits will be discussed in detail in the following paragraphs. Refer to the schematic diagram while you read about these circuits (Fig. 5-14).

Preamplifier

Since the operation of both preamplifier channels are identical, only the right channel will be described here.

The signal from the record—playback head is coupled through capacitor C3 to the base of transistor Q1. Here the signal is amplified and direct-coupled to the base of transistor Q2 for further amplification.

From the collector of transistor Q2, the signal is coupled through a frequency-sensitive network consisting of capacitor C7 and resistors R9 and R13. This network provides standard equalization of the signal. This signal is then coupled to the emitter of transistor Q1. Resistors R11 and R17 form a voltage divider that provides dc feedback from the emitter of transistor Q2 to the base of transistor Q1.

The signal is also coupled through capacitor C11 to the base of transistor Q3. Transistors Q3 and Q4 form a complementary amplifier circuit with feedback. Resistors R25 and R27 make up a voltage divider circuit to provide the proper feedback voltage to the emitter of transistor Q3.

From the collector of transistor Q4, the signal passes through a high-frequency rolloff network consisting of resistor

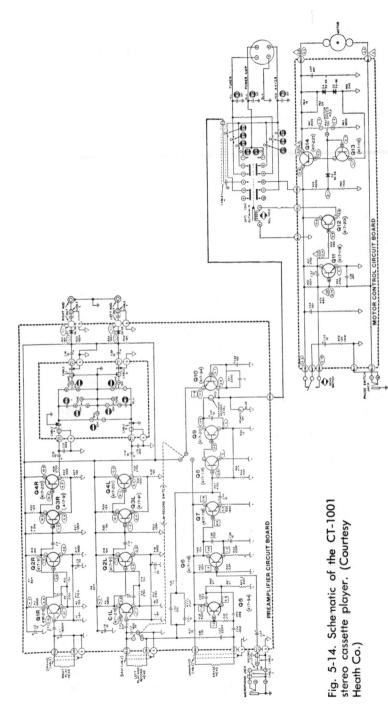

Fig. 5-14. Schematic of the CT-1001 stereo cassette player. (Courtesy Heath Co.)

143

R29 and capacitor C15. From this network the signal goes to the balance, tone, and volume controls. The signal is coupled from the volume control to the output jack through capacitor C19 and diode D1. Diode D1 acts as a switch when the CR-1000 FM tuner is part of the system and the tuner is on. The diode prevents the balance, tone, and volume controls from interfering with the controls on the tuner.

Record Circuit

The following circuits are activated when the record bar is pushed in, which operates the slide switch on the preamplifier circuit board.

Transistor Q5, its associated resistors and capacitors, and the erase head form the bias oscillator, which is a grounded-collector Colpitts oscillator. This oscillator produces a signal with a frequency of about 100 kHz and erases any information on the tape and "preenergizes" the tape for recording.

The signal to be recorded comes from the microphone, through the *record level* control, and is coupled to the base of transistor Q6 through capacitor C27. Transistors Q6 and Q7 make up a 2-stage amplifier which operates in the voice-frequency only, since the record feature is for dictation only. The signal is amplified by this amplifier and coupled from the emitter of transistor Q7 through capacitor C30 and parallel trap RFC1 and C22 to the record—playback head. The parallel trap prevents the 100 kHz bias signal from reaching the base of transistor Q8.

Transistors Q8 and Q9 form a multivibrator circuit. Peak audio signals which would saturate the record—playback head are passed through resistors R47 and R48, which biases the base of transistor Q8. This turns transistor Q8 on and biases transistor Q9 to turn the *record level* light on. Resistor R50 keeps the light either "full on" or "full off."

Transistor Q10 is an amplifier which adds more capacitance across the supply line than the 100μF of C32.

Reject and Sensing Circuit

When a tape cassette is inserted into the tape transport, power is switched on. A square cam or the idler reel (located on the tape transport) opens and closes the sensing switch, which charges and discharges capacitor C33. This capacitor discharges through resistors R54 and R56 and biases transistor Q11. The bias voltage keeps transistor Q11 turned on. This causes a voltage drop across resistor R58 which biases transistor Q12 on. Transistor Q12 acts as a switch in the supply line of the latching solenoid. When Q12 turns on, the solenoid is activated and holds the tape transport on.

Capacitor C35 and resistor R55 form a timing circuit which keeps some bias on transistor Q11 so that any abrupt voltage or torque changes do not release the solenoid.

When the tape reaches the end of the cassette, the idler reel stops turning. This stops the square cam from operating the sensing switch. When the sensing switch stops working, transistor Q11 loses its bias voltage and turns off. This removes the bias voltage from transistor Q12, which opens the supply line to the solenoid. The solenoid then releases the tape transport mechanism. Since the mechanism is spring-loaded, it ejects the cassette and turns the power switch off, which removes power from the player.

Motor Speed Regulations

Transistors Q13 and Q14 form a voltage- and current-sensing regulator. Any variation in the supply voltage changes the voltage drop across resistor R59 and diode D3, which changes the bias on transistor Q13. This changes the bias on transistor Q14 and increases or decreases its collector voltage. This keeps the current constant through the motor. Any torque change on the motor is seen as a current change through resistors R64 and R65. The voltage change across these resistors is coupled to the base of transistor Q13 through resistor R61 and *motor speed adjustment* control R62. The same voltage change is coupled back to the emitter of transistor Q13 through diodes D4 and D5. The motor speed adjustment control sets the proper voltage across the motor for the correct tape speed.

Ferrite beads FB1 through FB8 and capacitors C38 through C40 form filter networks that eliminate any possible ignition noise on the power source lines.

TAPE PLAYER MAINTENANCE

The only maintenance required on tape players is periodic cleaning of the tape player head. This service should be performed every 100 hours of operation. The head cleaning is done by swabbing the head (unit still installed in car) with a cotton swab that has been dipped in alcohol.

No lubricants should be used since they will cause the player to operate improperly, especially at extreme temperatures.

Do not bring any magnetized tools near the tape head. If the head becomes magnetized, every cassette played in the player will sound hissy.

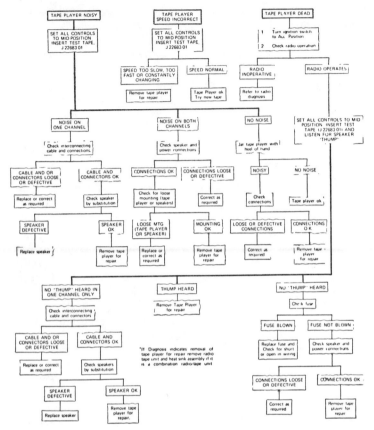

Fig. 5-15. Stereo 8 tape player troubleshooting chart. (Courtesy Chevrolet Motor Div. of General Motors Corp.)

A complete troubleshooting chart for a combination radio and tape player is given in Fig. 5-15. This chart is handy for checking most auto radios and tape players.

ELECTRONIC SIREN—PA

The Heathkit model GD-18 electronic siren (Fig. 5-16) functions as an automatic wail or yelp siren, a manually operated wail siren, a public address (PA) system, and a radio-monitoring amplifier all in one compact unit for emergency service vehicles. The siren is powered by a 12V storage battery system and is capable of delivering adequate sound levels on all of its five functions.

Solid-state circuitry with a temperature- and voltage-compensated stage is used in the siren amplifier. The

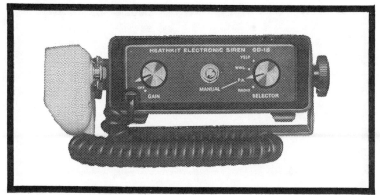

Fig. 5-16. Electronic siren and PA system. (Courtesy Heath Co.)

amplifier is transformer coupled to the speaker output to provide pretection against short circuits or accidental grounding of the speaker cables. The amplifier chassis is also isolated from the circuitry so the siren may be used with either a negative or positive electrical system ground.

Electronic Siren

Refer to the block diagram (Fig. 5-17) and the schematic diagram (Fig. 5-18), while reading the following circuit description.

The electronic siren consists of amplifier, tone multivibrator, sweep generator, and switching transistor

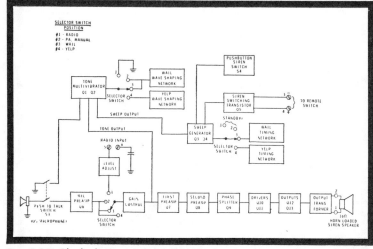

Fig. 5-17. Block diagram of the GD-18 electronic siren. (Courtesy Heath Co.)

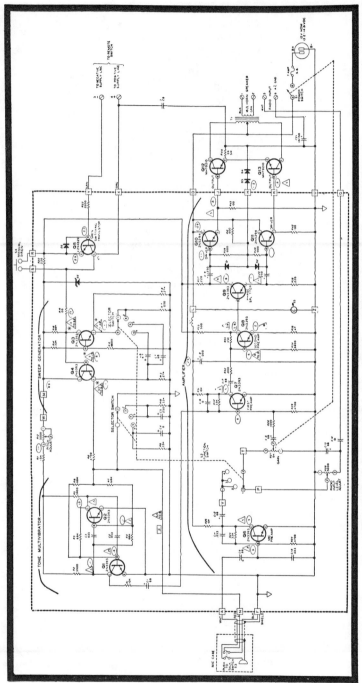

Fig. 5-18. Schematic of the GD-18 electronic siren. (Courtesy Heath Co.)

circuits. In either the YELP or WAIL mode, the tone generator varies this frequency to obtain either the yelp or wail siren sound. The amplifier then amplifies this siren sound. In either the RADIO or PA mode, the amplifier amplifies the signal from either the 2-way radio speaker or the microphone, depending on the position of the selector swtich.

Tone Multivibrator

Transistors Q1 and Q2 comprise a common multivibrator circuit. The free-running frequency of the multivibrator is determined by the RC time constant of the feedback networks R3−C2 and R4−C3. The frequency of the multivibrator can be varied +10 percent by adjusting the pitch adjust control, R12, which varies the supply voltage to the multivibrator.

Sweep Generator

The sweep generator varies the bias of Q1 and Q2, which turns on the tone multivibrator and varies its frequency to produce a characteristic motor-driven siren sound.

When the selector switch is in the PA position, transistor Q3 is biased on because of the low resistance of resistor R17 in the emitter circuit. While Q3 is conducting, Q4 is biased off due to the voltage drop across resistor R16. Q4 will remain off until either the pushbutton siren switch or switching transistor Q5 applies a positive voltage to the base of Q4. (Q5 can be turned on by closing the remote switch.)

As Q4 turns on, its emitter voltage will increase and start charging capacitor C5. Since the varying emitter voltage of Q4 is coupled to the bases of Q1 and Q2, the bias and, consequently, the frequency of the tone multivibrator will also vary siren sound when the button is pushed, or when the remote siren switch is closed.

When the selector switch is in the WAIL position, resistor R17 is removed and capacitor C7 is connected to the emitter circuit of Q3. The increased resistance in the emitter circuit causes Q3 to shut off and Q4 to turn on. When Q4 turns on, two things will happen: C5 will begin to charge, which will turn on the tone multivibrator and vary its frequency at the charging rate of C5. Also, C7 will begin to charge, which will eventually raise the emitter voltage and turn on Q3. When Q3 conducts, Q4 will shut off. Both transistors will remain in this state until the voltage on C7 discharges, which will reduce the emitter voltage of Q3 to the point where Q3 shuts off.

Therefore, the frequency of the tone multivibrator will vary at the charging rate of C5, and the sweep will cycle at the charging and discharging rate of C7. The resulting sound will be a wailing siren sound.

In the YELP mode, the circuit operates basically the same. However, capacitor C4 is used instead of C5, and capacitor C6 is used instead of C7. The sweep cycle rate will increase to produce a yelp sound.

Amplifier

Audio signal from the microphone is passed through the push-to-talk switch on the microphone and is coupled through capacitor C9 to the base of preamplifier transistor Q6. Capacitors C10 and C11 attenuate higher frequencies to minimize acoustic feedback. They also suppress high-frequency ignition noise.

When the selector switch is in the PA, WAIL, or YELP positions, the output of Q6 is coupled to transistor Q7, through capacitor C12, gain control R27, capacitor C15, and resistor R28. High frequencies are also attenuated by capacitor C16.

When the selector switch is in the WAIL or YELP position, the output of Q1 is applied to the base of transistor Q7 through capacitor C1 and resistor R1; therefore, gain control R27 does not affect the siren volume.

The amplified output of Q7 is coupled through capacitor C17 and R32 to the base of transistor Q8 for further amplification. The higher amplitude signals from the tone multivibrator have been clipped before arriving at this stage. Amplification by additional amplifiers clips these signals still further, producing a square-wave output to drive the speaker.

Amplifier phase-splitter Q9 is directly coupled to the collector of Q8. In addition to amplification, Q9 also provides two nearly identical, but 180 degrees out-of-phase signals which are capacity coupled to the bases of driver transistors Q10 and Q11 through C19 and C20.

Driver transistors Q10 and Q11 are connected as emitter followers and are directly coupled to output transistors Q12 and Q13. Bias for the driver transistors Q10 and Q11 is provided by R41, R39, R40, R44, and by diodes D1, D2, D3, and D4. Diodes D3 and D4 are physically mounted to sense the temperature of Q12 and Q13. Therefore, they can adjust the bias of these transistors for changes in temperature as well as for changes in voltage.

Output transistors Q12 and Q13 are connected for push-pull operation. Output transformer T1 couples the output from Q12 and Q13 to the speaker load.

Choke L1, capacitor C18, resistor R20, and zener diode D5 decouple and filter the power supply voltage.

The audio signal from the voice coil of the 2-way radio speaker is coupled through capacitor C14 and attenuated by R26 (radio level input adjust). This signal is switched into the amplifier by selector switch S2. Gain control R27 controls its volume. C15 and R28 couple the signal to the amplifier. An ac reference ground for the radio input at terminal 6 is maintained by capacitor C21.

WIRING YOUR CAR FOR SOUND

Basically, there are three different speaker hookups for audio systems in cars; these are illustrated by Fig. 5-19.

Part A shows a typical rear-seat speaker hookup for a single-channel (monaural) radio. Note how the negative and positive terminals are connected together, each to the like terminal on the other speaker. Connecting the speakers thusly is necessary to insure that they will be *in phase*; i.e., working together.

In Fig. 5-19B and C, typical hookups of stereo tape players are shown. In the hookup in B, it is important to have a wire

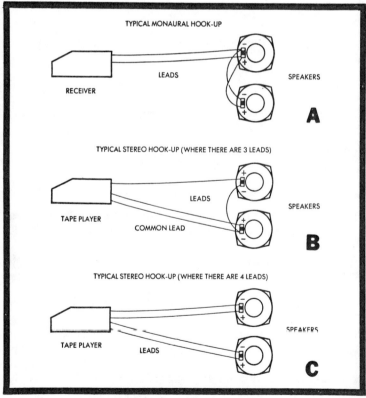

Fig. 5-19. Speaker hookups.

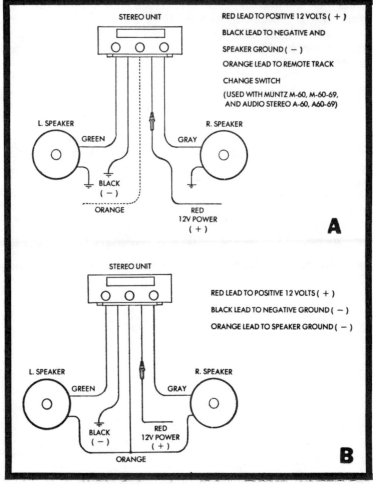

Fig. 5-20. Stereo connector configurations.

from the plus terminal of one speaker connected to the plus terminal of the other. In the hookup in C, the two wires running to the speaker plus terminals are usually the same color.

The two complete stereo hookups in Fig. 5-20 are typical. The hookup in Fig. 5-20A is used with Muntz, Audio Stereo, Automatic Radio, Ranger, Kraco, Tenna, Bowman, and Auto-Sonic units. The orange wire is present only in the case of those Muntz and Audio Stereo units having a remote track-change feature, and leads to the remote switch. Note that the black lead and one lead of each speaker must be connected to a good chassis ground (in a negative-ground car), and the red

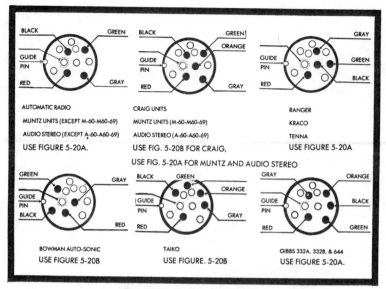

Fig. 5-21. Stereo unit hookups.

power lead must be fused. This lead may be connected to the accessory terminal of the car's ignition switch of fuse block.

Figure 5-20B shows another common hookup, used for Craig, Taiko, and Gibbs (332A, 332B, and 664) units. Note that in this installation the speakers are not grounded.

The pin configurations for the wiring plugs used with various stereo units are shown in Fig. 5-21. In using the drawings, imagine that the pins of the plugs shown are projecting toward you.

6 Comfort and Convenience Group

Most of the automotive accessories in the comfort and convenience category are electrically operated, but do not involve electronic circuitry. That is, they use no vacuum tubes, diodes, transistors, or other electronic devices. However, there are a few comfort and convenience accessories that do employ electronics. Discussed in this chapter are an air conditioner control offered by Chevrolet, a Ford speed control, and an automatic transmission control by Renault.

BASIC AIR CONDITIONER

An air conditioning unit always has a set of coils or a finned radiator core through which the air to be cooled passes. This is known as the *evaporator*. (Refer to Fig. 6-1.) The *refrigerant* (Freon) boils in the evaporator. In boiling, of course, the

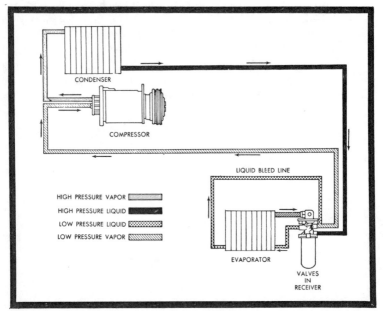

Fig. 6-1. Basic refrigeration cycle. (Courtesy Chevrolet Motor Div. of General Motors Corp.)

refrigerant absorbs heat and changes into a vapor. By piping this vapor outside the car, the heat that created the vapor can be carried out.

Once the vapor leaves the evaporator, the heat it contains has to be removed. Since heat is the only thing that expanded the refrigerant from a liquid to a vapor in the first place, removal of that same heat will let the vapor condense into a liquid again. Then the liquid refrigerant can be returned to the evaporator to be used over again.

Actually, the vapor coming out of the evaporator is very cold. The liquid refrigerant boils at temperatures considerably below freezing, and the vapors arising from it are only a shade warmer, even though they do contain quantities of heat. Consequently, the heat can't be expected to be removed from subfreezing vapors by "cooling" them in air temperatures that usually range between 60 and 100 degrees...heat refuses to flow from a cold object toward a warmer object.

But with a pump, the heat-laden vapor can be squeezed into a smaller space. And, when the vapor is compressed, it also concentrates the heat it contains. In this way, the vapor is made hotter without adding any heat; it can be cooled in comparatively warm air.

That is the responsibility of a *compressor* in an air conditioning system. Not intended to be a pump just for circulating the refrigerant, its job is to exert pressure for two reasons. Pressure makes the vapor hot enough to cool off in warm air. At the same time, the compressor raises the refrigerant's pressure above the condensing point at the temperature of the surrounding air, so it will condense.

As the refrigerant leaves the compressor, it is still a vapor, although it is now quite hot and ready to give up the heat it absorbed in the evaporator. One of the easiest ways to help refrigerant vapor discharge its heat is to send it through a radiator-like component known as a *condenser*.

The condenser really is a very simple device having no moving parts. It does exactly the same job as the familiar radiator in a typical home steam-heating system. There, the steam is nothing more than water vapor. In passing through the radiator, the steam gives up its heat and condenses back into water.

The purpose of the condenser, as the name implies, is to condense the high-pressure, high-temperature refrigerant vapor discharge by the compressor into a high-pressure liquid refrigerant. This occurs when the high-pressure, high-temperature refrigerant is subjected to the considerably cooler metal surfaces of the condenser. This is due to

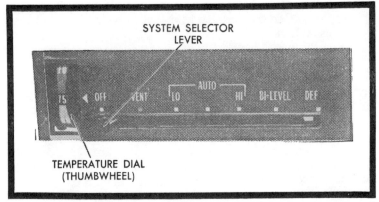

Fig. 6-2. Comfortron control head. (Courtesy Chevrolet Motor Div. of General Motors Corp.)

fundamental physical laws—heat travels from a warmer to a cooler surface, and when heat is removed from vapor, liquid is produced.

When the refrigerant condenses into a liquid, it is again ready for boiling in the evaporator, and is directed by a pipe from the condenser back to the evaporator.

These three units, then—the evaporator, the compressor, and the condenser—are the main working parts in any typical air conditioning system. In the evaporator the refrigerant boils and changes into a vapor, absorbing heat as it does so. A pump, or compressor, puts pressure on the refrigerant so it can get rid of its heat. And a condenser outside the car body helps discharge the heat into the surrounding air.

AUTOMATIC AIR CONDITIONING SYSTEM

The Chevrolet *Comfortron* air conditioning system is basically the same as the standard Chevrolet *Four-Season* system, but with the additional feature of completely automatic control. To the driver, the most noticeable difference between the two systems will be in the control panel (Fig. 6-2). In place of the 2-lever, 1-switch panel of the Four-Season system, the Comfortron has a single control lever plus a temperature dial similar to that found in a home thermostat. After the dial is set to the desired temperature and the lever is moved to place the system in operation, the Comfortron will automatically control the heating and air conditioning functions to maintain the selected interior temperature regardless of changes in outside air temperatures.

Most Comfortron parts are located in the passenger compartment (Fig. 6-3).

Programer

The programer (Fig. 6-4) controls the blower speeds, the air mix door, and vacuum diaphragms. Contained in the programer are the following components.

Vacuum Motor. The vacuum motor moves as a result of the modulated vacuum from the transducer (Fig. 6-5), which in turn controls the position of the output shaft of the programer, the programer vacuum valve, the amplifier feedback potentiometer, and the blower speed.

Vacuum-Checking Relay Valve. This relay valve will shut off transducer vacuum to the vacuum motor whenever the vacuum from the engine intake manifold falls below the vacuum in the vacuum motor supply line (engine stopped or operating at low manifold vacuum for long periods). This causes the vacuum motor to be held in position when the vacuum supply falls too low to maintain control.

Vacuum Valve. This valve is controlled by the vacuum motor and supplies vacuum to the control head and other components in the system, according to input requirements.

Transducer. The transducer (Fig. 6-5) will produce a varying vacuum output in response to the input voltage provided by the amplifier. An increase in the applied voltage results in a reduced vacuum output. The vacuum output controls the movement of the vacuum motor.

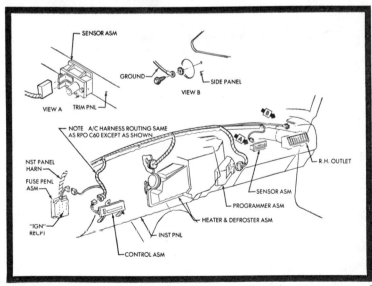

Fig. 6-3. Instrument panel wiring. (Courtesy Chevrolet Motor Div. of General Motors Corp.)

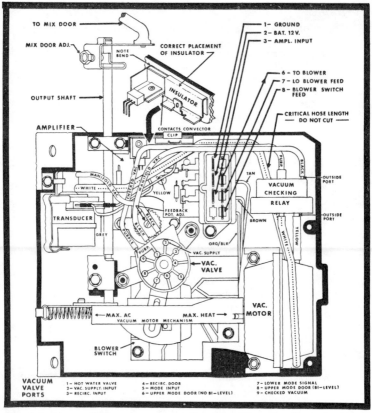

Fig. 6-4. Air conditioner programer schematic. (Courtesy Chevrolet Motor Div. of General Motors Corp.)

Amplifier Circuit Board. This circuit board (Fig. 6-6) amplifies the dc signal supplied from the sensor string. The output of the amplifier controls the operation of the transducer.

Feedback Potentiometer. The feedback potentiometer indicates to the amplifier system the position of the temperature door. Movement of the vacuum motor changes the resistance of this potentiometer.

Resistor Assembly. The blower resistors are located in the programer. The printed circuit board switch in the programer determines which of the resistors are being used, and as in conventional systems, the resistors control the blower speed.

Blower Switch

This set of contacts is located in the programer and moves as the vacuum motor moves. These contacts (of varying

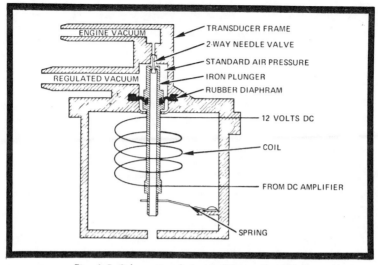

Fig. 6-5. Schematic of air conditioner transducer.

resistance) complete the electrical circuit to the blower motor and vary the blower speed.

Control Head

A thumb-wheel is provided to select the desired temperature. A control lever performs the following functions:

1. Operates a switch that allows the driver to select the type of blower program desired.
2. Operates the control-head vacuum switch.

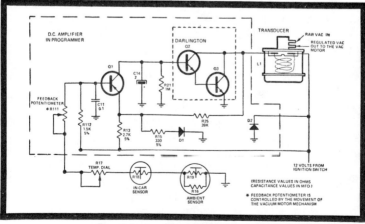

Fig. 6-6. Amplifier circuit schematic.

3. Operates the defroster through the control head vacuum switch. The defroster door is partially opened in all positions, and fully open in the DEF position.

Sensors and Switches

The function of the *in-car sensor* is to determine the temperature of the interior of the automobile. It is located on the right trim moulding of the instrument panel (Fig. 6-3).

The *ambient sensor* measures the temperature of the air entering the evaporator core.

The *ambient switch* operates the air conditioning compressor switch. When the temperature *at the switch* is above 40°F, the compressor must be on. When the temperature *at the switch* is below 25°F, the compressor must be off. This switch is mounted on the blower side of the evaporator case.

The override switch is located on the control head. When the temperature at the switch is above 73°F, this switch overrides the engine thermal switch and turns the system on immediately.

Mode-Door Diaphragms

Located behind the ductwork, the mode-door diaphragms operate the mode doors and direct the air flow out of either the air conditioning outlets, the heater floor outlet, or both the heater and air conditioning outlets. These are pull-type diaphragms; actuated by vacuum with a spring return, they are controlled by the programer vacuum switch.

Outside Air Diaphragm

When there is no vacuum applied to the outside air diaphragm, the air door is positioned to admit all outside air. With vacuum applied, a mixture of inside air and outside air enters the system.

Defroster Door

The defroster door is a 3-position door; sealed in the OFF position, it directs all air out the heater outlet. Partially open approximately 45 seconds after starting the engine in LOW, MAIN, HIGH-AUTOMATIC and BILEVEL position, and fully open in the DEF position, it directs most of the air out the defroster outlets.

Engine Thermal Switch

This switch delays the initial operation of the system in cool weather to allow the engine coolant to warm up, so the occupants will not be subjected to an excessive amount of cold air from the heater outlet.

Restrictors

The restrictors are small porous plugs that are installed in the vacuum harness in the outer port of the defroster vacuum diaphragm, and the line to the outside air diaphragm. This produces a delay in vacuum being applied to the diaphragms.

Auto Relay

This relay is energized whenever the engine thermal switch or the A/C OVERRIDE switch is closed and the control head is in AUTO, HIGH, or DEF positions. It is immediately energized in the DEF position. This allows the system to automatically vary the blower speed from low to high.

Low Relay

This relay is located on the evaporator case in the engine compartment and is energized whenever the control head is in VENT or DEF or whenever the engine thermal switch or the A/C override switch is closed. This allows the blower motor to operate at low blower speed. It is possible for the *low* relay to be energized whenever the ignition switch is on or the control head selector lever is in the OFF position.

Aspirator Assembly

The aspirator is located on top of the heater—defroster assembly and is designed to draw a sample of passenger compartment air through the in-car sensor grille and across the in-car sensor assembly to give the sensor a more responsive temperature signal. It is connected to the in-car sensor assembly by a ½ in. diameter vinyl hose which incorporates a noise-reducing chamber. Disconnection of this hose will result in erratic or slow response to changes in vehicle interior temperatures.

Electronic Circuit

Two temperature sensors (thermistors), the feedback potentiometer, and temperature control dial are all connected in series, and are located so as to sense the temperature of the outside air, inside air, system output air, and the desired temperature.

The resistance of each sensor varies according to its temperature. The control head temperature dial varies in resistance as it is adjusted by the operator to suit his comfort requirements.

Thus, temperature differences in the sensor string, plus the requirements fed into the system by the operator, cause changes in total circuit resistance which allow a varying current flow through the circuit.

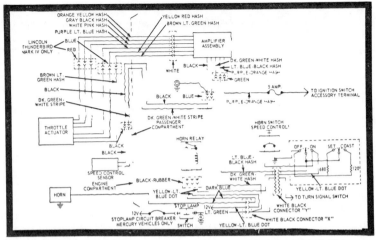

Fig. 6-7. Speed control system wiring diagram. (Courtesy Ford Customer Service Div.)

In accomplishing automatic control, the system follows three steps to transform an electronic signal into mechanical energy through which the control is achieved.

Changing the Electronic Signal to Electrical Voltage. Current flow from the sensor-string temperature-dial circuit is fed into the amplifier (Fig. 6-6) where it is transformed into a usable amplifier output voltage, the strength of which is determined by the strength of the original amplifier input signal. This voltage is then supplied to the transducer.

Changing the Electrical Voltage to a Vacuum Signal. Amplifier output voltage, varying according to temperature requirements, is converted by the transducer into a modulating transducer output vacuum. This modulated vacuum is applied to the vacuum motor.

Changing the Vacuum Signal to Mechanical Energy. The vacuum motor, controlled by the modulated transducer-output vacuum, operates the vacuum, electrical, and mechanical components of the system as required to provide automatic control of system operation.

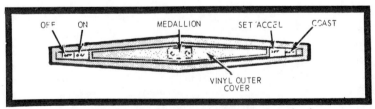

Fig. 6-8. Speed control switches on steering wheel.

Other major system components are mounted conventionally in the engine compartment. Underhood components and system air-flow remain much the same as in the Four-Season system except for the addition of the automatic control provisions. The system operates on outside air and a mixture of outside and inside air depending on the demands of the system.

SPEED CONTROL SYSTEM

Ford Motor Company's speed control system is composed of an ON–OFF switch and the SET–ACC and COAST switches, a servo (throttle actuator) assembly, a speed sensor, an amplifier assembly, and the necessary wires, linkage, check valve assembly, vacuum reserve tank, and vacuum hose to connect the components. The wiring diagram is given in Fig. 6-7. The switches are located in the steering wheel spokes (Fig. 6-8). The amplifier assembly and speed sensor are located under the instrument panel, and the servo assembly (throttle actuator) is attached to the dash panel under the hood on Ford, Meteor, and Mercury models (Fig. 6-9), and to the engine intake manifold on Thunderbird, Lincoln Continental Mark IV cars. To operate the speed control system, vehicle speed must be between 30 and 80 mph. Manifold vacuum is constantly supplied when the engine is running. When the ON-OFF switch in the

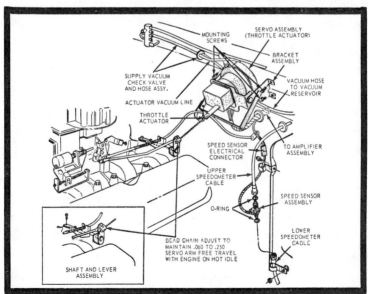

Fig. 6-9. Speed control sensor and servo assembly. (Courtesy Ford Customer Service Div.)

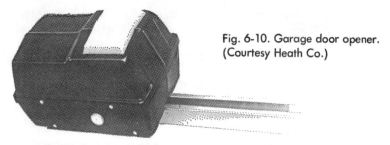

Fig. 6-10. Garage door opener.
(Courtesy Heath Co.)

steering wheel is actuated, the system is made ready to accept a set speed signal. When the vehicle has been accelerated and stabilized at a speed over 30 mph and the switch is engaged, the operator may quickly depress and release the SET–ACC (set-accelerate) button. This speed will be maintained until a new speed is set by the operator, the brake pedal is depressed, or the system is turned off.

Decreasing Set Speed

The rate of set speed may be reduced by applying the brake and resetting the speed or by depressing the COAST switch. When the vehicle has slowed to the desired speed, the COAST switch is released and the new speed is set automatically. If the vehicle speed is reduced below 30 mph, the operator must manually increase the speed and reset the system.

Increasing Set Speed

The vehicle set speed may be increased at any time by depressing the accelerator until the higher rate is reached and stabilized, then depressing and releasing the SET speed button.

Speed may also be increased by depressing the SET–ACC button (at speeds over 30 mph) and holding it in that position. The vehicle will then automatically increase speed. When the desired speed is attained and the button is released, that new speed will be maintained.

Amplifier Testing

Do not use a test lamp to perform the following tests, as excessive current will damage electronic components inside the amplifier. Use only a voltmeter of 5000 ohm/volt rating or higher.

ON CIRCUIT TEST

Turn on the ignition switch and connect a voltmeter to the lead at the amplifier terminal of the green connector. The voltmeter should read 12V when the switch on the steering wheel is depressed and held. If voltage is not available, check the horn relay circuit and control switch. Release the button; 12V should remain at the blue wire indicating the circuit is engaged. If the voltage does not remain, check the ground connection on the amplifier, inspect the fuse, and check for good circuit continuity.

OFF CIRCUIT TEST

With the ignition on and the voltmeter still connected, depress the OFF switch on the steering wheel. Voltage on the blue wire should drop to zero, indicating the ON circuit is deenergized. If the voltage does not drop to zero, perform the control switch test. If the switches work properly, mount a known good amplifier and recheck the OFF circuit as above.

GARAGE DOOR OPENER

The Heathkit garage door opener model GDA-3209-1 (Fig. 6-10) is a sturdy, quiet device which will open and close all types of overhead residential garage doors up to 7½ feet high. When used with the optional Heathkit garage door transmitter (Fig. 6-11), leaving the car to open the garage door is unnecessary. Pressing the button on the transmitter will open or close the garage door. This is especially convenient during bad weather or when it is late at night.

The door opener not only opens and closes a garage, but provides positive locking. Once closed, the garage door cannot be opened by hand from the outside of the garage. Should a power failure occur, the quick-release arm latch can be easily disengaged from inside the garage, permitting the door to be opened by hand.

A clutch and safety switch feature returns the door to its fully open position if it becomes obstructed while the door is

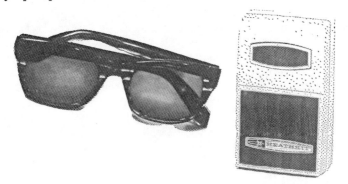

Fig. 6-11. Garage door opener transmitter, shown with eyeglasses for size comparison.

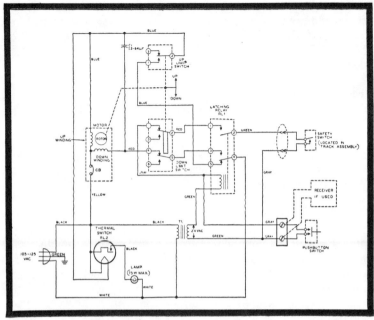

Fig. 6-12. Schematic of a garage door opener. (Courtesy Heath Co.)

being closed. Other safety features include circuit overload protection and a safety lamp. A time delay circuit turns on the safety lamp for 1 to 3 minutes when the garage door is opened or closed, to prevent fumbling in the dark for garage lights.

DOOR OPENER CIRCUIT

Refer to the schematic diagram (Fig. 6-12) while you read this circuit description. The schematic diagram shows the position of all switch and relay contacts when the garage door is open, the motor is not running, and the lamp is turned off.

To automatically open and close a garage door, it is necessary to use a mechanism that can start, stop, and reverse the direction of the drive motor. These functions are obtained by using a power circuit, a switching circuit, and a motor that has both forward and reverse windings. The power circuit supplies the necessary line voltage to operate the motor, while a 24V switching circuit controls the latching relay which directs power to the appropriate limit switch and motor winding.

Line voltage is applied to transformer T1, to the yellow (common) motor lead, and to contact 4 of latching relay RL1. The motor has an internal thermal circuit breaker for overload protection. This circuit breaker automatically resets after any circuit overload problem has been corrected.

The externally mounted pushbutton switch connects 24V across the coil of relay RL1 and causes the relay contacts to latch in a reversed position (opposite that shown on the schematic). Power is then applied through contacts 4 and 3 of relay RL1, through contacts 5 and 4 of the *down* limit switch, and through the down winding of the motor. The motor will run until either the down limit switch, the safety switch, or the pushbutton switch is actuated. When the door reaches its closed position, contacts 4 and 5 of the down limit switch will open and remove power from the down winding.

Capacitor C1 is, at one time, parallel with the up winding of the motor, and at another time in parallel with the down winding. This capacitor causes an approximate 90-degree phase shift in the power applied to the motor windings, allowing the motor rotation to be reversed as required to operate the door in the proper direction.

If an obstruction prevents the door from closing, the safety switch contacts will close and apply 24V through contacts 2 and 1 of the down limit switch, to the coil of RL1. This will happen when the drive screw has stopped and the clutch has slipped one revolution. Relay RL1 will now latch in the position shown on the schematic. Whenever the door is not fully open, contacts 1 and 2 of the *up* limit switch are closed. Power is now coupled through contacts 4 and 5 of RL1, and through contacts 1 and 2 of the up limit switch, to the up winding of the motor. The motor will drive the door opener to open the door until contacts 1 and 2 of the up limit switch are opened. Also, the safety switch circuit is disabled by the open contacts (1 and 2 of RL1) when the door is opening.

Due to the extra closing force required to properly seal most garage doors during the last 2 or 3 in. of travel, contacts 1 and 2 of the down limit switch open to disable the safety switch from interpreting this extra force as an obstruction and reopening the door.

Whenever the motor is running, the heater coil of the thermal switch draws current from the power line. This action heats a bimetallic strip and causes one of its contacts to bend and touch a stationary contact. The lamp is now placed across the power line and will remain on for 1 to 3 minutes after the motor stops.

ELECTRONICALLY CONTROLLED TRANSMISSION

Renault, Inc. offers an electronically controlled automatic transmission. In this unit, vehicle speed and engine load are electrically sensed and the resulting signal is applied to an electronic computer unit. The computer develops appropriate

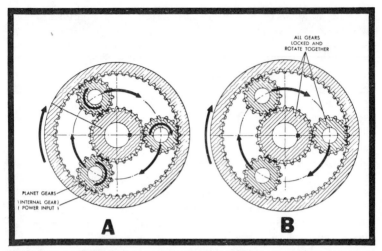

Fig. 6-13. Planetary units in reduction (in A) and in direct drive (in B).

electrical signals, depending on the vehicle speed and engine load, and sends them to two solenoid valves, which take the place of hydraulically operated valves in conventional automatics, and cause the gears to shift.

Gear Train

Like conventional automatics, the Renault automatic is based on planetary units. The planetary units (see the simplified drawing in Fig. 6-13) consist of *planet* gears that encircle the center, or *sun* gear, as the earth and the other planets circle the sun. The planetary gears are meshed with the sun gear and the *ring* gear, which encircles them. One member of this planetary unit can be kept from rotating by a hydraulic *brake*. As in a coaster brake on a bicycle, braking action results from increased friction when the discs in the brake are pressed together. Each unit also includes a multiple-disc clutch that is applied by oil pressure.

Engine power is applied to the planetary unit through a type of turbine called a *torque converter*. When engine power is applied to the ring gear through a clutch and the sun gear is held stationary by a brake, the planet gears are forced by the driving gear to "walk around" the stationary gear (Fig. 6-13A) at a reduced speed. The ratio between the speed of the ring gear and the speed at which the planet gears orbit the sun gear is the *gear reduction* ratio.

When the brake of the sun gear is released and the clutch is applied, power will be applied directly to both it and the ring gear. Since both gears are driven by the engine at the same speed, the entire unit is locked together and rotated as a unit providing direct drive, or 1:1 ratio (see Fig. 6-13B).

Each planetary unit is a complete 2-speed transmission in itself, as it can operate in either reduction or direct drive. The transmission contains two of these planetary units to provide the desired range of gear ratios.

Transmission Hydraulic System

The hydraulic system of the Renault transmission is illustrated in Fig. 6-14. The internal-tooth oil pump applies oil pressure to the torque converter (conv), gear box (G), pressure regulator (R), manual valve (VM), selection valve (VP), relay valve (VR), control clutches (E1 and E2), control brakes (F1 and F2), and two solenoid ball valves (E11 and E12).

The *manual valve* is worked mechanically by placing the gear shift lever in one of six positions: P, R, N, A, 2, or 1. (The A position corresponds to D on American transmissions.) The manual valve sends hydraulic signals to E1 and VP that depend on the position of the gear shift lever.

The *selector valve* routes oil pressure from the manual valve to the control sections of the gear train either straight (in the case of clutch E2) or by way of the relay valve (F1 and F2). It has three positions, which depend on the opening or closing of the two solenoid ball valves, E11 and E12.

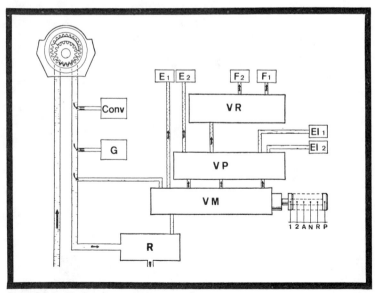

Fig. 6-14. Hydraulic components of automatic transmission. (Courtesy Renault, Inc.)

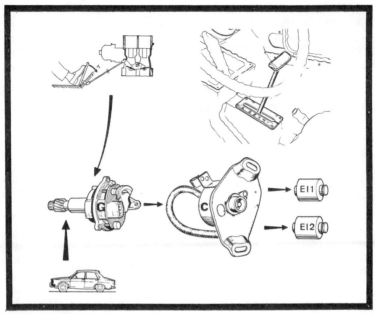

Fig. 6-15. Electrical parts of an electronically controlled transmission. (Courtesy Renault, Inc.)

The *relay valve* controls the switching over between second and third speed by allowing the release of brake F2 only after the pressure on clutch E2 has reached sufficient pressure.

Transmission Electrical Components

The electrical parts and their interrelationship are illustrated in Fig. 6-15.

The gear changes in the transmission are determined by three positions of the selection valve which are, in turn, determined by the two solenoid valves in Fig. 6-15. Their action is set by an electronic assembly whose function is to give circuit orders dependent on the speed of the car and the amount of opening of the carburetor butterfly valve.

The electronic assembly consists of the governor (G) and computer (C). The governor senses vehicle speed and engine load and fends this information in the form of a varying current to the computer unit. The latter, depending on the governor, accelerator pedal, and selector lever signals received, sends instructions to the solenoid ball valves, E11 and E12.

The solenoid ball valves (Fig. 6-16) are electrohydraulic components. Each has a central passage connecting to the selectiowlve. A cutoff ball can open or close the passage. With current passing through the coil, the ball cuts off the passageway; with no current through the coil, the ball moves to open the passageway. The function of the two solenoid ball valves is to guide the selection valve to one of three positions. In selection valve position1, both ball valves are closed and the pressure applied at the right side of VP is able to keep the piston in VP at equilibrium at point 1. In selection valve position 2, no current is applied to E11. It opens, pressure in the right side of VP is reduced, and the piston moves to position 2. When both ball valves open, the piston is able to move to position 3. As the piston in VP thus moves, it covers and uncovers ports leading to the appropriate brake and clutch.

Governor

The governor (Fig. 6-17) is a low-power alternator that produces about 1W. The rotor consists of a permanent magnet (1) with three pairs of poles. This magnet is turned by the gear (2) and worm wheel (3), which are integral with the transmission drive shaft. The rotation of the rotor is, therefore, proportional to the speed of the car.

The stator (4) consists also of three pairs of poles, plus a field coil (5). This coil, as shown, has a current flow along two wires of equal length, the center point of which is ground. This arrangement allows sufficient current to be retained at the terminal for recovery purposes, in case one side of the coil is open.

Of the three stator poles, two can be offset by a control lever (6) attached by a cable to the accelerator. In light-throttle

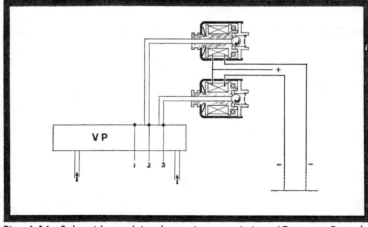

Fig. 6-16. Solenoids used in electronic transmission. (Courtesy Renault, Inc.)

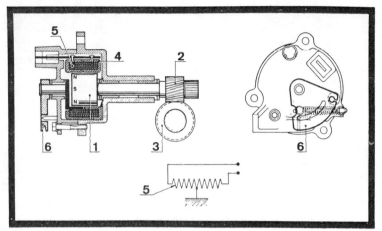

Fig. 6-17. Governor of electronically controlled transmission. (Courtesy Renault, Inc.)

operation, the poles are in the normal setting (Fig. 6-18A). Figure 6-18B shows that the current output increases linearly with speed to an amplitude designated as **x**.

By means of the accelerator, the lever turns the two moving poles. When the carburetor butterfly valve is wide open, the two poles are at maximum offset, as shown in Fig. 6-19A. Current is then produced according to the graph in Fig. 6-19B. It still increases with speed, but at 3000 rpm, the current has a value of x/3; it is one-third of the current at light throttle.

From the foregoing you can see that the governor current output depends not only on the speed of the car, but on the engine load, as represented by the accelerator setting.

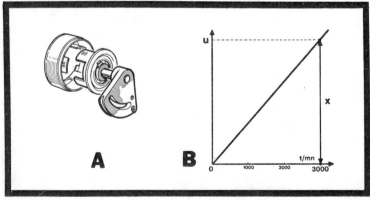

Fig. 6-18. In A, the stator poles in the normal position; in B, the current output for this condition is shown. (Courtesy Renault, Inc.)

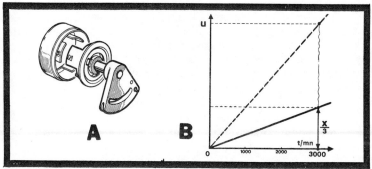

Fig. 6-19. In A, with the carburetor butterfly wide open, the stators are at maximum offset; B shows the current output for this condition. (Courtesy Renault, Inc.)

Electronic Computer Unit

In Fig. 6-20, the varying alternating current is seen to be fed to the electronic computer at T. The electronic section of the unit consists of a circuit for rectifying the governor current and two electronic grounding devices for the solenoid ball valves, E11 and E12.

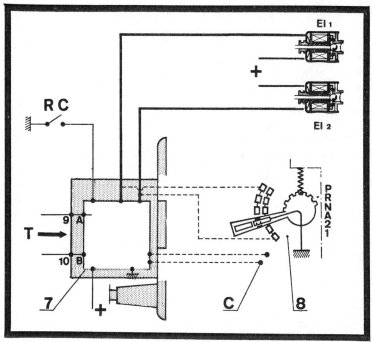

Fig. 6-20. Control circuitry of the Renault automatic transmission.

The alternating current (T) on the two governor coils is fed to terminals 9 and 10 on the electronic computer unit. After passing through the rectifier (diodes and capacitor) this current, now dc, is fed to points A and B for the solenoid ball valves. Two currents are fed into the computer—a fixed battery current and the variable current from the governor.

The grounding of the current for the solenoid ball valves is carried out inside the unit. When the variable governor current reaches certain values at A and B, the unit starts working, initiating or cutting off the grounding of the solenoid ball valve concerned.

A lower gear can be selected within certain limits of the vehicle speed by using a *kickdown* switch (RC) operated by the accelerator at the end of its travel. This switch, by a grounding procedure, alters the characteristics of the control unit for the solenoid ball valves and sets them working instantaneously.

The *first-gear-hold* circuit (C) insures retaining first gear as speed increases and works as a safety measure in slowing down the car. In fact, with decreasing vehicle speed at light throttle, the engagement of first gear comes into effect only at about 21 mph. At full throttle, it is "advised" not to select first gear above about 37 mph.

Switch 8 in Fig. 6-20 is positioned by the gear selector lever in one of the six positions P, R, N, A, 2, or 1. Mechanically, it insures the position and locking of the manual valve for each position of the selector lever, this by means of a 3-ball lock. Electrically, it connects the different circuits of the electronic computer unit as follows:

- In position P, R, or N, the switch immediately grounds the two solenoid ball valves (E11 and E12).
- In position A, the switch has no effect. The ball valves are automatically controlled by the electronic system.
- In position 2, the switch gives overriding grounding of solenoid ball valve E12.
- In position 1, the switch immediately grounds solenoid ball valve E12.

Automotive Test Equipment

Gone forever are the days when all a mechanic needed to tune up or troubleshoot a car was a good pair of ears, a good set of eyes, and a good feel for vibrations. Today's sophisticated cars require sophisticated techniques for their maintenance. Sophisticated electronic test instruments act as extensions of the serviceman's innate senses, providing far deeper insight into a car's operation than a man's unaided senses ever could. For checking the timing...for testing ignition system components...for analyzing the exhaust gases, electronic test equipment is indispensable.

ELECTRONIC TIMING LIGHT

the Heathkit model CI-1040 12V automotive timing light (Fig. 7-1) is a self-contained, solid-state flash unit that is powered by the vehicle battery and features a new triggering method. A high-impact plastic housing is proportioned to allow aiming the timing light in narrow spaces while keeping hands at a safe distance from moving engine parts. A special low-voltage trigger pickup coil permits connecting the timing light while the engine is running. This also eliminates direct connections to the spark plug.

The flash from this unit is many times brighter than the flash from timing lights that operate from only the spark plug voltage. This extra brilliance is created by a circuit board that steps up the battery voltage to provide the high output. The high-intensity flash is easy to use even under full daylight conditions.

Many timing lights receive their triggering signal directly from the spark plug voltage. However, in this timing light, a portion of the spark plug current is inductively coupled into the pickup coil to provide the low-voltage triggering signal. Also, because an indirect triggering method is used, the timing light does not interfere with other test instruments that may be connected to the engine.

A special, built-in neon lamp allows accurate adjustment of the high-voltage circuit without using special instruments.

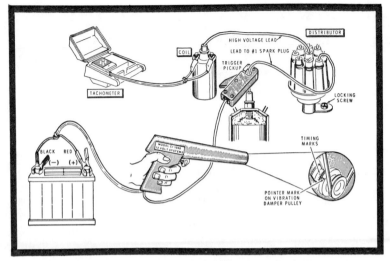

Fig. 7-1. Using a timing light. (Courtesy Heath Co.)

USING A TIMING LIGHT

Refer to Fig. 7-1 for an illustration of the operation and use of the timing light on an automobile engine. Obtain the timing specificatims for your car's engine (see owner's or service manual) before attempting any timing adjustments.

Precautions

While doing engine timing, avoid personal injury or damage to the timing light, its power cord, and the trigger pickup lead by observing the following precautions: (1) Avoid touching any high voltage points on the engine ignition system. (2) Keep away from the fan and the fan belt. (3) Be sure the timing light, its power cord, and the trigger pickup cable are correctly positioned as shown in Fig. 7-1 so they are clear of the fan and fan belt. (4) Avpd touching the exhaust manifold of the engine. (5) Do not lay the timing light on the engine. (6) Do not look directly at the lens of the timing light when it is operating. (7) Do not let the triggered clamp snap shut.

Operating Considerations

The timing light can be used in daylight at a range of up to 2 feet from the timing marks. The pushbutton switch should not be taped down. Use the pushbutton switch only when doing timing adjustments or when checking the timing. Do not attempt to do timing adjustments until other engine tuning work has been completed. Operating the engine at over 2000 rpm should only be intermittent. The timing light should not be used in temperatures below 0°F; otherwise the electronic components may be damaged.

Timing Procedure Example

Refer to Fig. 7-1 for an illustration of the hookup of the timing light to an automobile ignition system. *Note:* the following basic step-by-step procedure is only an example.

Refer to the engine timing specifications.

Start the engine and allow it to warm up to normal operating temperature.

Us a tachometer to set the engine to the specified idle speed.

Connect the trigger pickup around the No. 1 spark plug lead.

Connect the battery clip with black insulation to the negative (−) battery terminal. Connect the battery clip with red insulation to the positive (+) battery terminal.

Refer to the engine timing specifications for your particular engine and disconnect the vacuum line if required. *Warning:* The stroboscopic effect of the timing light that causes the timing mark to appear stopped also causes other revolving parts (fan, fanbelt, and pulleys) to appear stopped. *Do not* place your hands near these supposedly stopped parts.

Aim the timing light at the timing marks and press the pushbutton switch.

If the timing reference mark lines up with the specified timing mark, no adjustment is necessary. Turn the engine off. However, if the reference mark does not line up with the timing mark, the engine needs timing.

The following steps show how to time it. *Note:* Do not rotate the distributor after loosening the lock screw. (If you wish, mark the position of the distributor before loosening the screw so you can return it to the original adjustment point.) Turn the engine off. Then carefully loosen the locking screw on the distributor clamp. Leave the screw tight enough so that the distributor will not change position by itself while the engine is running.

Start the engine.

Rotate the distributor until the timing reference mark lines up with the specified timing mark.

Tighten the distributor locking screw and then recheck the engine timing using the timing light.

Note: If the distributor of your engine has a centrifugal spark advance, perform this step. If it does not have a centrifugal spark advance, disregard this step and proceed to the next step. Increase the engine speed smoothly and observe the timing marks with the timing light aimed at them. The matching

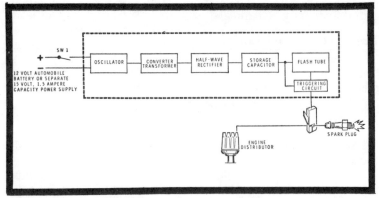

Fig. 7-2. Block diagram of timing-light circuit. (Courtesy Heath Co.)

timing mark should move as the engine speed is increased. The direction of movement of the timing mark should be opposite to the direction of rotation of the damper pulley.

Reconnect the vacuum line if it was disconnected and plugged as required by the engine timing specifications.

Set the engine speed at a higher-than-normal idle speed. While the timing light is aimed at the timing marks, open the throttle suddenly and then let it spring closed. The matching timing marks will momentarily move in the direction of rotation of the engine (retards spark) when the engine is suddenly speeded up. With normal speed increases, the vacuum control advances the spark and adds to the spark advance caused by the centrifugal advance mechanism. A sudden increase in engine speed causes the intake manifold vacuum to drop to a low value which momentarily retards the spark.

HOW THE TIMING LIGHT WORKS

The strobe tube of the timing light is fired by the current induced into the trigger pickup coil when the No. 1 spark plug fires. The flash of the timing light illuminates the rotating damper pulley and the timing marks when the firing voltage for the No. 1 spark plug occurs at the distributor. As the pulley will appear to align with one of the timing marks. If the engine passes the timing marks, the pointer mark on the pulley needs timing, the distributor is adjusted (by rotating the distributor housing) so that the pulley mark then aligns with the proper timing mark as specified by the engine manufacturer. On some engines, the timing marks are located on the vibration damper pulley and the reference mark is a stationary pointer located near the pulley. Refer to the block diagram (Fig. 7-2) and the schematic (Fig. 7-3) as you read the following descriptions.

Timing Light Circuit

The voltage from the storage battery of the car is applied through switch SW1 to oscillator transistor Q1. R1, the 100 ohm control in the base circuit of Q1, varies the bias voltage of Q1. This bias voltage controls the oscillation frequency of Q1 and thus Q1's output, a pulsating dc to the primary winding of converter transformer T1, is controlled. This pulsating dc induces 600 volts ac in the secondary winding of T1.

The output voltage of T1 is applied to diodes D1 and D2, which operate as half-wave rectifiers and change the 600 volts ac to a pulsating dc voltage. The 2 μF capacitor, C3, charges to the 600 volts, which is also applied to strobe tube V1. The tube does not fire at this time because the voltage is less than the self-ionization voltage of the tube. A voltage in the form of a trigger pulse is taken from the No. 1 spark plug lead of the engine when the plug fires.

A trigger pulse applied to the gate (G) of the SCR (D3) causes it to conduct. Capacitor C4 then discharges through trigger transformer L1. L1 steps up this voltage to the potential necessary to ionize the strobe tube. The tube then conducts, which allows capacitor C3 to discharge through the tube. A brilliant flash is produced that is approximately 10 microseconds in duration.

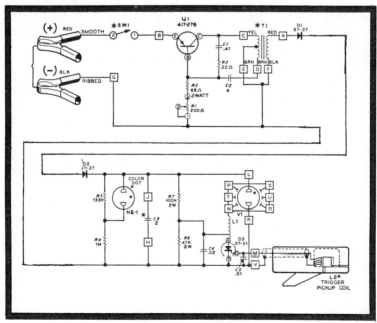

Fig. 7-3. Circuit of timing light. (Courtesy Heath Co.)

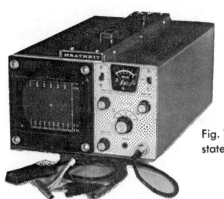

Fig. 7-4. Heathkit CO-1015 solid-
state ignition analyzer.

Resistors R4 and R5 form a voltage divider network for the voltage adjustment using the neon lamp and control R1.

Ignition Analyzer

The Heathkit CO-1015 solid-state ignition analyzer (Fig. 7-4) is a test instrument for use by garage mechanics, service station operators, and auto hobbyists. A pickup cable assembly transfers the electrical pulses produced by the engine ignition system into the analyzer where they are displayed on a crt (cathode-ray tube) screen. This display enables the operator to determine if each component in the ignition system is operating properly. Both conventional and capacitive-discharge ignition systems may be checked by turning the selector switch to the appropriate position. The connection procedure is the same for both systems.

The function switch also allows a display of secondary or primary patterns of either ignition system.

This analyzer has two special features, as follows:

A built-in calibration signal to properly adjust the sweep length of the pattern.

A sweep length of the pattern that is maintained regardless of engine rpm.

The flat-faced crt provides a clear in-focus pattern over the entire viewing area. The screen (graticule) has two scales marked in degrees. The upper scale is used to check 3- or 6-cylinder engines; the lower scale, to check 4- or 8- cylinder engines. This provides rapid checking of distributor dwell angle regardless of the number of engine cylinders. A special alloy shield around the cathode-ray tube shields the tube from stray magnetic fields that could have an effect on the displayed patterns.

The ignition analyzer should be regarded as a special tool to rapidly check or troubleshoot the operation of an ignition system. As with many other special tools, ability to use the analyzer to its greatest advantage will come with continued use. Interpretation of the patterns obtained will indicate if the ignition system is operating properly. If a malfunction is indicated, careful examination of the area of the pattern that is incorrect should indicate the system component that is the cause of the trouble.

This analyzer is actually two instruments in one—an ignition scope and a tachometer. The ignition scope is similar to the *oscilloscope* used by electronics personnel (also called a "scope" for short).

THE OSCILLOSCOPE

An oscilloscope is a measuring instrument capable of displaying a wide variety of rapidly changing electrical phenomena—even phenomena occurring only once and lasting for a fraction of a millionth of a second.

The oscilloscope graphs changes in voltage with time. The amplitude of the voltage is graphed along a vertical axis, and the time is graphed along a horizontal axis. Because the graph of a voltage often takes the form of a wave, the graph is called a *waveform*.

PROFILE OF THE OSCILLOSCOPE

A simplified block diagram of an oscilloscope is given in Fig. 7-5. The *cathode-ray-tube circuit* consists basically of a

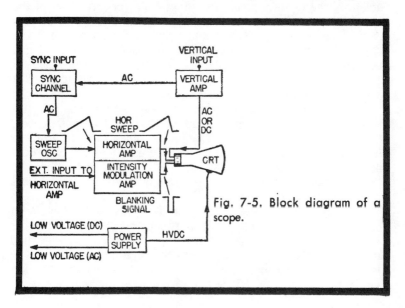

Fig. 7-5. Block diagram of a scope.

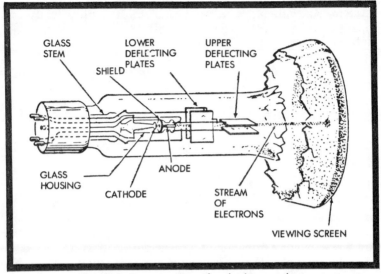

Fig. 7-6. Cutaway view of cathode-ray tube.

cathode-ray tube (crt) and its related controls, the *intensity* control and the *focus* control. The crt, the visual display device of the oscilloscope, operates in the following manner: a beam of electrons leaves the cathode of the tube, is accelerated through the tube, and strikes a phosphor-coated screen that glows at the point of impact. This beam is focused to a sharp point by the action of the focus control. The magnitude (or intensity) of the beam is controlled by the intensity control. The beam sweeps the screen in the horizontal and vertical directions when the appropriate voltages are applied to the horizontal (lower) and vertical (upper) *deflection plates*. (See sketch of crt in Fig. 7-6.) The resultant trace left by the beam is a visual presentation of a voltage waveform in the circuit being examined.

The voltage waveform to be examined may be applied ditly to the vertical deflection plates of the crt. In most cases, hwever, the voltage to be presented is either too small or too large in amplitude to be examined. It must be either *amplified* or *attenuated*. The amplification or attenuation of the input to the vertical deflection plates is accomplished by the vertical deflection amplifier circuit.

The purpose of the horizontal deflection amplifier is to establish the desired amplitude of sweep voltages applied to the horizontal deflection plate of the crt. The sweep voltage will control the beam deflection across the face of the screen. The input to the horizontal amplifier may be selected from the sweep oscillator (Fig. 7-5) or from some external source.

If a voltage is applied to the vertical deflection plates without a voltage applied to the horizontal deflection plates, only a thin vertical line will appear at the face of the scope. If only the sweep is observed without a vertical signal applied, only a horizontal line would be present on the screen. The length of the horizontal line is dependent upon the amplitude of the sweep voltage applied to the horizontal deflection plates. The amplitude of the sweep voltage applied to the horizontal deflection plates is controlled by the *horizontal gain control*.

The sweep circuit oscillator provides a voltage which is applied to the input of the horizontal amplifier. In order for the time base across the face of the tube to be linear, thus preventing a distorted signal on the screen, the rise of voltage of the sweep circuit, which is a sawtooth generator, must be linear with respect to time.

A type of sweep circuit often used in an oscilloscope is a free-running sawtooth generator. This type of circuit is not a particularly stable type. To observe a signal on the face of the scope, the sweep frequency and the frequency of the signal to be observed must be synchronized. In order to achieve synchronization of the sweep oscillator and the frequency under observation, a synchronizing signal must be obtained from the signal under observation and applied to the sweep circuit. This operation will insure that the sweep will always start at the same position in the observed cycle. The synchronizing signal may also be obtained from the line frequency or some outside source.

ENGINE ANALYZERS

The most common use of the "scope" in engine analysis is for displaying the operation of the ignition system. Scopes used for this purpose are similar to conventional scopes, but often the controls are called by different names. Instead of a sweep frequency or sweep rate control, the engine analyzer may have a *stability* control. There may be an *expand* control instead of a horizontal gain control, and a *parade* control instead of a horizontal position control. Instead of a vertical gain control, there may be a *height* control. The names of the controls on an engine analyzer of this type are actually more descriptive than names of conventional scope controls, and are practically self-explanatory.

There is a surprising amount of information about engine operation that may be obtained with an engine analyzer. In fact, the information to be gained is limited mainly by the ability of the operator to interpret the meaning of observed waveform deviations from the normal wave patterns.

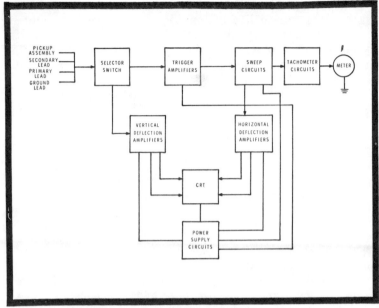

Fig. 7-7. Block diagram of ignition analyzer. (Courtesy Heath Co.)

IGNITION ANALYZER CIRCUIT

Refer to the block diagram (Fig. 7-7) and schematic diagram (Fig. 7-8) while you read this circuit description.

The Heathkit CO-1015 solid-state ignition analyzer is composed of the following circuits: trigger, calibrating signal, sweep, vertical deflection amplifier, horizontal deflection amplifier, tachometer, and power supply.

Trigger Circuit

The trigger circuit consists of transistors Q301 through Q304 and their associated circuitry. With selector switch SW1 in the SEC position (either STD IGN or C-D IGN mode) and SW3A in the PARADE mode, the signal from the No. 1 spark plug wire is picked up by the clamp-on pickup assembly and fed to the base of Q301 through lug 2 of the cable connector socket, C301, R301, and R302. The signal is then amplified by Q301, Q302, and Q303. The output of Q303 triggers the sweep circuit. At the same time, the signal from the secondary lead T-clip passes through SW1, to C801, R801, and to the base of Q802, the vertical deflection preamplifier.

With Selector switch SW1 in the PRI position (either STD IGN or C-D IGN mode) and SW3A still in PARADE mode, the signal from the breaker points is picked up by the primary lead and

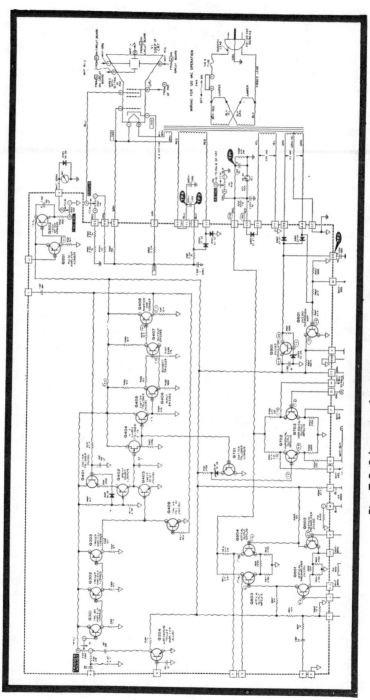

Fig. 7-8. Schematic of ignition analyzer. (Courtesy Heath Co.)

185

applied through lug 4 of the cable connector socket to SW1. From SW1, this signal again passes to Q802 and the signal from the clamp-on pickup assembly again passes to Q301, Q302, Q303, and triggers the sweep circuit.

With selector switch SW1 in the standard ignition SEC position and switch SW3A pushed in (superimposed mode), the signal from the primary lead passes through R2 and R12 to SW1R and SW3A; then to the base of Q304. From Q304, the signal passes through C302 and R302 to Q301, Q302, and Q303. The output of Q303 triggers the sweep circuit. At the same time, the signal from the secondary lead T-clip passes through switch SW1F to C801, and the base of Q802. In the C-D IGN mode of SW1, the signal from the primary lead passes directly to SW1R lugs 1 and 12; then to SW3A and Q304. The signal from the secondary lead passes through SW1F lugs 2 and 6, to Q802. With tz selector switch SW1 in standard ignition PRI position, and SW3 pushed in, the signal from the primary lead is applied through R2 and R12 to SW1R and through SW3A to the base of Q304. At the same time, this signal also passes through SW1F lugs 5 and 6, C801, and R801 to Q802.

Sweep Circuit

The sweep circuit is designed to maintain a constant horizontal width regardless of the frequency of the incoming signal. This eliminates the necessity of recalibrating the sweep width every time the engine speed changes. To prevent the horizontal width (sweep amplitude) of the trace from changing when the engine speed varies, the charging current to seeep-forming capacitor C401 is adjusted automatically. This compensates for engine speed variations because the voltage across C401 does not change and the sweep width stays the same.

To change the charging current of C401, the sweep circuit generates a ramp voltage of contant amplitude and variable repetition rate. As shown in the partial schematic, the sweep circuit consists of a current source (Q402), a Schmitt trigger circuit (Q406, Q407), an integrator circuit (C402, R412), the sweep forming capacitor (C401), and a reset switching transistor (Q403).

When the circuit operates at a given reset pulse repetition rate (engine speed constant), the voltage developed across the sweep-forming capacitor, C401, is a linear ramp voltage with a peak voltage of E. The Schmitt trigger is designed to have a firing point at $E/2$. This results in a symmetrical square wave at the output of the Schmitt trigger.

For any particular reset pulse repetition rate (F), the Schmitt trigger establishes $1/F$. With the firing voltage $E/2$ of the Schmitt trigger constant, E/2 must occur at time F/2 to maintain a symmetrical square wave at the output of the Schmitt trigger (Q407). The square wave output of Q407 is applied to the integrator circuit which converts the square wave to a dc output (used to control the current source) proportional to the duty cycle of the square wave. This allows the gain of the current source to be high. As the current from the current source is changed, the change in duty cycle due to frequency changes will decrease and the peak voltage across the sweep-forming capacitor can be held constant.

Q409 prevents the trigger circuit from operating on any signal pulse other than the actual plug firing signal.

Vertical Deflection Amplifier

The preamplifier and output stages of the vertical deflection amplifier operate as differential amplifiers. A signal pulse from either the secondry lead T-clip or the primary lead is routed to the base of Q802 by selector switch SW1. Q802 conducts and its emitter voltage increases. This increased voltage is applied to the emitter of Q801 and reduces the forward bias of Q801 and increases its collector output voltage. The signal at the collector of transistor Q801 is 180 degrees out of phase with the signal at the collector of Q802. This then forms the push-pull type of preamplifier required to drive the vertical output amplifier. SW2, the vertical expand switch, places R14 between the emitters of Q801 and Q802 when the switch is pulled out. This doubles the vertical amplitude of the trace. With the *vertical expand* switch in its normal pushed-in position, emitter resistors R804, R805, and R806 establish the dc gain of the vertical output amplifier, Q803 and Q804.

Horizontal Deflection Amplifier

The operation of the horizontal amplifier is similar to that of the vertical amplifier. However, the horizontal amplifier does not have a preamplifier stage.

The sweep signal from the sweep circuit and emitter follower Q701 is amplified by the horizontal differential amplifier, Q702 and Q703. The push-pull output of Q702 and Q703 is applied to the horizontal deflection plates of the crt. This causes the electron beam to sweep across the face of the crt and produce a trace. The horizontal sweep rate of the electron beam is determined by the frequency of the trigger signal.

R6, the horizontal position control, varies the dc voltage applied to the base of Q703. This causes a dc unbalance in the horizontal amplifier and determines the horizontal position of the trace.

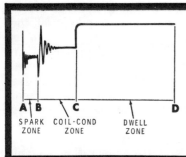

Fig. 7-9. Primary pattern standard ignition. (Courtesy Heath Co.)

A   B   C   D
SPARK   COIL-COND   DWELL
ZONE   ZONE   ZONE

Horizontal expand control R5 varies the coupling between the emitters of Q702 and Q703 which determines the gain of the horizontal amplifier. Therefore, horizontal deflection (sweep width) is determined by the setting of the *horizontal expand* control.

IGNITION ANALYSIS

The various components of the engine ignition system produce complex voltage signal pulses. The ignition analyzer converts these signal pulses into a visual pattern on the crt screen. Comparison of the acutal displayed pattern with the normal pattern produced by a properly operating ignition system enables the detection of any deviation from normal and the isolation of the trouble area. Therefore, it is necessary to know how each part of the ignition system will affect a normal pattern.

The analyzer will display a superimposed primary or superimposed secondary pattern in which the firing patterns of all engine cylinders are shown simultaneously, one on top of the other. It will also display a primary or secondary "parade" pattern in which the firing patterns of all engine cylinders are shown from left to right across the screen in their normal firing order. The primary superimposed pattern is most useful in locating troubles that may occur due to a poor connection anywhere between the vehicle battery and the grounded side of the breaker points in the distributor. The secondary superimposed pattern is most useful in locating troubles that may occur in the high-voltage circuits between the ignition coil and the spark plugs. The parade pattern is used to determine if one or more firing patterns are not normal and, if so, which engine cylinders are involved.

The patterns shown in Fig. 7-9 through 7-12 show patterns obtained from an engine with a negative-ground electrical system. That is, the negative (−) terminal of the battery is connected to the vehicle frame. A positive-ground system (positive battery terminal connected to the vehicle frame) will produce a primary pattern that is inverted from those shown in the various primary pattern figures.' The secondary patterns will be the same for both negative and positive ground systems.

Primary Pattern

At point A in Fig. 7-9 (points-open signal), the breaker points open. This produces a high voltage in the coil secondary winding and the spark plug fires. At A—B (spark zone), the high voltage is directed by the distributor to the correct spark plug for firing. At B—C (oil—condenser zone), the spark plug stops firing. The coil—condenser oscillations show unused coil energy being dissipated to ground. At C (points-closed signal), the start of current flow through the coil primary occurs. At C—D (dwell zone), the current flow through the coil primary rebuilds the magnetic field around both windings. This completes the firing cycle for one cylinder. At D the breaker points open again and the firing pattern sequence is repeated for the next cylinder in the firing order.

Secondary Pattern

At point A in Fig. 7-10 (plug firing signal), the breaker points open. This produces a high voltage in the coil secondary winding and the spark plug fires. Interval A—B (spark zone) is the firing time the spark plug. Once the spark is started at A, a lower voltage sustains the firing to B.

Because the coil—condenser oscillations that occur in the primary circuit are not reflected, the secondary pattern shows a horizontal line during the time that the spark plug fires. This line, called the *spark line*, is very important since any deviations in this zone reflect difficulties in the high-voltage circuits.

At B—C (coil—condenser zone), the spark plug stops firing. Coil—condenser oscillations show unused coil energy being

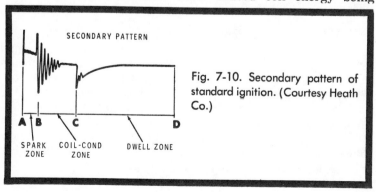

SECONDARY PATTERN

Fig. 7-10. Secondary pattern of standard ignition. (Courtesy Heath Co.)

A | B   C   D
SPARK ZONE   COIL-COND ZONE   DWELL ZONE

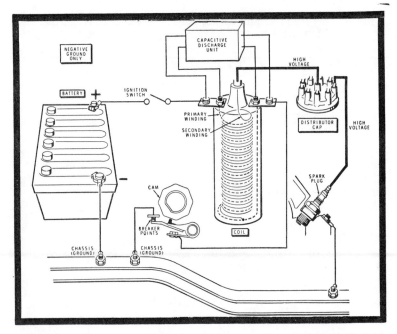

Fig. 7-11. Capacitive discharge ignition system. (Courtesy Heath Co.)

dissipated to ground, just as in the primary display. At C (points-closed signal), the start of current flow through the coil primary occurs. When the breaker points close there is a voltage induced in the secondary winding which oscillates for a short period of time. This signal, which is shown in the secondary pattern, is very important since it reflects the proper closing of the points. The position of point C indicates the setting (degrees of dwell) of the distributor breaker points. At C–D (dwell zone), current flow through the coil primary rebuilds the magnetic field around both windings. As before, this signals the end of the firing cycle for one cylinder.

Capacitive-Discharge Ignition System

In addition to the vehicle battery, coil, distributor, and spark plugs, a capacitive-discharge ignition system contains an electronic unit that is triggered by the points-open signal from the vehicle distributor (Fig. 7-11). Each time the capacitive-discharge system is triggered, approximately 400V dc is discharged into the primary winding of the vehicle ignition coil. As a result of this high-voltage pulse, which creates a much more intense field in the ignition coil, a much higher voltage is available to fire the spark plugs.

When the Heath analyzer is used on an engine equipped with a capacitive-discharge ignition system, the analyzer should be operated with its selector switch in the C-D IGN mode. With the selector switch in the capacitive-discharge SEC position, the display on the crt screen will be a superimposed secondary pattern. With the selector switch in the PRI position, the display on the crt screen will be a superimposed primary signal.

Although the analyzer's primary lead is connected to the breaker points as for a standard ignition system, the only signal present will be the points signal (a rectangular waveform). This is because in a capacitive-discharge system the breaker points are not connected to the primary winding of the ignition coil.

CD Breaker Points Pattern

At point A in Fig. 7-12, the points-open signal triggers the capacitive-discharge unit. At A—B)spark zone), there is a very short spark plug firing time. The plug stops firing at B. At B—C (coil zone), since the analyzer primary lead is not connected to the ignition coil no signal is present to cause vertical deflection of the sweep signal. The timing of C—D (dwell zone) indicates the setting (degrees of dwell) of the distributor breaker points.

CD Secondary Pattern

At point A in Fig. 7-13, (points-open signal), an output pulse from the capacitive-discharge unit produces a high voltage output from the vehicle ignition coil to fire the spark plug. At A—B (spark zone), again you see the very short plug firing time. The plug stops firing at B. Zone B—C (coil zone) shows rapid decay of coil energy to essentially zero at C. At C—D is the dwell zone. The dwell zone will be the same as that shown in Fig. 7-12. Point C can hardly be seen in the secondary pattern of the capacitive-discharge ignition system.

ANALYZER OPERATION

The amount of information you obtain from your analyzer depends to a great extent upon your knowledge of the controls.

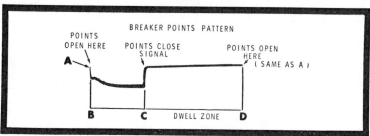

Fig. 7-12. Breaker points pattern for CD ignition.

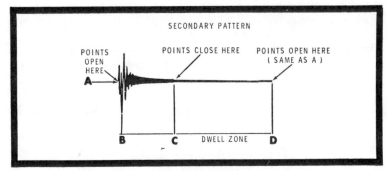

Fig. 7-13. Secondary pattern for CD ignition.

Refer to Fig. 7-14 and read the information about each control function of the Heath CO-1015 ignition analyzer.

Always perform the following adjustments before you start an ignition analysis.

Push the power switch to off.

Push the TAC switch to the LO position.

Push the HORIZ POS control in.

Plug the line cord into an ac outlet of the proper voltage (120 or 240V ac).

Push the power switch on. The power lamp should light and the meter pointer momentarily read full scale. This is normal.

Turn the selector switch to the CAL position. Allow two to three minutes for warmup.

Turn the HORIZ POS control until the trace is horizontally centered on the screen.

Push the VERT POS control in.

Turn the VERT POS control until the trace is vertically centered on the screen.

Pull or push the HORIZ EXP control to match the number of cylinders in the system being tested. (Pull out for 3 and 6 cylinder engines; push in for 4 and 8 cylinder engines.)

Turn the HORIZ EXP and HORIZ POS controls as necessary to adjust the length of the trace to the limits of the appropriate dwell angle scales.

Analyzer Connection Procedure

Use the following procedure to connect your solid-state ignition analyzer to the ignition system you want to test. Refer to Fig. 7-15 as you perform the following steps. (1) Place the analyzer in a convenient position near the ignition system. (2) Connect the cable connector end of the test cable to the analyzer. (3) Clip the black lead coming from the pickup assembly to a good engine ground. (4) Clip the secondary lead

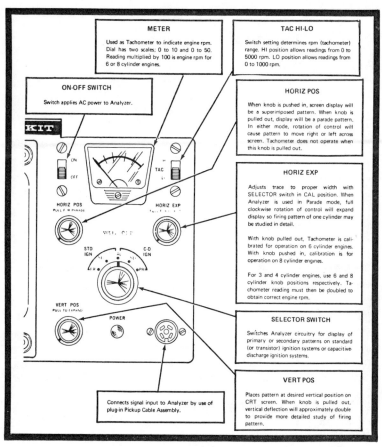

Fig. 7-14. Controls of the Heathkit CO-1015 ignition analyzer.

T-clip over the insulation of the high-voltage lead between the ignition coil and the center terminal of the distributor cap. Be sure this clip does not touch any metal surface and that the high-voltage lead is seated in the curved halves of the T-clip.

Note: The following connection starts the parade pattern with the No. 1 cylinder. The remaining cylinder patterns are displayed in their normal firing order. For example, on a 6-cylinder engine with a firing order of 1-5-3-6-2-4, the parade pattern on the crt screen will be *displayed* in the same order. On this same engine, if the pickup assembly is clamped around the No. 3 spark plug wire, the parade pattern will start with the No. 3 cylinder, and will be *displayed* on the crt screen in a 3-6-2-4-1-5 order. Only the display *sequence* of the firing patterns will change.

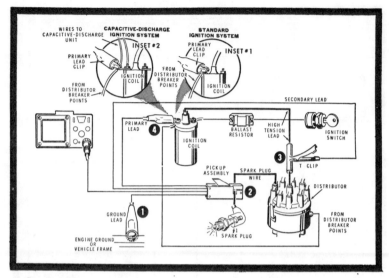

Fig. 7-15. How to hook up an ignition analyzer. (Courtesy Heath Co.)

Ignition Tests

This section contains two ignition test procedures based on the Heath CO-1015 analyzer. Read the general information presented in the following paragraphs; then proceed with the ignition test procedure that corresponds to the type of system you want to test.

Tuneup specifications can be found in your car owner's manual, or you can obtain a specification book from your local automotive parts store.

General

The ignition analyzer can be used to check the ignition system of an improperly operating engine, to verify work done on the ignition system, or to check the condition of various components for preventive maintenance.

When you perform these checks, the answers to the following four questions will help you arrive at a satisfactory analysis.

Are the patterns normal in all respects?

If something is not normal, is it common to all cylinders?

How does the pattern differ from the normal?

In what zone does this difference occur?

In order to help answer these questions, you may find it necessary to observe some portion of the ignition pattern in greater detail. This can be accomplished by pulling the VERT POS control out and turning the HORIZ EXP control in a clockwise direction. If you wish to view the ignition patterns of all the cylinders simultaneously, push the HORIZ POS control in. This produces a display on the screen that represents all of the cylinder firing patterns superimposed one on top of the other. These superimposed primary and secondary patterns provide an overall display of the complete ignition system. The SEC mode displays patterns of he high-voltage ignition circuits, while the PRI mode displays patterns of the low-voltage ignition circuits.

Each cylinder firing pattern can be viewed separately by pulling the HORIZ POS control out. This provides a parade display on the screen that will show each cylinder pattern, from left to right, in its normal firing order when the pickup assembly is clamped around the No. 1 spark plug wire. If you want to start the parade display with another cylinder, simply move the pickup assembly to the desired spark plug wire.

With the analyzer in the parade mode, you can adjust the HORIZ EXP and HORIZ POS controls to display a horizontally expanded view of each firing pattern. If the VERT POS control knob is pulled out, the firing patterns will also be vertically doubled in size. This can prove very important to your analysis and provide a highly detailed view of any desired area of one of the firing patterns.

Dwell angle in degrees can be measured using the dwell scales printed on the screen. Dwell readings should be taken with your analyzer set up for a superimposed primary pattern. With this pattern, variations (such as cam wobble) can be easily identified by a multiple points-closed indication.

The various test procedures described in this chapter have been tried and found completely satisfactory on many internal combustion engines.

Ignition Test Procedure

Connect your analyzer to the ignition system you want to test. Perform the preoperation adjustments as outlined earlier. Start the engine and adjust it to the idle speed listed in the manufacturer's specifications. Set the analyzer's controls to give a superimposed secondary display, with the pattern centered on the screen, and spread between the lines marking each end of the dwell scales.

Compare the display pattern produced by the system under test with that of a normally operating system. If the ignition system is operating correctly, there will be no outstanding discrepancies over any portion of the displayed pattern. If one or more discrepancies are noted, compare the displayed pattern with the normal standard ignition or capacitive-discharge ignition system patterns (Fig. 7-9, -10, -12, and -13).

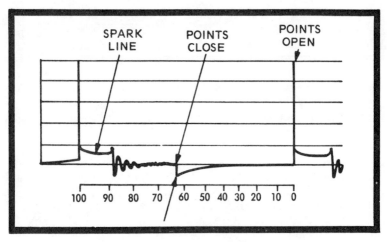

Fig. 7-16. How dwell is measured on a scope.

If every cylinder appears to be affected, the difficulty will be in a part of the ignition system that is common to all cylinders. In this case, push in the HORIZ POS control to obtain a superimposed primary or secondary pattern. Then adjust the HORIZ EXP and HORIZ POS controls to spread and position the pattern so the trace covers the screen. The VERT POS control may be pulled out for an even more detailed view.

After the difficulty has been diagnosed, repair the system. After repairs have been made, check with the analyzer to insure that no additional difficulties exist.

If all cylinders do not appear to be affected, the difficulty will be located in that part of the ignition system that is common to the affected cylinder(s). In this case, pull the HORIZ POS control out to obtain a parade pattern of all cylinders. The first pattern on the left side of the screen is for the No. 1 cylinder, provided the pickup assembly is clamped to the No.1 spark plug wire. The remaining patterns are presented in their normal firing order. Detailed examination of the firing pattern for the affected cylinder may be accomplished in the following manner:

1. Center the affected pattern on the cross mark at the center of the crt screen.
2. Adjust the HORIZ EXP control fully clockwise; then pull out the VERT POS control knob. This will provide maximum expansion of the pattern.
3. Determine the cause of the trouble by careful and detailed examination of the affected area of the pattern. Then make the necessary repairs to the ignition system.

4. Check each firing pattern by adjustment of the HORIZ POS control to make sure no additional trouble exists.

It is not necessary to disconnect the analyzer from the engine while you make adjustments on the engine under operating conditions. In this way, any ignition adjustments can be monitored on the scope while the adjustments are being made.

INTERPRETING IGNITION WAVEFORMS

Using the expand and parade controls, the pattern of one cylinder can be centered on the bottom scale of the screen. The dwell time, which is the time during which the points are closed, can be measured on the scale (Fig. 7-16), and should be between 60 and 70 percent for all engines regardless of the number of cylinders. On some engine analyzers, the scale may be calibrated in terms of dwell angle. In any case, very accurate dwell measurements are possible with this type of scope.

An open circuit anywhere between the distributor cap and a spark plug can also be detected. First adjust the expand control to crowd the cylinder patterns together at the left side of the screen. Next, adjust the height control so that the peaks register around the 50 percent line. Compare the heights of the peaks, and if any varies over one division (10 percent), it indicates a gap between the distributor and the spark plug. This shows up as a higher-than-normal peak, and it may be caused by a plug wire being open or not making contact in the distributor cap.

A test of ignition reserve is made by removing any spark plug wire except No. 1, where the analyzer is connected, and adjusting the height control until that cylinder peak reaches the top line. Fig. 7-17 shows how the voltage of the inoperative cylinder (the available secondary voltage), may be compared with the operating plug voltages. The reserve is the difference between the high peak and the other peaks, and should be 60 percent or more. Insufficient reserve may be caused by any of the following: wide plug gaps, a burned distributor rotor, burned distributor cap points, the center coil wire improperly seated, the condenser leaking, high resistance between the breaker points, or a defective ignition coil (to test plug 1, of course, you repeat the test with the analyzer connected to another plug).

REGULATOR TESTER

The Heath CTW-1170 solid-state voltage regulator tester (Fig. 7-18) allows extensive testing of GM integral charging

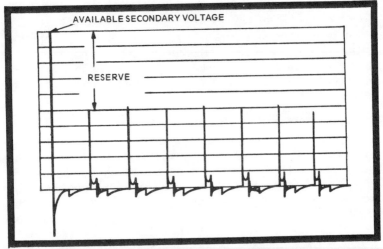

Fig. 7-17. Measuring ignition reserve on a scope.

system regulators. When the regulator is placed in the special heated regulator holder, it is tested at near maximum operating temperature.

Regulator Functions

The block diagram (Fig. 7-19) shows the relationship between a typical automotive charging system and the following four basic regulator circuits:

Fig. 7-18. Tester for solid-state voltage regulators. (Courtesy Heath Co.)

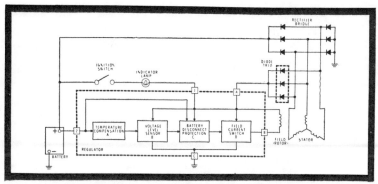

Fig. 7-19. Block diagram of VR tester. (Courtesy Heath Co.)

Temperature Compensation. Causes the maximum charging voltage to vary with temperature to insure the optimum voltage for charging the battery.

Voltage Level Sensor. Monitors the battery voltage and then controls the generator field current switch circuit (D) which, in turn, controls the generator output.

Battery Disconnect Protection. Prevents the voltage level sensor circuit (B) from turning on the field current switch circuit (D) when the battery and the generator are disconnected from sense terminal 2.

Field Current Switch

Allows current to flow through the generator field winding, causing the generator to produce an output.

The accessory cable set consists of two test cables that connect to the tester front-panel accessory socket. These cables permit in-car generator and regulator circuit tests and continuity tests. The in-car test accessory cable allows quick tester connection to the generator regulator circuit while it is still mounted in the vehicle (Fig. 7-20A). A second accessory cable (Fig. 7-20B) provides for continuity tests of generator components (diodes, windings, etc.).

In-Car Test of VR

This in-car test procedure aids in the quick determination of an existing problem in the generator regulator circuit. If the proper results are not obtained in this test, the generator must be dismantled and the regulator removed for further testing.

First turn the tester off and make sure a regulator is *not* installed in the tester regulator holder. Plug the testing accessory cable into the accessory socket on the tester front panel. Disconnect the regulator connector from the generator. Then plug the testing accessory cable in its place. Connect the

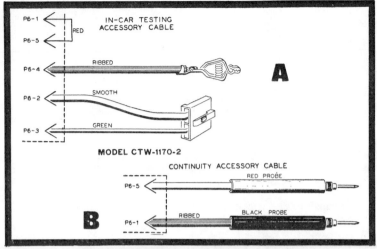

Fig. 7-20. Cables for VR tester: in A, the continuity cable; in B, the in-car-testing cable. (Courtesy Heath Co.)

ground lead (alligator clip) to the generator case. Test the generator regulator circuit using the steps 1, 2, 3, and 4. If the lamp and voltmeter give improper indications, or if either or both lamps flicker on and off when these steps are performed, the regulator must be removed from the generator for further testing to determine whether the problem is in the generator or in the regulator.

1. Turn the tester knob clockwise until it clicks. The voltmeter should read 0 volts. If it does not read 0 volts, the internal connection within the regulator between terminal A and terminal 1 is open, or the regulator is not making good contact with the tester terminals. Inspect both the regulator and the tester terminals to make sure they are making good contact. The field lamp should remain off. If the field lamp is on, the field current switch circuit in the regulator may be shorted.

2. Continue turning the knob clockwise until the voltmeter reads about 5V. Note: Do not pause or leave the voltage set between 0.5V (first short line on voltmeter scale) and 5V. The field lamp should be on If the field lamp is not on, one or more of the regulator circuits have opened at normal operating temperature, or the voltage level sensor circuit is defective.

3. Continue turning the knob clockwise until the field lamp turns off. The voltmeter should read between 14 and 15.5V. If the field lamp does not turn off or if the voltage is not

within limits, the voltage level sensor circuit in the regulator is defective.

4. Turn the tester off and open the holder cover. *Caution*: The regulator is *hot*; allow it to cool before removing it from the tester.

Continuity Test

The continuity test accessory cable is used in conjunction with the meter on the tester. A high meter reading indicates an open circuit (no continuity) while a zero meter reading indicates continuity.

When a continuity test is made, keep the following points in mind:

- Make sure a regulator is *not* installed in the holder.
- The knob is turned clockwise only until it clicks.
- All components must be removed from the generator for testing.
- Make sure external voltage is not applied to the component being tested.

VR TESTER CIRCUIT

Refer to the schematic (Fig. 7-21) while reading this circuit description.

Diodes D1 and D2 form a full-wave rectifier for the transformer secondary voltage. The dc output voltage from this circuit is filtered by capacitor C1.

Transistors Q1 through Q5 form a series-pass regulator circuit that maintains and regulates the output at 16.5 volts dc. Transistors Q1 and Q2 form a Darlington series-pass transistor combination that is driven by the current through resistor R1. As the output voltage tends to increase, the voltage at the wiper of control R4 also increases, causing the Darlington combination of Q3 and Q4 to conduct harder. This reduces the base current to Q2 and Q1 which, in turn, reduces the output voltage. Also, if the output voltage tends to decrease, transistors Q3 and Q4 will conduct less, thus allowing the base current through Q2 and Q1 to increase. Zener diode D3 and transistor Q5 form an amplified zener circuit that establishes the reference voltage for transistor Q4.

Transistor Q6 limits the output current to approximately 4A by lowering the output voltage as required. This happens when the current through and the voltage across R2 increases to the point that transistor Q6 turns on and reduces the drive to transistors Q2 and Q1.

Transistor Q7 forms a current foldback circuit that *folds back* (reduces to zero) the current when the output voltage falls

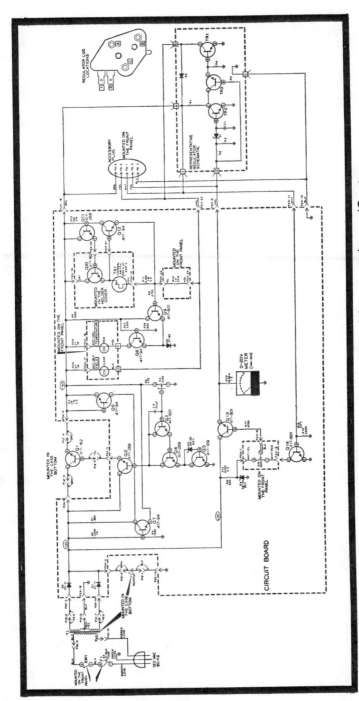

Fig. 7-21. Schematic of the tester for solid-state regulators. (Courtesy Heath Co.)

below approximately 10V. Resistors R5 and R6 make up a voltage divider that holds the base of Q7 at a fixed value. Then, when the emitter voltage of Q7 (output voltage) decreases below the base voltage, Q7 turns on and decreases the drive to Q2 and Q1. The turn-on of Q7 is regenerative, so it happens very rapidly and removes all drive to Q2 and Q1.

A constant-current source, Q10, Q11, and Q12, supplies the current (3.5A) to the regulator under test through connector B to ground. Transistor Q10 also serves as the heating element to raise the regulator temperature to 240°F. When the temperature reaches 240°F, thermal switch TS1 opens and reduces the current to 0.26A.

Transistors Q8 and Q9 function as switches to turn on the temperature lamp when the heater reaches maximum temperature (240°F) and the thermal switch opens. When the thermal switch is closed, the current through resistor R12 (3.5A) produces a voltage drop large enough to turn on transistor Q9. This holds the base of Q8 low to keep it turned off. However, when the thermal switch opens, the voltage drop across R12 decreases and allows Q9 to turn off. A positive voltage is then applied through resistors R8 and R25 to the base of Q8, turning it on. Transistor Q8 then turns on the temperature lamp, indicating the regulator is up to temperature (240°F).

The field lamp is on whenever terminal B is placed at or near ground by the internal circuitry of the regulator.

Transistors Q13 and Q14 and resistor R14 supply an adjustable output voltage. Resistor R14 provides overload protection by limiting the current if the output is shorted. Control R16 controls the output voltage by setting the base current through series-pass transistor Q13. Transistor Q14 places one end of control R16 at ground, providing the regulator has continuity between terminals 1 and A.

Computers and Cars Today

The computers are coming! It's nothing to call the Marines about, but it is exciting. The marriage of the computer—with all its revolutionary potential—and the automobile, which is the world's No. 1 manufactured item, has staggering implications.

The joining together of the computer and car may be likened to a shotgun wedding. The aerospace market, the prime market of the computer industry, petered out just at the climax of pressure on the auto industry to do something about emissions, safety, and service problems. These problems are being dealt with mainly by a number of tack-on solutions. In the cars of tomorrow, as you shall see in Chapter 10, computers will provide many of the solutions. In some of the cars of today—in what may be termed the "first generation" of computerized cars—we have some inklings of the future issue of the car—computer marriage.

The computer systems discussed in this chapter are used to monitor service areas such as lights, fluid level, and brake condition. Both types of automotive computer applications—on-board and fixed—are represented.

ESP

In terms of alerting the driver to potentially unsafe conditions in his car, Toyota's ESP, or *Electro Sensor Panel*, is the next best thing yet to extrasensory perception. The panel, pictured in Fig. 8-1, warns of such things as low oil level, a worn brake pad, or low radiator coolant level.

System Operation

The system consists of 11 sensors (Fig. 8-2), a computer, and an overhead panel with a main warning light and separate indicator lights that warn the driver if brake, head, tail, or license lights go out; if windshield washer, battery water, radiator coolant, brake fluid, or engine oil levels are low; if brake vacuum booster loses pressure; or if front brake pads are worn and need to be checked.

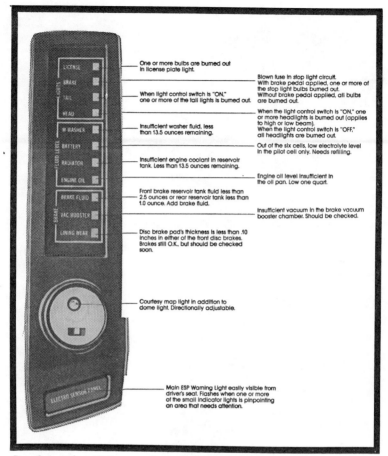

One or more bulbs are burned out in license plate light.

When light control switch is "ON," one or more of the tail lights is burned out.

Insufficient washer fluid, less than 13.5 ounces remaining.

Insufficient engine coolant in reservoir tank. Less than 13.5 ounces remaining.

Front brake reservoir tank fluid less than 2.5 ounces or rear reservoir tank less than 1.0 ounce. Add brake fluid.

Disc brake pad's thickness is less than .10 inches in either of the front disc brakes. Brakes still O.K., but should be checked soon.

Courtesy map light in addition to dome light. Directionally adjustable.

Main ESP Warning Light easily visible from driver's seat. Flashes when one or more of the small indicator lights is pinpointing an area that needs attention.

Blown fuse in stop light circuit. With brake pedal applied, one or more of the stop light bulbs burned out. Without brake pedal applied, all bulbs are burned out.

When the light control switch is "ON," one or more headlights is burned out (applies to high or low beam). When the light control switch is "OFF," all headlights are burned out.

Out of the six cells, low electrolyte level in the pilot cell only. Needs refilling.

Engine oil level insufficient in the oil pan. Low one quart.

Insufficient vacuum in the brake vacuum booster chamber. Should be checked.

Fig. 8-1. What ESP can tell you. (Courtesy Toyota Motor Sales, USA, Inc.)

When the ignition switch is first turned on, the ESP warning light and all indicator lights go on. If all the lights do not go on at this point, an ESP malfunction is indicated. Thus, the system is self-checking. As soon as the engine is started, all indicator lights will go out if the systems monitored are normal.

If any monitored item is not normal, the main warning light will flash and the appropriate indicator light will go on.

ESP Readout

Standard on all new *Corona* hardtops, the ESP is a built-in feature located above the driver (Fig. 8-3) with the main warning light easily visible to him. If something needs attention, that light starts flashing and one of the smaller lights

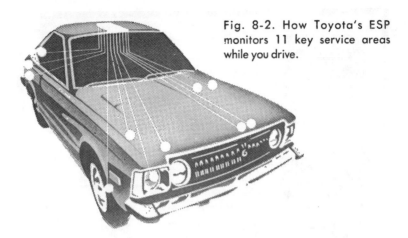

pinpoints the problem. In addition, ESP-equipped models have all the standard warning lights. The indications of the various ESP lights are explained in Fig. 8-1.

VOLKSWAGEN'S COMPUTER ANALYSIS

Computer analysis is a breakthrough for Volkswagen research. Using a socket built into all new VWs, and a digital computer connected to the car, more than 70 items can be checked in less than half an hour. Results of the checks are compared electronically with standard factory specifications and printed out on a diagnosis sheet (Fig. 8-4). The sheet shows

Fig. 8-3. Location of the monitoring-system panel. (Courtesy Toyota Motor Sales, USA, Inc.)

Test		Measured Value			+/−	U	R	Operation	Description
18 Battery Voltage	Volts	1	1	O	+				
19 Battery Voltage Under Load	Volts	O	O	O	−				
20 Stop Lights	units	U	O	O	+				
21 Battery Electrolyte—level		O	O	O					
22 Turn Signal Lights Left	units	U	O	O	+				
23 Turn Signal Lights Right	units	U	O	O	+				
24 Rear Window Defogger	units	U	O	O	+				
25 Oil Temperature	Degrees Centigrade	Y	6	9					
26 Starting Current	units	O	O	O	−				
27 Cylinder No. 1-compression	units	O	1	O	−				
28 Cylinder No. 2-compression	units	O	1	2	−				
29 Cylinder No. 3-compression	units	O	1	O	−				
30 Cylinder No. 4-compression	units	O	1	1	−				
31 Dwell Angle	Degrees	5	2	4	+				
32 Horn		C	O	O	+				
33 Charging Voltage	Volts	1	1	8	−				
34 Charging Current	units								
35 Kick-down Switch									
36 Kick-down Solenoid		O	O	O	−				
37 Basic Ignition Timing	Degrees BTDC								
38 Basic Ignition Timing	Degrees ATDC	U	O	O	+				
39 Ignition Timing Advance	Degrees BTDC	U	C	O	+				
40 Ignition Timing Advance	Degrees ATDC								
41 Headlight Aiming		O	O	O	+				
42 Total Toe-in Front	Degrees/Min.	O	1	3	+				
43 Total Toe-out Front	Degrees/Min.								
44 Pos. Camber Frt. left	Degrees/Min.	O	3	7	+				
45 Neg. Camber Frt. left	Degrees/Min.								
46 Pos. Camber Frt. right	Degrees/Min.	O	3	6	+				
47 Neg. Camber Frt. right	Degrees/Min.								
72 Water Drain Flaps									
73 Drive Shaft Boots		O	O	O	+				
74 Parking brake, plate, cable incl. lube									

Test drive by _____

Additional observations

U=Urgently required   Total Cost Estimate $
R=Recommended

Typical interpretation of Values and (+ −) Indicators
Test 19: Batt. volt. under load Volts 104 + can be read as "10.4 volts" which is O.K.
Test 27-30: Compression is acceptable if the lowest measured value, in units, is at least 50% of the highest measured value, and all four cylinders show a plus (+) indicator.
Test 31: Dwell angle Degrees 472 + can be read as "47.2°" which is also O.K.
To maintain the best possible performance and safe operation, and to protect the value of your Volkswagen, we urge you to have all of the checked (✓) items corrected as soon as possible.

Customer's Signature_____Date_____

Fig. 8-4. Printout of the Vokswagen computer analysis system. (Courtesy Sharrett Volkswagen, Inc.)

the owner and the mechanic the condition of the car's major components and indicates any service that might be necessary.

How It Works

A VW, equipped with a central socket (Fig. 8-5) in the engine compartment, is connected to an in-dealership computer by means of an umbilical cord (multiconductor cable). A plastic program card, containing standard specification data for the year and model car being checked, is inserted into the computer's program card reader. The technician, using a hand-held input unit, follows the progression of the test sequence.

Testing progresses automatically until a visual or manual test must be made. At this point, a film strip in the hand-held

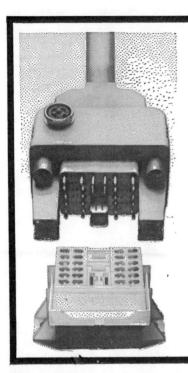

Fig. 8-5. How the umbilical cord connects to the central socket of the VW to be tested. (Courtesy Volkswagen of America, Inc.)

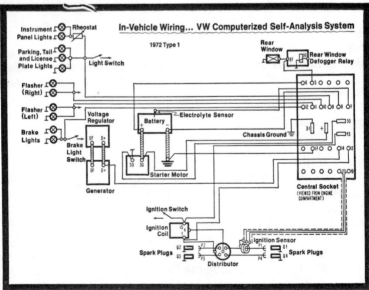

Fig. 8-6. In-vehicle wiring of the VW computerized analysis system. (Courtesy Volkswagen of America, Inc.)

unit tells the technician what to check. If the item checks okay, he presses the plus-sign button; if it doesn't, he presses the minus-sign button. This advances the sequence to the next item to be checked. The technician continues to perform tests indicated on the film strip as it advances, until another automatic sequence is reached.

The film then advances automatically as checks are completed, until another manual check is indicated. This procedure continues until all of the more than 70 tests are completed.

The result of each test (okay or not okay)—together with measured values—is printed on a diagnosis form. Data is likewise visually displayed on the computer console front panel.

The state or condition for each item tested is compared with standard factory specifications coded into the program card.

Sensors and test wiring (Fig. 8-6), built into the car, supply data to the computer by way of the central socket for many of the tests (25 at present). Example: A probe built into the battery measures electrolyte level without visual inspection. Some test sequences are performed automatically, with the computer doing the evaluation. Examples: compression reading; state of the ignition system; charging voltage; parking, stop, and turn signal lights; and operation of the electric rear window defogger.

Front-end alignment is measured automatically by optical electronic equipment utilizing mirrors attached to the front wheels, a light beam, and a photosensitive diode detector.

Reflected light signals from the mirrors are decoded by an electronic circuit and fed into the computer module for evaluation and for printout.

VW Computer Equipment

The computer analysis system consists of the following components, shown in Fig. 8-7:

1. Central socket with associated test wiring and sensors built into all VWs produced since mid-1971. The mechanic uses an umbilical cord (multiconductor cable) to connect the vehicle's central socket to the computer. This cable also contains the oil-temperature sensor line (sensor replaces dip stick during diagnosis).
2. Digital computer processes data from vehicle and compares it with nominal values (factory standard specifications) for vehicle being checked, and displays test results.
3. Program card reader.

Fig. 8-7. The VW computer analysis setup. (Courtesy Volkswagen of America, Inc.)

4. High-speed printer that records go/no-go information and measured values.
5. Hand-held input unit containing film strip that displays test operations in sequence. Go/no-go buttons, used for visual inspections only, report technician's findings to computer.
6. Optical electronic front-end alignment reader connected to computer.
7. Headlight tester to check headlight adjustment.
8. Positioning pads to insure proper setting of the car for wheel alignment and headlight tests.
The following parts not shown in Fig. 8-3 are also included:

Chassis contact hoist for under-vehicle inspections.

Special diagnosis hand tools for manual tests.

Observation mirrors for visual check of lights for older cars without socket.

Adapter to allow use of computer analysis system for VWs not equipped with central sockets.

Simulator (with program card) for checking system performance and calibration.

Portable tire inflator.

Adaptability to the Future

The existing system can handle approximately 150 test operations; of these, only about 70 are used now. Modular design of the computer permits updating to accommodate additional programs as necessary.

Dealers are able to lease the equipment at a moderate monthly rate. Virtually all VW dealerships were computer equipped by mid-1974.

The existing equipment is designed for VWs which have the exclusive built-in sensors and central socket. With an adapter cable, earlier VWs with 12V electrical systems can be diagnosed using the new system.

Volkswagen says the system improves shop efficiency and customer satisfaction. Computer analysis cuts diagnosis time approximately in half. This means more VWs can be checked in a day, and customer waiting time is reduced. In addition, the equipment virtually eliminates the chance of human errors—either in evaluating complicated systems and recording of data, or in inadvertently skipping items that should be checked. For the VW owner, this means he knows exactly what work needs to be performed to bring his car to standard specifications; mechanics can go right to work on those items, and the customer need buy no more parts or shop time than is necessary.

Computer Basics

This chapter will serve as a computer introduction to some readers and a review to others. In either case, it will provide information requisite to understanding the automotive applications of computers discussed in the next chapter.

COMPUTER CHARACTERISTICS

The term "computer" is a catchall (and often something of a misnomer) for a wide range of complex electronic systems, only some of which are used for computing answers to mathematical problems. Computers are also very often used for such data-processing functions as printing monthly bills, taking inventories, compiling payrolls, sorting address labels for magazines, and controlling machinery. The last-named application—controlling machinery—is the one of interest here; the automobile is the machinery to be controlled.

Versatile as they are, computers do have their limitations. They know only what they are told by humans in a *computer program*, and they must be very carefully instructed (programed) in their jobs. A computer program typically consists of coded instructions on a magnetic tape or on punched cards. In small computers, the program is often "wired into" the computer by the use of logic gates (discussed earlier) combined and organized to perform the logical functions required of the computer. Programs wired into computers are said to be "hard" wired, and indeed they are hard to change. General-purpose computers have changeable programs onmrtic tapes or on punched cards; special-purpose computers have hard-wired programs.

No matter how carefully they are instructed, or programed, problems often arise when computers are called on to perform tasks requiring critical judgment...tasks such as translating languages. One computer, for example, when asked to translate from Russian to English the sentence, "The men were low in spirits," translated it as, "The men's supply of whiskey was low." Small wonder computers are often called "fast idiots."

What computers lack in judgement, however, they more than make up for in speed. Some modern computers are capable of performing tens of millions of computations per minute. Therein lies their applicability to automobiles. A computer is able to compute, for example, almost instantaneously, the optimum air—fuel ratio for an engine under constantly changing load and speed conditions.

DIGITAL SIGNALS

Digital signals consist of *pulses*, or brief surges of voltage. An example is to be found in your automobile engine, where pulses are used to fire the spark plugs. Every time a cylinder is ready to fire, the distributor delivers a high-voltage pulse to the spark plug. This high-voltage pulse may be thought of as a *signal*, or message—a digital signal to ignite the air—fuel mixture. That brings up two key points about the successful use of digital signals: They must be delivered to the right place, and they must be delivered at precisely the right time. Reverse the spark plug wires and the signals go to the wrong plugs; the engine will run poorly, if at all. Or if the engine timing is off, the signals do not get to the plugs at exactly the right time; again the engine will run poorly.

BINARY ARITHMETIC

Mathematics is said to be the language of technology. The language of computers is a specialized form of mathematics called binary arithmetic. In the binary system of arithmetic, there are only two digits, *1* and *0*. Numbers are represented in a computer by pulses. Binary 1 may be represented by a pulse, and binary 0 by the absence of a pulse—a pause or space. Combinations of 1s and 0s can, in turn, be represented by pulses and pauses. The binary numbers and pulse equivalents of the 10 digits of the decimal system are shown in Table 9-1.

Calculations in a computer are performed by means of logic circuits built with logic gates. The most basic calculation that can be performed is the addition of two binary digits. The circuit that accomplishes this, the *adder*, is shown in block form in Fig. 9-1.

The two digits to be added are applied to terminals A and B. If a 1 and a 0 were to be added, a positive pulse representing 1 would be applied to terminal A, and no pulse would be applied to terminal B (Fig. 9-1A). The absence of a pulse at B would represent a 0. The sum of 1 and 0 is, of course, 1, so a pulse representing a 1 would appear at the output terminal (C) of the adder, as shown in Fig. 9-1A.

If two 1s are added, the sum is 2, but there is no such digit in the binary system. A similar situation occurs in everyday

Table 9-1. Binary and Pulse Equivalents of the Decimal Digits.

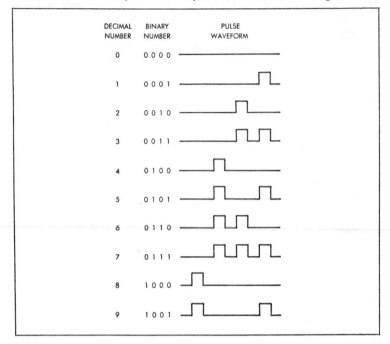

DECIMAL NUMBER	BINARY NUMBER	PULSE WAVEFORM
0	0 0 0 0	
1	0 0 0 1	
2	0 0 1 0	
3	0 0 1 1	
4	0 1 0 0	
5	0 1 0 1	
6	0 1 1 0	
7	0 1 1 1	
8	1 0 0 0	
9	1 0 0 1	

decimal arithmetic when you add 1 to the highest digit in that system, 9. There is no single digit in the decimal system to represent the sum of 1 and 9, so you write a zero and carry the 1 one *place*, or position, to the left. The word for what you have thus written is "ten," of course. You do the same thing in binary arithmetic. The binary sum of 1 plus 1 is 0 with a carry. As shown by Fig. 9-1B, this result is indicated by the digital adder as a pulse at its carry terminal, and an absence of a pulse at its output terminal. Binary 10 (for the quantity 2) is spoken as "one-oh."

It is possible to construct a table showing the state of the adder's output and carry terminals for every possible combination of inputs. Such a table, called a *truth* table, is shown in Fig. 9-1C.

COMPUTER ORGANIZATION

The organization of the digital computer is illustrated by Fig. 9-2. Part A shows the organization of a factory, which is analogous to the organization of a computer, shown in part B.

In the factory, a number of steps take place; these are keyed to the numbers in Fig. 9-2A:

1. The customer expresses his needs to the salesman and places an order.
2. The salesman writes up the order so that the specifications of the customer will be met and so that the production department will have the information it requires to meet them. He passes this data along to the production manager.
3. The production manager is obviously a very busy and important fellow—look at all the arrows he has. The production manager adds to the specifications of the order some "specs" of his own, and sends all of this data to the production staff with instructions to get to work.
4. If the product is a complex one, the production staff assembles it in stages. It puts together some subassemblies and sends them to be held in the storeroom until needed for the final assembly of the product.

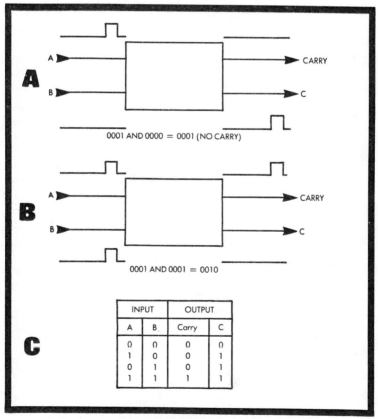

Fig. 9-1. The binary adder.

5. As work progresses, the production staff will need to obtain some parts, tools, and blueprints from the storeroom. And eventually, it will need to recall the subassemblies it sent to the storeroom. So the production staff asks the production manager to requisition the needed materials from the storeroom.
6. The production manager instructs the storeroom to send down the required parts, blueprints, and assemblies.
7. The parts, prints, and subassemblies are sent to the production staff.
8. The production staff completes the final assembly and informs the production manager, who checks it:
9. If the product meets his original specifications and is satisfactory, he has it sent to the shipping clerk for delivery to the customer.

Obviously, not all factories operate exactly as explained above, but the above plan is a realistic one. Consider now how it compares to the organization in a computer. In the typical digital computer (Fig. 9-2B), the following steps take place:

1. The computer operator (analogous to the customer) feeds the problem to be solved and the data needed for its solution into the input device (analogous to the salesman).
2. The input device (salesman) converts the problem and data into the language of the computer (order) and passes them along to the control section (production manager) of the computer.
3. The control section sends the central processor (production staff) the problem and data bearing on the problem. It also instructs the processor to get to work on a solution.
4. The processor performs some partial solutions of the problem, which will be needed later, and sends them to the memory (storeroom).
5. The processor will require some constants (tools and parts), such as *pi* (3.14159...), and some standard procedures (blueprints) stored in the memory. It will also require the partial solutions (subassemblies) sent to the memory. To get these, it asks the control unit to release them from the memory.
6. The control unit instructs the memory to release the constants, standard procedures, and partial solutions required by the central processor.
7. The constants, procedures, and partial solutions are sent to the central processor.
8. The central processor completes the solution and sends it to the control center for checking.

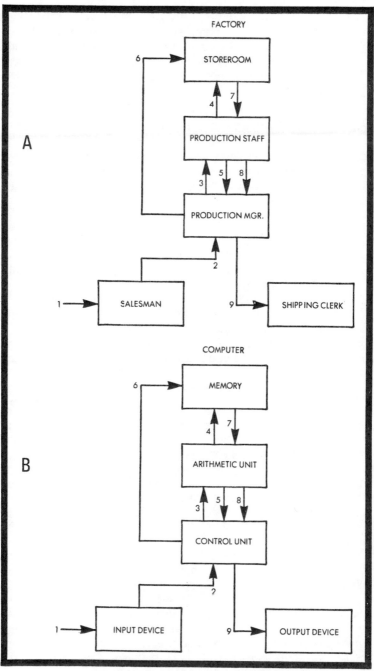

Fig. 9-2. Factory-vs-computer analogy.

9. After satisfying itself that the solution (finished product) is okay, the control center sends it to the output device (shipping clerk). The output device converts the solution from computer language, or "computerese," into a form understandable to humans, and delivers it, often on a printed page.

The computer just described is a general-purpose one capable of performing a wide range of computations and other functions. A special-purpose computer—such as one used to control the air—fuel ratio in a car—is organized similarly. A general-purpose computer has been described here, since that type seems to represent the ultimate solution to many of the technological problems facing auto makers.

COMPUTERS FOR CARS

There are three main approaches to computerizing a car:

- Replace each existing electronic unit with a special-purpose processor using the latest integrated-circuit technology.
- *Combine* the functions of the existing electronic units into one or more special-purpose processors.
- Build a computerized vehicle from scratch. Convert as many vehicle functions as possible to electronics, and combine them into a single, *general-purpose* reprogrammable processor.

Operationally, today's automobile consists of a number of independent systems—a charging system, braking system, ignition system, etc. The first approach would preserve this compartmentalized concept of car building. This approach would be the simplest to implement, but it would lose the advantage an integrated system would have in minimizing hardware. Also, since each new processor would require its own highly regulated power supply or a lead to a single central power supply, the complexity of a car's wiring harness would be increased.

The second approach is a compromise designed to gain the benefits of integrating the vehicle electronics without radically changing the machinery. Under this plan, existing electronic systems would be greatly changed, but there would be no radical redesign of the machinery and no substitution of electronics for mechanical actuation. The system would not attempt to replace nonelectronic processes such as fuel mixture control or shift-point control, since that would require that the vehicle mechanisms be modified.

The third approach is the most radical one and the one that would produce the most benefits. At first the system would take over some of the vehicle control functions—enough to justify its cost. This system could be expanded later to cover more functions without redesign of the processor. All that would be required would be to add appropriate sensors (input devices) and actuators (electrical "muscles," or output devices), and to reprogram the processor to accommodate the added functions. To reprogram the processor, formulas would have to be devised to relate signals from the sensors to the forces and other responses required of the actuators. The formulas, called *algorithms*, would be simplified as much as possible to take up a minimum of space in the computer memory. Space in a memory, like space in a warehouse, costs money.

The third approach seems the most promising, since it has the most potential for expansion and could be changed without redesigning the processor. Also, since a general-purpose computer is very powerful in terms of the amount of computations it can handle, the processor in the third approach could even handle the diagnosis and isolation of a wide range of vehicle defects.

DIGITAL COMMUNICATIONS

Since the computer is a digital (pulse signal) system, it is natural that the communications between the processor and the sensors and actuators in a computerized car be by means of pulses. In this type of communication, a continuous series of pulses, or pulse *carrier*, is generated. The pulses of the carrier have the same height, width, repetition rate, shape, etc. They are more alike than bumps on a log.

The carrier is made to convey intelligence, or a signal, by the process of *modulation*. In pulse modulation, the signal to be transmitted is sampled during brief periodic intervals, and the samples are made to modify in some way, or modulate, the carrier. The carrier is varied in some manner in accordance with the instantaneous value of the modulating signal at the moment of sampling. It may be varied in a number of ways. For example, the amplitude, frequency, or spacing of the pulses may be varied.

Pulse Modulation Characteristics

Pulse modulation can be used for *multiplexing*, or simultaneous transmission of more than one data signal on a single line. Pulse modulation permits the transmission of many types of data in a short time and with a minimum of equipment.

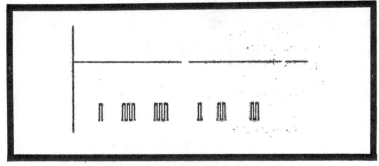

Fig. 9-3. Pulse code modulation.

The simultaneous transmission of multiple channels may be accomplished by *time-division multiplexing*. In this system, the instantaneous amplitude of the signal is sampled from one channel (sensor) at a time and transmitted in a regular sequence until all channels have been transmitted. The process is then repeated in the same sequence until all the desired data has been transmitted.

Pulse Code Modulation

The type of modulation considered most applicable to automotive computer systems is pulse code modulation (PCM).

Pulse code modulation is produced by using the signal voltage to vary the bias of a *keying circuit*. In its normal, no-signal, unmodulated operation, the keying circuit produces groups of pulses that are uniform in number and concentration. The keying circuit may contain a one-shot multivibrator.

The keying circuit is designed so that a positive-going signal voltage increases the number or concentration of the pulses in the normal group, as illustrated in Fig. 9-3. Also, a negative-going signal voltage *decreases* the number or concentration of pulses in proportion to the amplitude of the modulating signal. Note that the frequency of the carrier is not changed in the PCM system. The intelligence is conveyed by the number of pulses contained in each signal-modulated group as compared to the number of pulses in the normal group.

Advanced
Automotive Technology 10

On-board computers...semiautomatic steering...an anti-jackknifing system for heavy trucks...radar speed control...personal rapid transit—these advanced systems are not remote will-o'-the-wisps. They are already on the drawing boards, and in some cases, practical models have already been demonstrated. These are the electronic marvels that will make the late 1970s and the '80s and '90s among the most exciting years in the history of the automobile--the *electronic* age of the automobile. The purpose of this chapter in reaching into the outer limits of automotive technology is to prepare you and readers after you for the opportunities and wonders to come.

COMPUTERS AND THE CARS OF TOMORROW

How the cars of tomorrow will be computerized is as uncertain as how they will look. But one thing is certain—they will be computerized. This chapter will report on the most significant developmental efforts aimed at putting computers in cars—efforts that continue in the laboratories and on the proving grounds of the auto makers and their suppliers.

GENERAL MOTORS' ALPHA CARS

General Motors' Alpha vehicles were built to test several versions of a car computer. Computers of increasing sophistication were tested in the Alpha I, II, and III experimental cars.

One of the features of the cars of the 1980s will probably be a digital display from the on-board computer. The Alpha I version is shown in Fig. 10-1. The futuristic instrument panel includes a digital clock, speedometer, and gas gage. On the right is a sobriety keyboard. Before the car will start, the right buttons must be pressed in the right way—supposedly an impossible task for a would be drunken driver.

Alpha I

The Alpha I system was organized along product lines rather than for optimum computer utilization. Note that the system, diagramed in Fig. 10-2, includes a stability and control

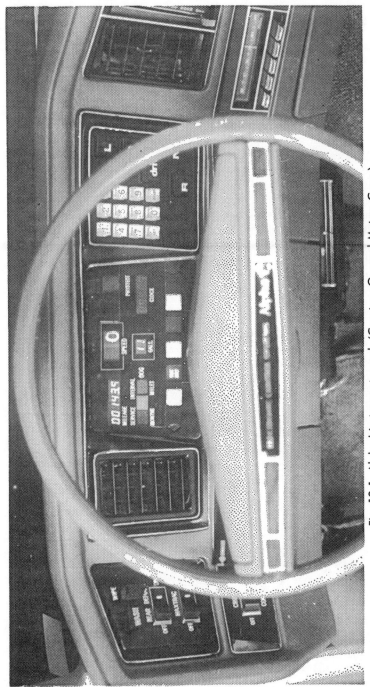

Fig. 10-1. Alpha I instrument panel. (Courtesy General Motors Corp.)

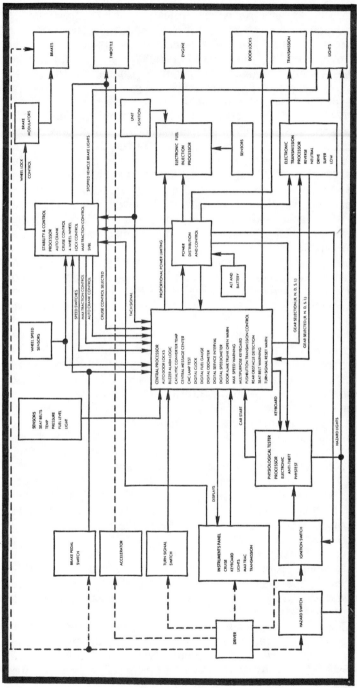

Fig. 10-2. Block diagram of the Alpha I system.

223

processor, an electronic fuel injection (EFI) processor, a physiological tester processor, a central processor, an electronic transmission control, and the instrument panel. This system corresponds to the second computer approach discussed in the last chapter under the heading "Computers for Cars." Existing electronic functions were integrated using a central processor and a number of specialized processors.

The first of the five processors is a stability and control processor used in providing cruise control, wheel slip control (during acceleration), wheel lock control (during braking), and so on. This processor is primarily involved in providing stable lateral and longitudinal control; that is, it keeps the car in the lane and pointed straight ahead when on a straight stretch of road. Four-wheel lock control is achieved by a technique described earlier. Wheel speeds are sensed and the signals thus derived are used to modulate the application of the brakes so as to prevent skidding.

Acceleration slip control is also provided by comparing driven wheel speeds with true vehicle speed as represented by undriven wheel speeds, limiting the power applied to the driven wheels when the deviation exceeds a preset limit and threatens wheel slip.

The same processor also provides automatic cruising-speed control. The desired speed is selected by a fingertip control and a corresponding signal is sent to the processor. A *true vehicle* speed signal is also sent to the processor. The processor uses these signals to regulate a throttle actuator to cause the true vehicle speed to increase or decrease at a rate determined by a formula programed into the processor. The formula, or algorithm, is designed so that the car will approach the desired speed with dispatch, but without laying down a strip of rubber.

With the addition of an *engine speed* sensor, the processor is able to provide an automatic cranking command in case of a stall. The cranking function provides hydraulic power after a stall, so that the such hydraulically operated systems as power steering and braking continue to operate normally.

As an indication of the advantages of integrating (combining) the car's electronics, several functions became easily available because of the variety of speed signals in the processor. Speed signals are used to operate switches providing automatic locking of the doors at 5 mph, brake light control, and transmission gear selection.

The next processor provides electronic fuel injection. Manifold pressure, engine speed, and engine and ambient temperatures are used to meter fuel to eight injectors in General Motors' experimental EFI system. The fuel injectors,

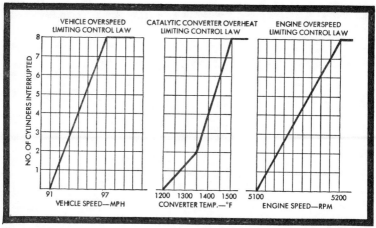

Fig. 10-3. How the Alpha I EFI system provides various kinds of protection.

and the capability of providing very rapid control of them, made possible a function called proportional power limiting. This function limits engine top speed, controls acceleration wheel slip, and prevents catalytic converter overheating. To provide these features, fuel injection to the cylinders is interrupted as safe conditions are exceeded. The number of cylinders thus interrupted depends on the extent to which safe conditions are exceeded. For example, when the vehicle speed reaches 92 mph, one cylinder is interrupted. When it reaches 97 mph, all eight cylinders are interrupted (refer to Fig. 10-3). Adding catalytic converter and engine overspeed protection is also a simple matter (Fig. 10-3)

Another processor is used to provide electronic control of the automatic transmission. Gear selection signals are created in response to pushbutton selection at the instrument panel. Gear ratio selection is provided by the processor, providing better shifting than the best human driver. Shift schedule control is also provided, which means that it is impossible to inadvertently switch the transmission from a forward mode to park or reverse.

The physiological tester processor is an experimental device intended to evaluate driver performance. This processor, in conjunction with the instrument panel keyboard, also provides a combination lock feature to deter theft of the car. Any integrated processing system will require data entry and display equipment. The digital keyboard and display in the Alpha I physiological tester system are examples of such equipment.

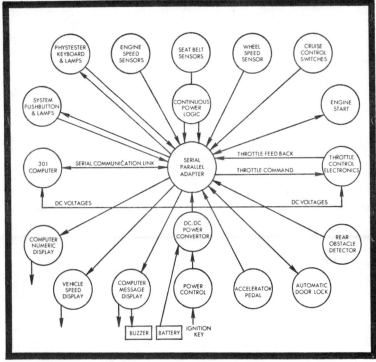

Fig. 10-4. Alpha II block diagram.

The central processor of Alpha I combines data from special sensors with data already available from the other processors. This processor provides for routing of data between other processors. It also combines the processing of system controls and displays, and provides for the compact display seen in Fig. 10-1.

Alpha II

Alpha II represents the third approach to car computerization discussed in the last chapter. This system uses a small, general-purpose aerospace computer manufactured by GM. The block diagram of Alpha II in Fig. 10-4 shows that it provides functions similar to those of Alpha I. Some functions were removed on Alpha II, however; for example, the electronic transmission. A *throttle servo* was added. In this function, the accelerator position becomes a signal input to the computer, which then calculates an appropriate throttle position. The computer then issues a signal to the throttle-positioning motor, which then operates the carburetor linkage. One purpose in including this feature was to show what the computer could do in terms of converting a mechanical control to electronics.

The computer used in Alpha II is serially organized. That means that the computer cannot accept and process signals from all the sensors at once. Rather, it is designed to process signals from the sensors one at a time; i.e., serially. The function of the parallel-to-serial adapter is something like that of an appointments secretary. It allocates the time of the computer among the various sensors. It does this by sequentially sampling the various sensors in a PCM multiplex operation such as that discussed in the last chapter.

In summary, Alpha I and II have provided some important inklings as to the cars of the future—inklings far more significant than the Batmobile renditions of the Sunday supplements. Whatever the cars of the future will look like, their most distinctive features will be the marvelous new functions provided by on-board computers.

ADAPTIVE STEERING FOR CARS[1]

Adaptive steering is an automotive accessory developed by Bendix Corp. that provides automatic, limited power-steering to combat the lateral-motion effects of wind gusts and similar disturbances. Its purpose is to prevent large undesired course deviations and to relieve the driver of certain course-keeping chores imposed by automobile wander and road camber.

The conventional automobile steering system is operated by manual positioning. Turns of the steering wheel are directly related to turns of the front wheels. In most cars the effective gear ratio is approximately twenty to one. Power steering relieves the driver of a greater part of the steering effort by providing hydraulic assistance, but manual positioning is still required; the driver must sense all demands for steering action and apply all input steering commands. This type of steering control is obviously adequate for most driving conditions. The human operator is a versatile control system and can satisfactorily "close the loop" between the road and the steering wheel for normal maneuvering and road following. He may find it more difficult, however, to sense and control unexpected deviations from the established path caused by external lateral forces from wind gusts or road irregularities.

Such a disturbance is illustrated in Fig. 10-5, where an automobile is shown traveling down a road through a cut, a fill, and then another cut. In a prevailing cross wind, the automobile is in wind shade while in the cut, but in the filled portion of the

[1]This section is based on a contribution by J.T. Kasselmann and T.W. Kerenan to **Bendix Technical Journal.**

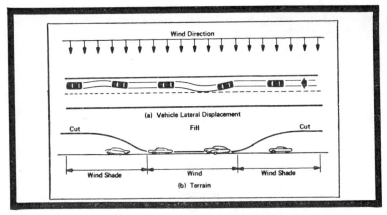

Fig. 10-5. Crosswind travel through cut-and-fill terrain. (Courtesy Bendix Technical Journal.)

road it is suddenly exposed to the full force of the wind and driver action is required to maintain course stability. Similar lateral disturbances may result from passing large trailor trucks or from road irregularities such as sudden camber changes, ruts, or holes. These disturbances may be so severe, or may occur so unexpectedly, that the driver cannot respond before the automobile is thrown seriously off course—possibly into the path of an oncoming vehicle.

To reduce or eliminate vehicle course deviations resulting from lateral disturbances, an adaptive steering system based on servo-system technology has been conceived. Servo systems are used extensively in aircraft to provide autopilot control and stability augmentation. They relieve the the pilot of certain navigational and altitude-control chores by sensing disturbances and applying appropriate corrections to rudder, elevator, and aileron. The technology behind these systems has now been applied to automobile steering. Adaptive steering operates independently of the driver to automatically correct for lateral disturbances of established vehicle course; i.e., undesired lateral motion is sensed, the sensor signal is amplified, and the amplified signal is applied to a hydraulic servoactuator which steers the front wheels. The actuator has limited stroke capability and can always be overridden by the driver.

The following goals were established for the pioneering development program of Bendix Corp.:

1. Automatic correction for lateral course disturbances caused by aerodynamic, road, or inertial forces or vehicle-component malfunctions such as brake-pull or tire blowout.

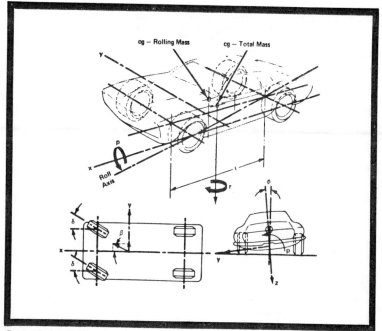

Fig. 10-6. Axis reference for automobile. (Courtesy Bendix Technical Journal.)

2. Allowance for simultaneous manual steering and limited-authority automatic steering at all steering angles.
3. Noninterference between automatic straight-line steering and manually directed turns.

Like an airplane, an automobile has a tendency to rotate around two axes, x and z in Fig. 10-6. The motion about these axes is described as *roll* and *yaw*. Roll is what makes a car tend to tip over in a fast turn and yaw tends to make a car wander from side to side. A third motion, in the plane of y in Fig. 10-6, tends to make a car skid sideways off the road—this is called *sideslip*.

Of all the quantities that could be sensed and used for automobile directional control, Bendix engineers decided upon *yaw rate*—how much yaw changes with time.

SYSTEM OPERATION

The electrohydraulic adaptive steering system which was designed and tested by Bendix contains an electronic *rate gyro* (described later) which senses vehicle yaw rates. The yaw-rate gyro electric-output signal is amplified and used to control the hydraulic *servovalve* (Fig. 10-7). The servovalve hydraulic

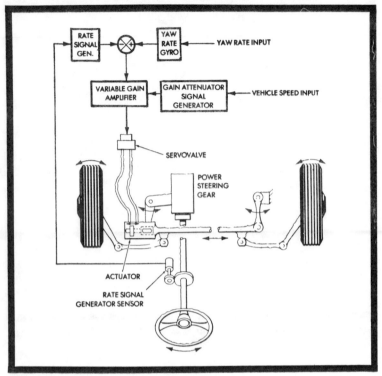

Fig. 10-7. Pictorial schematic of adaptive steering system. (Courtesy Bendix Technical Journal.)

output is used to drive the adaptive-steering actuator which is attached to the vehicle steering linkage. Electric feedback is used to control actuator position.

A gear-driven potentiometer senses steering-wheel position, and electronic processing produces an electric signal that results from driver-induced vehicle motions. This circuit prevents the adaptive steering system from opposing driver-steering commands.

To improve adaptive steering performance at low vehicle speeds, a *gain attenuator* is used to reduce the magnitude of the servovalve input. The gain-attenuator sensor is a speedometer-driven dc tachometer generator whose output is electronically processed to reduce the gain of the amplifier. In the test installation, the servovalve was mounted stationary to the frame of the automobile, and flexible tubing was used to transmit hydraulic oil to the actuator that travels with the steering linkage. Three possible locations for the servoactuator were studied—one in the steering column, one integral with the

Fig. 10-8. Servovalve and actuator installed in test vehicle. (Courtesy Bendix Technical Journal.)

power-steering gear, and one in the steering linkage. The linkage location was accepted because good actuator dynamic response could be achieved without upsetting the driver. The poor dynamic characteristics and mechanical advantages of the power-steering gear also served to isolate the driver from actuator reaction forces. The servovalve and actuator installations on the test vehicle are shown in Fig. 10-8.

The hydraulic circuit of the adaptive steering system is represented schematically in Fig. 10-9. Hydraulic power is provided by an engine-driven, modified power-steering pump. The output pressure of the pump is controlled by an adjustable

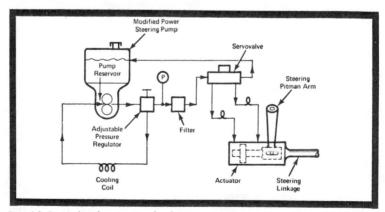

Fig. 10-9. Hydraulic circuit of adaptive steering system. (Courtesy Bendix Technical Journal.)

Fig. 10-10. Hydraulic pump and pressure regulator installed in test vehicle. (Courtesy Bendix Technical Journal.)

pressure regulator. The oil (type A transmission fluid) is filtered before it enters the servovalve-actuator system. The pump and pressure regulator are shown in Fig. 10-10, installed on the test vehicle.

Operational amplifiers and standard electric components were used to build the electronic signal processor. This unit contains circuitry for the rate gyro, the rate-signal generator, the electronic amplifier, the servovalve, the actuator-feedback potentiometer, and the speed-gain attenuator. Circuitry is also provided to scale parameters for recording. The design of the electronic signal processor was based on information obtained in an analog computer study. System component specifications are detailed in Table 10-1.

ADAPTIVE BRAKING COMPONENTS

There are a number of functions that a control system such as this must perform:

- It must set up fixed reference lines in space, from which deviations in direction can be measured. This requires a *gyroscope*, or *gyro*, for short.
- It must provide a mechanical or electrical means of operating the controls of the car as required. A device for this is a *servo*.
- It must provide a means of measuring the magnitude and direction of the angular deviations the car makes from the reference lines and which the servos make in position of the steering mechanism. This requires a *pickup*, or *synchro*.

Table 10-1. Components of Adaptive Steering System. (Courtesy Bendix Technical Journal.)

Component	Specifications
Yaw-Rate Gyroscope	Bendix Model 19101-1A Gain: 0.2 volt/(deg/sec) Natural frequency: 19 Hz
Rate-Signal-Generator Sensor	Wire-wound Helipot Potentiometer (1000-ohm, 10-turn) Gear-driven off steering-gear input shaft Gear Ratio: 2:1
Speed-Gain-Attenuator Sensor	Servo-Tech d.c. Tachometer Generator Gain: 20.8 volts/1000 rpm Driven off speedometer drive cable Gear ratio: 1:1
Electronic Signal Processor	Centralized Electronic Circuitry containing operational amplifiers for adaptive steering
Servovalve	Moog 16-101B Servovalve Full-stroke electric input requirement: ± 20 ma Hydraulic input: 1.71 in^3/sec Supply pressure: 600 psig
Actuator	Integral with steering linkage Steering inputs limited to within ± 3 deg of front-wheel movement (independent of normal steering-linkage operation) Effective area: 2.0 in.^{2} Stroke: ± 0.3 in. Output force: 1255 lb Supply pressure: 600 psig
Hydraulic Power	Power-Steering Pump with blocked-flow control valve Vickers C7-06-B Regulator for output pressure
Electric Power	115-Volt, 400-Hz Inverter for yaw-rate gyro and electronics 115-Volt, 60-Hz Inverter for data-recording instrumentation Special Power Supply (115-volt d.c.) for operational amplifiers

Gyroscope: the Basic Sensor Unit

Before discussing the application of gyroscopes in a control system, first consider some basic gyroscopic terms and definitions.

A gyroscope is a mechanical device containing an accurately balanced rotor. The rotor spins about its central or

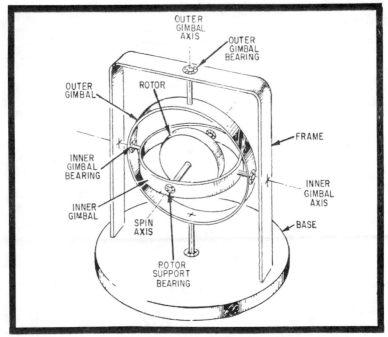

Fig. 10-11. Free gyroscope.

spin axis, which passes throught the center of gravity. A free gyroscope is so mounted that it can tilt or turn in any direction about this center of gravity. Figure 10-11 shows such a gyroscope. When the rotor is rotated at a high speed, it assumes the characteristics of a gyroscope, that is, rigidity in space.

The characteristic of rigidity in space makes the gyroscope useful as a reference or sensor unit in controlling the motion of a car.

Rigidity of Gyroscopes

Rigidity, gyroscopic inertia, or angular momentum, is that property of a gyroscope which resists any force tending to displace the rotor from its plane of rotation. Three factors determine a gyroscope's strength or amount of rigidity. These factors are (1) the weight of the rotor, (2) the distribution of this weight, and (3) the speed at which the rotor spins.

Gyroscopic Precession

There are two types of gyro precession: real or *induced* precession and *apparent* precession.

Real Precession. Real precession is movement of the gyro spin axis from its original alignment in space. This precession

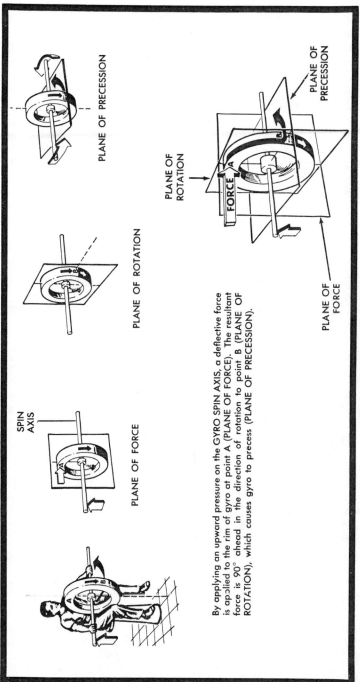

SPIN
AXIS

PLANE OF FORCE

PLANE OF ROTATION

PLANE OF PRECESSION

PLANE OF
ROTATION

FORCE

PLANE OF
PRECESSION

PLANE OF
FORCE

By applying an upward pressure on the GYRO SPIN AXIS, a deflective force is applied to the rim of gyro at point A (PLANE OF FORCE). The resultant force is 90° ahead in the direction of rotation to point B (PLANE OF ROTATION), which causes gyro to precess (PLANE OF PRECESSION).

Fig. 10-12. Real precession.

is caused by a force applied to the spin axis and can be predicted if the point to which the force was applied is known. Spin axis precession occurs 90 degrees from the point of applied force, in the direction of rotor rotation, and in the same direction as the applied force (refer to Fig. 10-12).

It is apparent from the preceding explanation of gyro precession that if a force were applied to the gyro at the center of gravity, it would not act to tip the gyro spin axis from its established position. No precession would take place. A spinning gyroscope can be moved in any direction, provided its axis remains parallel to its original position in space. The gyro provides stability only against tipping its spin axis. For complete stabilization in aircraft, for example two gyroscopes which have their spin axis at right angles to each other are required.

Rate Determination

A gyro having two gimbals may be used to determine the rate of deviation of a sensor from its established reference. By restraining one of the gimbals with springs or a similar means, the force exerted on the restraint by the precession of the gyro may be measured, giving an indication of rate.

Rate Gyro

A rate-of-deviation signal is supplied by a rate gyro. A rate gyro has a restricted gimbal, free to rotate about one axis only. It is a true gyroscope, conforming otherwise to the same basic principles as other gyros. The spin axis of a yaw-rate gyro is mounted with its spin axis parallel to the car's direction of travel.

The rate gyro used is similar to a free gyro in that it has a high gyroscopic momentum while the rotor is spinning. It differs in that it is free to rotate about one axis only and in that it is sensitive only to angular rates of movement; that is, angular movement of its cradle in excess of a certain rate causes its spin axis to change its position in relation to space. Such changes occur 90 degrees in the direction of rotation from the angular movement applied and in the direction of movement.

Selsyn Pickoffs

A selsyn (*self syn*chronizing) pickoff (also called synchro, autsyn, microsyn, etc.) usually consists of a pair of selsyns wired as a generator and a control transformer. They give an accurate electrical identification of angular movement, can be made small and light, and have a constant phase for a varying displacement. They lack sensitivity for minute variations in displacement.

Two typical selsyn pickoff systems are shown in Fig. 10-13. Note the similarity of the selsyn to an alternator. Of course, the selsyn rotor turns through only part of a circle. When a selsyn generator and a selsyn control transformer are properly connected, they form a complete pickoff system.

The schematic represents the electrical zero position. For a control transformer, electrical zero is defined as that position of the rotor in which no voltage is induced in the rotor windings from the stator windings. This condition occurs when the axis of the rotor is perpendicular to the axis of the S_1 winding.

Operation of a Control Transformer. A control transformer and a selsyn generator are connected in the electrical zero position. Note the relative positions of the two rotors in the diagrams. No voltage is induced by the S_1 coil since the rotor and coil are perpendicular. The currents of S_2 and S_3 coils are equal and opposite and induce voltages in the rotor which are equal and opposite. The net effect is that no voltage is induced in the rotor in this position.

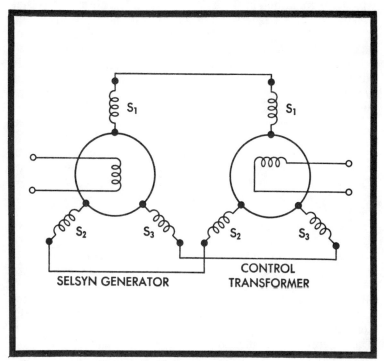

Fig. 10-13. Selsyn hookup.

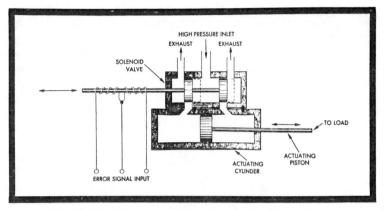

Fig. 10-14. Schematic of basic electrohydraulic actuator.

When the shaft of the control transformer is turned 90 degrees clockwise or counterclockwise, the position of S_1 and the rotor is such that maximum voltage is induced in the control transformer rotor. The currents in the S_2 and S_3 coils are equal and in the same direction, and they induce voltages in the rotor which are equal and of the same polarity. The net result is that maximum voltage is induced in the rotor in these positions, and the induced voltage is either in phase or 180 degrees out of phase with the voltage of the rotor of the selsyn generator.

The output voltage obtained from a control transformer is called an *error signal*, because the magnitude and phase of this voltage are an indication of how much and in what direction the two rotors are out of correspondence.

When the two rotors are connected by suitable mechanical linkage to a yaw-rate gyro, the precession of the gyro moves the rotors relative to each other. The relative motion, in turn, produces an electrical error signal that is analogous to the yaw rate. This signal is translated into action by a *servoactuator*.

Energy Transfer System

In some instances, actuators for control devices employ two different methods of energy transfer to achieve the desired results. For example, an electrohydraulic actuator consists essentially of a hydraulically operated piston whose direction of motion is determined by an electrically positioned selector. Actually, this device could be considered a controller—actuator combination. The electrically positioned valve acts as the controller, and the hydraulically driven piston is the actuator. The compact arrangement of the components of this combination—actuator justifies an explanation of it in this section.

Figure 10-14 illustrates the arrangement of the components of a typical electrohydraulic actuator unit.

Notice that the solenoid valve controls the input and output of hydraulic fluid to and from the actuating cylinder. The position of this valve is determined by the polarity of the error signal input. Also, the length of time that the valve remains in a certain position depends on the time interval during which the error signal of a certain polarity exists.

As illustrated in Fig. 10-14, the valve and piston occupy neutral positions. Assume that an error signal of a given polarity exists that will cause the valve to move toward the right as indicated by the dotted lines. This new valve position permits high-pressure fluid to pass through the valve into the actuating piston. The actuating piston is forced toward the left, and at the same time, fluid on the left side of the piston is forced out through the valve by way of the left exhaust port. During this action, the exhaust port located on the right is closed. When the error has been corrected, the valve and actuating piston will again be in neutral positions.

When an error signal of opposite polarity exists, the solenoid valve moves toward the left. High-pressure fluid now enters the actuating cylinder on the left side of the piston and forces it toward the right. Fluid forced from the right section of the actuating cylinder passes through the valve and escapes by way of the right exhaust port.

Remember, a hydraulic system is a closed loop. If the rest of the system were shown in the illustration, the exhaust ports would be connected to the hydraulic reservoir. The fluid displaced by movement of the actuator piston would be returned to this reservoir.

ADAPTIVE-STEERING SYSTEM PERFORMANCE

The main performance objectives of adaptive steering are reductions in the frequency and order of magnitude of the driver steering commands that are required to maintain vehicle course under lateral-disturbance conditions. The Bendix system met these objectives in the evaluation tests discussed below. System performance was evaluated by comparing the course deviations experienced by a vehicle subjected to reproducible lateral effects simulating wind gusts, road ruts, and road curb obstructions, with and without adaptive steering.

Wind-Gust Performance

Reproducible disturbances of the wind-gust type were simulated by subjecting the test vehicle to reaction forces from a thrust nozzle. The simulated-wind-gust generator used (shown

Fig. 10-15. Wind gust generator installed on test vehicle. (Courtesy Bendix Technical Journal.)

in Fig. 10-15) can apply thrusts ranging in magnitude up to 270 lb and in duration up to 4 sec.

The effect of adaptive steering on vehicle performance in wind gusts simulated by 0.5 sec. thrusts of 210 lb was tested. For this test, the vehicle was driven straight ahead on a flat concrete road at a speed of 60 mph, the steering wheel was held stationary. In the absence of adaptive steering, the vehicle exhibited a maximum yaw rate of approximately 3.4°/sec. With adaptive steering, a maximum yaw rate of only 0.9°/sec was exhibited under the same conditions. Thus, adaptive steering reduced vehicle motion by a ratio of 3.6:1. Motion reductions of better than 4:1 have been observed in some tests.

Rutted-Road Driving

To evaluate this type of performance, the test car was driven under normal driving conditions over an asphalt road that had been rutted by heavy traffic. Runs were made over a specific section of the road at identical speeds and by the same driver, with and without adaptive steering operative. Test results, typical examples of which are presented in Fig. 10-16, indicate that both vehicle motion and driver inputs are greatly reduced by adaptive steering.

Road-Curb Obstructions

Normal driving frequently invloves obstruction-avoidance maneuvers which may cause the vehicle to veer onto the shoulder of the road or to strike or run over a curb. To determine the effects of adaptive steering on this type of vehicle handling, the test car was driven over a standard road curb at a speed of 30 mph and at an approximate approach angle of 10 degrees. Adaptive steering greatly reduced vehicle motion and driver steering inputs, eliminating much of the violent lurching that normally occurs under these conditions and providing the driver with a far more controllable vehicle. Similar results were obtained in analogous tests in which the vehicle was driven off the edge of the road onto a loose-gravel shoulder.

When the test car was driven on standard expressways, adaptive steering resulted in a 50% reduction in driver-steering inputs.

Conclusion

Experience indicates that adaptive steering has associated with it performance characteristics that can be interpreted in terms of safer automobile operation. It reduces driver fatigue, makes possible precise high-speed handling, and greatly increases vehicle stability. Based on road tests made under conditions varying from wind gusts and rutted roads to expressway driving, the Bendix system promises to provide a high degree of vehicle controllability, requiring driver-steering inputs that are fewer in number an smaller in magnitude than would otherwise be the case.

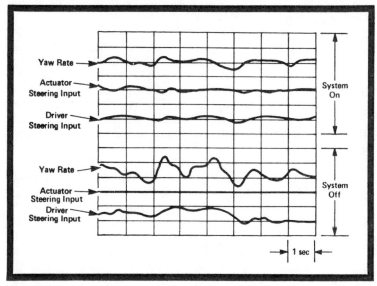

Fig. 10-16. Vehicle performance in rutted-road driving. (Courtesy Bendix Technical Journal.)

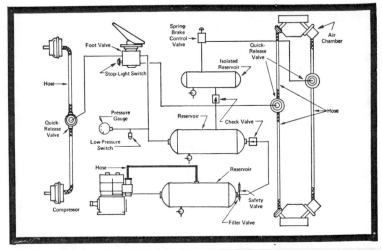

Fig. 10-17. Truck air brake system. (Courtesy Bendix Technical Journal.)

ADVANCED BRAKING SYSTEM FOR TRUCKS[1]

Two truck brake systems currently in use are described schematically in Fig. 10-17 and 10-18. Figure 10-17 shows a typical air brake system with wedge-type drum brakes and spring brakes on two wheels. Figure 10-18 shows a typical vacuum—hydraulic system having two Hydrovac power unit, one supplying the front brakes and half the rear brakes, the other supplying the other half of the rear brakes.

There are several limitations associated with current brake systems. Both air and vacuum—hydraulic systems have slow response times and therefore long stopping distances. The long pedal-travel distance in vacuum—hydraulic systems also increases stopping distance because the operator loses time in raising his foot to the high pedal. Size restrictions limit peak system output pressures and fluid displacements. Air systems suffer from relatively long recovery times in high altitudes because the volumetric efficiency of the air compressor is lowered.

The use of larger brakes on the front axle, which would make possible a more nearly equal brake distribution, and thus permit decelerations in the passenger-car range of 26 to 32 ft/sec, has been delayed by the directional instability that characterizes front drum brakes.

The low heat capacity of drum-type brakes causes fade on long downhill runs and limits deceleration capability. Brake

[1]This section is based on a contribution by R. T. Burnett, K. H. Fullmer, and F. G. Grabb to **Bendix Technical Journal.**

fade may also be accompanied in some cases by boiling of the brake fluid. Brake fluid has a high affinity for water, and any increase in its water content will lower its boiling point.

Drum brakes also suffer from the disadvantage of slow water recovery, because water remains trapped in the brake until it i evaporated by the heat generated during braking application and because drum-brake linings are more water-absorbent than are the hard, dense materials used on disc brakes.

Bendix Corp. has designed and is in the process of implementing an advanced braking system that promises to meet the general requirements and to overcome the limitations described above. The major elements of the system are caliper disc brakes with ventilated discs; a fully redundant, full-power hydraulic actuator system; and an electrohydraulic adaptive-braking control.

In designing the sysyem, Bendix placed particular emphasis on the following basic objectives:

- Deceleration rates comparable to those of passenger cars
- Extended brake service life
- Increased fade resistance
- Controlled braking under all conditions
- Improved performance under conditions of water exposure

Design criteria included equal brake capacity on all wheels and an equalized distribution of the total braking load. Brakes were to be rated for load capacity and were to be made in as few sizes as possible. Optimum split-system performance was

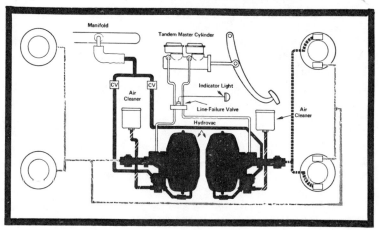

Fig. 10-18. Truck vacuum-hydraulic brake system. (Courtesy Bendix Technical Journal.)

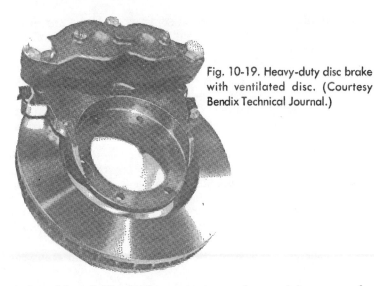

Fig. 10-19. Heavy-duty disc brake with ventilated disc. (Courtesy Bendix Technical Journal.)

to be achieved. The brakes were to require a minimum number of component changes for installation on existing vehicles and were to be capable of handling trucks weighing 16,000 lb or more.

The Disc Brake

The disc brake designed for this system evolved out of many years of work on passenger-car disc brakes and three years of brake development for heavy-duty trucks. The brake itself and a cross section through it are shown in Fig. 10-19 and 10-20, respectively. It is of the floating-caliper type, with actuating cylinders on the inboard side of the disc to apply the inboard shoe directly; the outboard shoe is attached to the caliper and is applied by the hydraulic reaction of the cylinders. This construction was dictated by cost and space considerations. The dual cylinders provide the reqred hydraulic area in a configuration that the vehicle can accommodate.

Brakes of four sizes have been designed, with two basic calipers and two cylinder sizes adapted to each caliper. The brakes are rated on the basis of torque and energy considerations in terms of the vehicle weight they can support per axle, these being 10,000 lb, 13,000 lb, and 19,000 lb.

Adjustment is fully automatic and very simply accomplished. As the brake lining wears, the pistons continue to move out to compensate. After each brake application, they retract a few thousandths of an inch because of the elasticity of the piston seals, which are contained in grooves specially contoured to promote this action.

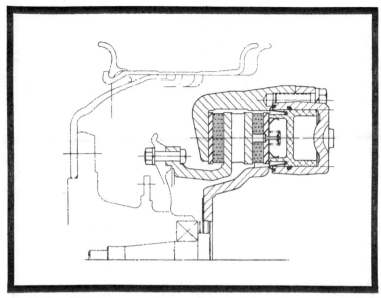

Fig. 10-20. Cross section of heavy-duty disc brake. (Courtesy Bendix Technical Journal.)

The Hydraulic Actuator System

To meet the basic program objectives, it was neccessary to design an actuator system having the following characteristics:

- Compatibility with either disc or drum brakes
- Improved response
- Reduced size and weight
- High reliability
- Acceptable cost
- Driver acceptance
- Increased hydraulic pressure and greater displacement

Bendix found that a *full-power hydraulic* system (Fig. 10-21) best met these requirements. In its simplest form, the system incorporates a fluid reservoir, a hydraulic pump, a high-pressure accumulator, and a control valve. The reservoir supplies brake fluid at ambient pressure to the pump. The pump charges the accumulator with brake fluid to a pressure somewh exceeding the maximum brake requirement. The control valve provides brake-fluid pressure to the brake in direct proportion to operator pedal pressure.

The term "full power" identifies the system as one in which only the force of the driver's foot actuates the control valve to direct brake fluid from the accumulators to the brake wheel cylinders. The amount of pressure metered through the valve is

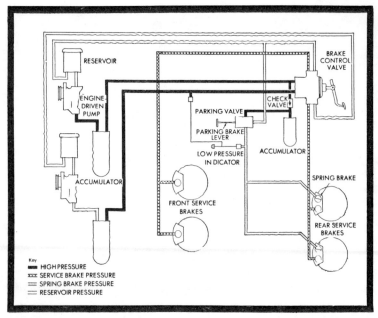

Fig. 10-21. Full-power hydraulic system with disc and spring brakes (split system). (Courtesy Bendix Technical Journal.)

directly proportional to the force applied to the pedal by the driver.

The system is a *dual* system in which all the major components are in duplicate; the control valve consists of two complete sets of valving elements in a single housing. Each circuit functions independently, and during normal operation the pressures in each are equalized via an internal equalizing lever. Should either system fail, the driver is immediately warned and the remaining system continues to function.

In each circuit, fluid flows from the sealed reservoir to the pump to the accumulator to the brake valve to the brakes and then back to the sealed reservoir. This cycle is described in detail in the paragraphs that follow.

The *pump* (Fig. 10-22), which is belt-driven by the engine, maintains the fluid in the accumulator at operating pressures. Fluid is supplied to the pump from the reservoir and passes through a filter screen into the crankcase or pump. From the pump, it flows into the intake groove of the cylinder. When the piston is in the extreme down position, fluid from the groove fills the cylinder cavity above the piston. As the piston begins its compression stroke, it displaces a small amount of fluid back to the sump until it reaches the edge of the cylinder intake groove. The fluid trapped in the cylinder cavity is pressurized as the piston completes its compression stroke and opens the check valve over the cylinder. The pressurized fluid is then discharged through the outlet fitting and hose into the accumulator. This cycle is repeated until a system pressure of 2300 psi is built up, the pressure being limited by a pressure-sensitive piston and valve inside the pump. When system pressure is reached, its force overcomes the spring and closes the valve with the rubber seal against the casting face, blocking any further fluid flow from sump to cylinder. Since no more fluid can enter the cylinder cavity, no more can be discharged, even though the pump continues to operate. In the configuration in Fig. 10-22, the regulator is open as it would be while system pressure is building.

The *accumulator* (Fig. 10-23) is a pressure-storage vessel in which a membrane or bladder separates the brake fluid from a precharged gas. Before any fluid is pumped into the accumulator, nitrogen gas pressure inside the bladder forces its walls into tight contact with the sides and domed end of the accumulator shell. As fluid is pumped in, the bladder flexes as

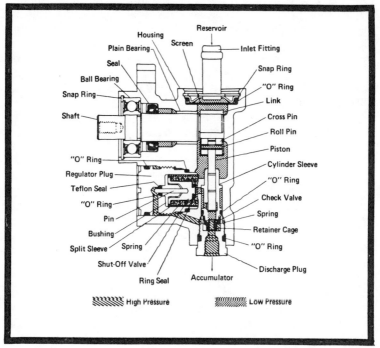

Fig. 10-22: Pump and pressure regulator. (Courtesy Bendix Technical Journal.)

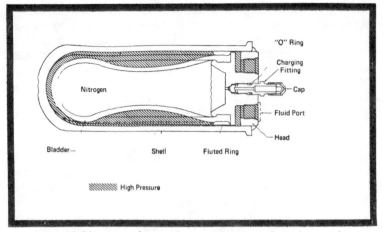

Fig. 10-23. Accumulator. (Courtesy Bendix Technical Journal.)

shown in Fig. 10-23, and the gas and fluid pressures rise and equalize. The fluid volume increases until it reaches 7 cubic inches at 2000 psi. This is the pressurized fluid that is available for braking when the pumps are not running. As the fluid is metered out by the brake valve, the pressure gradually drops to 1000 psi (the accumulator precharge pressure). At this point, the fluid is exhausted and fluid pressure suddenly drops to zero. It subsequently rebuilds by jumping initially from zero to the precharge pressure of 1000 psi and then increasing gradually to maximum system pressure.

The force applied to the brake pedal by the driver's foot is transmitted through the pushrod and lever (see Fig. 10-24) to the plungers and outlet valves. The initial movement seats the outlet valve against the ball in each side of the *control valve*, cutting off brake-system communication with the reservoir. Additional force and a slight movement unseats the ball from the inlet seat and meters high-pressure fluid from the accumulator to the brake system. The buildup of brake system pressure causes the transmission of an increased force through the rubber reaction disc to the end of the reaction plunger. Thus the force exerted on the pedal is in direct proportion to the brake system pressure supplied. As force on the pedal is withdrawn, the ball valve is seated on the inlet seat and the outlet seat is opened to release the pressurized brake fluid back to the reservoir. The control valve is shown in this released position.

System pressures are limited to approximately 3200 psi by two safety relief valves that operate in case of malfunction of either of the normal pressure-monitoring units.

The *reservoir* serves to accommodate fluid-level variations that result from temperature changes as well as fluid-volume changes that result from pressure changes in the accumulator.

The Adaptive-Braking Control

The combination of full-power hydraulic actuation and disc brakes can provide controlled 0.8g decelerations (or better) on high-friction-coefficient roads if braking power is appropriately distributed among the various axles. However, such a distribution can be appropriate only for one condition of loading—full loading, for example. Thus, empty trucks or trucks traveling on low-friction-coefficient roads may experience early wheel slide unless special preventive measures are taken. To provide this necessary added control, an *antiskid* or *adaptive-braking* system incorporating a hydraulic modulator controlled by electric signals is used. (A similar system for cars is discussed in Chapter 3.) Combined with the full-power hydraulic components, this system speeds response time to such an extent that far shorter stopping distances are achievable on low-friction-coefficient roads than can be achieved with vacuum or air systems.

To achieve maximum deceleration, brake distribution (that is, the distribution of torque and energy absorption among the

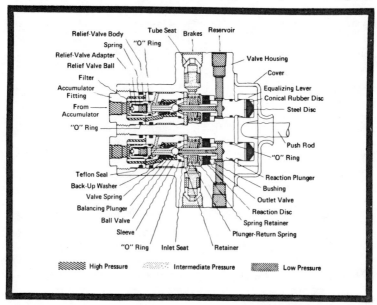

Fig. 10-24. Full-power dual control valve. (Courtesy Bendix Technical Journal.)

various wheels) should ideally be proportional to the weight carried by the individual wheels. Since weight distribution is far from constant, however, varying with deceleration and loading conditions, a compromise must be made. If braking is not in proportion to weight supported, some wheels will be overbraked and early wheel silde will occur, causing loss of control and limiting maximum deceleration. Adaptive braking can prevent wheel slide, and under these circumstances the best brake distribution is what we call a 50-50 distribution—one that divides the work evenly among all the brakes for all normal stops. In the case of a two-axle truck, 50% of the braking would be handled by the front axle and 50% by the rear; in the case of a tandem-axle truck, each of the three axles would handle one-third of the braking.

The 50-50 concept greatly lengthens lining life, not only because each brake is doing its share of the work, but because peak temperatures are much lower. It also results in a minimum number of brake sizes. To equip trucks ranging in weight from 16,000 to 48,000 lb, only four sizes are required, half the number that would be necessary if the conventional practice of relating brake size to axle rating were followed. This is obviously an important advantage in tooling for a new series of brakes.

System Performance

An adaptive-braking system with individual wheel control has been installed and demonstrated by Bendix Corp. On both high- and low-friction-coefficient surfaces, including ice, the system prevents wheel slide under panic braking conditions and permits steering maneuvers during maximum-braking stops.

As of this writing, the advanced braking system described above has been tested on the dynamometer and on five trucks ranging in size up to 35,000 lb. The decelerations achieved, 26 to 32 ft/sec, have been exceptionally high compared with conventional decelerations of 19 to 20 ft/sec. Fade is virtually nonexistent, and lining life promises to be up to twice that of lining on present brakes.

Pedal feel and controllability are excellent. A weight saving of approximately 150 lb per vehicle has been effected. Though costs have not yet been firmly established, they should represent a sizable saving over costs of air brake systems with either wedge or cam brakes.

The disc brakes have performed well in tests conducted on a very muddy course, with lining life about three times that of drum-brake linings. Although the discs are exposed, the linings continually scrape off mud, preventing it from packing inside

Fig. 10-25. Radar and optical sensors mounted in test vehicle grill. (Courtsey Bendix Technical Journal.)

the brake and producing rapid wear as is the case with drum brakes.

Bendix foresees the rather widespread use of this advanced braking system on heavy trucks within the next few years. It was introduced on some models in 1972. They believe that the inherent advantages of the braking system are so great as to guarantee its almost universal adoption within the next decade.

ADAPTIVE SPEED CONTROL FOR AUTOMOBILES[1]

An electronic speed control for automobiles was introduced in the 1969 model year. Intended as a driver convenience, it allows the driver to feed the speed he desires into the memory of a unique electronic memory circuit. The throttle is then smoothly controlled so that this speed is maintained whatever the highway grade, car load, or wind velocity. The driver can temporarily override the system by using the throttle; he can disconnect it by applying the brakes. The system is described in detail in Chapter 6.

This section describes a "next generation" speed control which is designed to increase the usefulness of the present device. The Bendix adaptive speed control (ASC) system adjusts the speed of an automobile so that a safe following distance is maintained with respect to a lead vehicle located in the same traffic lane and within range of a radar or optical sensor situated in the ASC-equipped automobile (Fig. 10-25).

[1]This section is based on a contribution by R. W. Carp, J. G. Elliott, and J. S. Weidman to **Bendix Technical Journal.**

The driver is thus relieved of the routine speed adjustments required to cope with the rapidly changing conditions in moderately dense expressway traffic. Although no collision avoidance capability is claimed for the device, the practical experience and information it provides should facilitate the development of still more advanced systems capable of upgrading both traffic flow and traffic safety.

System Description

The ASC system now being road tested has two distinct modes of operation. Under open-road conditions, with no lead vehicle within 250 ft, the driver-selected speed is maintained as in the present system via a vacuum-actuated linkage connected to the throttle. The throttle setting is either increased or decreased on the basis of difference between the memorized driver-selected speed and the actual speed as it is reported by a small pulse generator connected to the speedometer cable. When a vehicle in the same lane becomes close enough to be detected by the sensor, the ASC system enters a headway-control mode to maintain a safe headway. If this lead vehicle subsequently pulls out of the traffic lane or accelerates to a speed greater than the driver-selected speed, the ASC system reverts to the standard speed control mode of operation.

Though other criteria are possible, the number of feet that constitute a safe *headway*, or following distance, is generally considered to equal the car speed in miles per hour plus 30. In establishing this headway, no account is currently taken of the road surface condition, i.e., of the tire/road coefficient of friction. If this factor were to be considered, an additional input would be required, either from the driver or from another sensor.

A block diagram and sketch of the complete ASC system is shown in Fig. 10-26. The elements of the present speed control system are those below the broken line; those above the line are new elements. The system operates as follows: The sensor (microwave or optical) determines the range R, and relative velocity (range *rate*, R) of the lead vehicle, and the speedometer cable provides data on the controlled-automobile velocity. The safe headway for this set of conditions is computed and, based on a linear combination of present range, safe headway, and range rate, the throttle and brakes are automatically put into operation as required.

Both a microwave and an optical sensor are used in the system that is currently being vehicle-tested by Bendix; the operator is able to select either at will. Their comparative efficiencies over a wide range of road, traffic, and weather conditions will determine which will be incorporated into the final unit. Since most of the research so far has centered around the microwave (radar) sensor, that is the one to be discussed in detail here.

Throttle and Brake Actuators

Both in present speed control systems and in the adaptive system, an integrated vacuum modulator and actuator are used for throttle control (see Fig. 10-27).

A spring-loaded collapsible diaphragm is linked to the throttle plate and mounted in a chamber which houses two

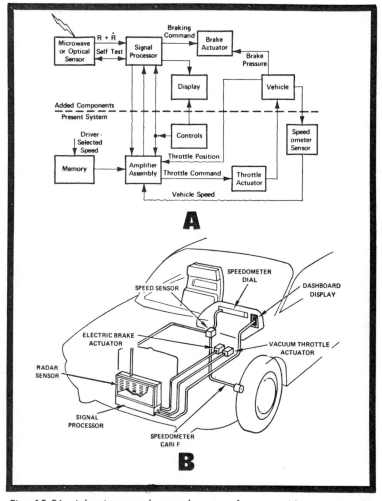

Fig. 10-26. Adaptive speed control system for cars. (Courtesy Bendix Corp.)

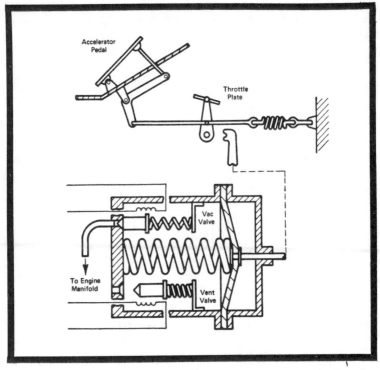

Fig. 10-27. Vacuum modulator and actuator. (Courtesy Bendix Corp.)

valves. One valve, which is normally open, allows communication between the chamber and atmospheric air. The other valve, which is normally closed, connected the chamber to engine-manifold vacuum when open. With both valves energized, the chamber is isolated from atmospheric air and ported to engine vacuum, causing the diaphragm to stroke. The diaphragm can be held at any stroke displacement by holding both valves in the closed position; it will return to the relaxed position when both valves return to their normal positions. Accurate throttle control is achieved via high servoloop gain and fast valve response, a mile-an-hour error resulting in a 30% change in throttle position. Automatic control is limited to about 70% of full throttle, since this is sufficient for proper speed control at normal highway speeds.

ASC SENSORS

The sensor must gather range and range-rate data on the vehicle ahead while ignoring vehicles in other lanes and false targets such as overpasses and bridges. Since a "noncooperative" system must be assumed, with no special marking of the lead vehicle required, discrimination is accomplished primarily through the sensor beamwidth.

DOPPLER RADAR

Doppler radar does not sense range as ordinary search radar does. Instead, it is *speed conscious*, It employs continuous carrier wave (cw) transmission energy and determines the forward velocity of a vehicle by using the principle known as *Doppler effect*.

The Doppler effect, or frequency change of a signal, can be explained in terms of an approaching and receding audio sound emitter. As shown in Fig. 10-28A, the sound emitter is on a moving ambulance and the receiver is the ear of a stationary listener. Assume that the frequency of the siren is 1000 Hz.

Notice the spacing between the waves from the stationary emitter, as illustrated in Fig. 10-28B. If the emitter and listener were standing still, then 1000 waves of sound energy would reach the listener in one second.

In Fig. 10-28C, the emitter is moving toward the listener (closing). The emitter moves a little closer to the listener between successive waves of energy, so each wave reaches the listener sooner than it would if the emitter were stationary. This

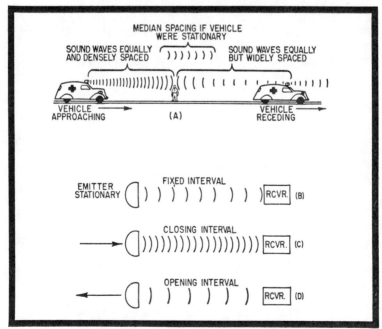

Fig. 10-28 Doppler effect with sound waves.

Fig. 10-29. Packaged radar sensor. (Courtesy Bendix Corp.)

means that the listener hears more than 1000 waves of energy in one second, and consequently the sound is higher in pitch.

The reverse is true in Fig. 10-28D. The emitter is moving away (opening), so the interval between sucessive waves is greater. Since the listener hears less than 1000 waves in one second, the frequency of the emitter seems lower than it actually is.

Doppler radar employs the frequency change phenomenon just described, except in the rf (radio frequency) range.

The radar emits cw energy at one frequency, and these waves of energy strike the target and are reflected. Energy waves returning from the target are spaced differently than the waves striking the target. A closing target moves a little closer to the radar between successive waves, and reflects the waves sooner than if it were stationary. The closer spaced waves mean that the frequency has increased slightly.

If the target moves toward the radar or if the radar moves toward the target faster, the waves of energy will be even closer together, causing a greater frequency change. The faster the closing speed, the higher will be the frequency of the returning waves.

The receiver of the Doppler radar system has two signal inputs—one from the transmitter, and one from the receiver antenna. The input signal from the transmitter is at all times the same frequency as the signal being radiated; the receiver antenna signal frequency will vary with the relative speed of the target and the radar. The two frequencies are compared in the receiver, and the difference frequency is a direct indication of the closing or the opening speed of the target.

The Doppler effect is present any time there is relative motion (opening or closing distance) between the radar and the target. Therefore, the radar could be moving toward a stationary target and the effect would be the same as if a target moved toward a stationary radar.

The Microwave Sensor

In general, the beamwidth of the ASC microwave sensor must approximate 3 to 4 degrees, and the sidelobes on the antenna pattern must be kept small. Since the average vehicle is a large radar target, good beamwidth control and a high signal acceptance threshold have given good results in road tests to date. Additional testing is in progress on the completed system.

In order to keep production costs low and reliability high, the choice of ranging techniques was restricted to those that could use a solid-state transmitter. Since this required a cw transmitter, Bendix decided to build a coherent system (one that could measure velocity via the Doppler shift) and to measure range by frequency modulating the transmitted signal. A high operating frequency, limited only by the availability of suitable solid-state sources, was needed to give a small beamwidth with minimum antenna size. The $K\mu$ band (16 gigahertz) was selected since all-weather operation is realized at this frequency. A $K\mu$ band radar sensor is pictured in Fig. 10-29.

If range resolution could be ignored, high range accuracy for a single target or vehicle could be achieved by any one of a number of simple modulation techniques. There is ambiguity in this range measuremnt, however, and care must be taken to prevent large distant objects from appearing to be close-in targets. The measurement technique selected for use is a dual-frequency modulation technique in which the two closely spaced frequencies are sequentially transmitted and received. Range in this case is proportional to the phase shift between the two Doppler signals that are obtained by mixing the transmitted and received signals. At $K\mu$ band frequencies, a Doppler shift of 32 Hz occurs for each foot-per-second of movement between target and radar; range information continues to be received until the relative closing speed drops below about 0.6 ft/sec. The fact that no range information is obtained if the target is stationary with respect to the radar has consequences that are currently under study.

A block diagram of the radar system is shown in Fig. 10-30. A single antenna is used for both transmission and reception to minimize the difficulty of installation on a standard automobile.

In general, the test results were encouraging. The system "acquires" typical vehicles at a range of approximately 250 ft and has good range accuracy at 200 ft. It ignores most roadside

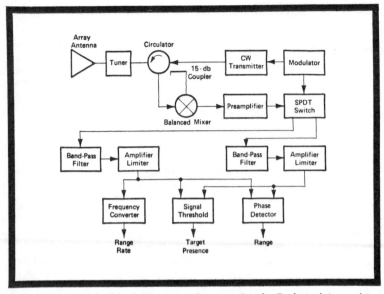

Fig. 10-30. Radar block diagram. (Courtesy Bendix Technical Journal.)

obstacles such as parked vehicles and signs and, once lock is attained on the vehicle ahead, also ignores vehicles in adjacent lanes. Some multipath and multiple-target errors do occur, mwever, and their effects on closed-loop system operation are now under study. Although the microwave sensor has high range accuracy, it does not have a correspondingly high range resolution; thus, multiple-target effects must be expected.

Problems

One of the major difficulties to be overcome involves system operation through curves. At present, both the optical and microwave sensors are body fixed and cannot be adjusted while the automobile is in motion. Because the sensor field of view cannot be manipulated, a roadside reflector or sign could be detected during a sharp-curve maneuver and interpreted to be another vehicle, with the result that the system would command the controlled automobile to stop. This problem is more serious in urban areas than on standard interstate highways and typical expressways where the minimum curve radius is about 1500 ft. A lead vehicle detected prior to entering such a curve can be tracked throughout in the headway control mode, and other potential targets will then be ignored. If the curve is entered with no target lock-on, however, false targets may be detected. One possible solution would be to provide for ASC system cutoff in the absence of a target when the wheels have changed direction by some preset amount; whether such a feature would meet with customer acceptance is questionable. A more suitable option might be to program the system to accept only moving targets during curve maneuvers.

A long-range solution to this problem and to others would be a "cooperative" system in which every vehicle would be marked with a special passive reflector, distinguishing it from roadside signs, markers, and the like. If such a system were universal, adaptive speed control could logically be extended to provide full automatic longitudinal control of the automobile. The driver would then no longer control motion in the lane of his selection, though lane-changing would still be done manually. In addition to upgrading safety, a system of this type could greatly increase present highway capacities.

PERSONAL RAPID TRANSIT SYSTEM[1]

A unique computer-controlled personal-rapid-transit (PRT) system is currently under construction and test at Morgantown, West Virginia. This people-mover system is planned to serve some 23,000 students and faculty members at two of West Virginia University's three campuses, as well as some 30,000 city residents. The system consists of small, driverless, automatically controlled vehicles designed to travel at speeds up to 30 miles per hour over exclusive rights-of-way having no road-level crossings or intersections. The rubber-tired, electrically powered vehicles carry up to eight seated and 13 standing passengers, providing security and privacy not usually found in larger, more common transit vehicles. The vehicles are switched to station platforms for passenger loading and unloading. All system functions—vehicle speed, nominal vehicle separation or headway, vehicle location, and vehicle tracking from origin to destination—are computerized. The system, when completed, will carry up to 3300 passengers per hour.

System Operation and Vehicle Management

In its normal mode of operation, the *demand mode*, the Morgantown PRT system provides vehicles for individuals or groups in response to passenger requests made through remote destination-selection devices located at the system stations. The system can be switched by the operator from this demand to a *schedule mode*, in which the vehicles automatically run from an originating station to a destination station in a predetermined origin-destination loop pattern within the route network. Alternatively, the vehicle can be run under the remote control of the operator in an emergency situation.

---

[1]This section is based on a contribution by V. E. Hutton and S. Bery to **Bendix Technical Journal**.

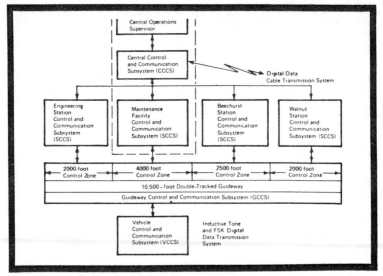

Fig. 10-31. Personal rapid transit system. (Courtesy Bendix Technical Journal.)

The control and communication system automatically controls vehicle movement and processes destination requests with a minimum of intervention on the part of the operator, who is responsible for monitoring total system operation. The central computer, through its supervisory programs, monitors and controls the operation of four similar computers housed at the various stations.

Vehicle-Position Monitoring

As shown schematically in Fig. 10-31, each station computer obtains information from vehicle-presence detectors located within its main-guideway control area and on its approach and departure ramps and its platform. Each station computer also transmits to the central computer at appropriate intervals individual-vehicle identification, position, and time at that location. In addition, the station computers monitor relative vehicle positions within their control areas with respect to assigned points, and report any time deviations to the central computer, which transmits them to the system operator. The operator can request and receive at any time the current position of any or all vehicles.

Vehicle Allocation

In the demand mode of operation, the vehicle-allocation portion of the software allocates vehicles in accord with passenger-destination requests. It also responds to operator inputs regarding operational vehicles, both in the demand mode and prior to activation of the schedule mode. Each station computer gives top assignment priority to vehicles already within its area of control; if no such vehicle is available, it requests a vehicle from the central computer. Should the central computer be unable to provide the required vehicle, the system operator is automatically alerted.

Dispatch Control

Discrete points representing nominal vehicle separations or headway intervals appropriate to the current guideway speed are maintained continuously as main-guideway positions eligible for vehicle assignment. When the central computer receives a dispatch request from a station computer, it selects an appropriate dispatch point far enough upstream with respect to time and distance from the station/departure-ramp merge point that it can be intercepted by the vehicle when it arrives at the merge area. After selecting this point, the central computer transmits a dispatch-time message to the station computer, and the station computer dispatches the vehicle at the time specified.

INDEX